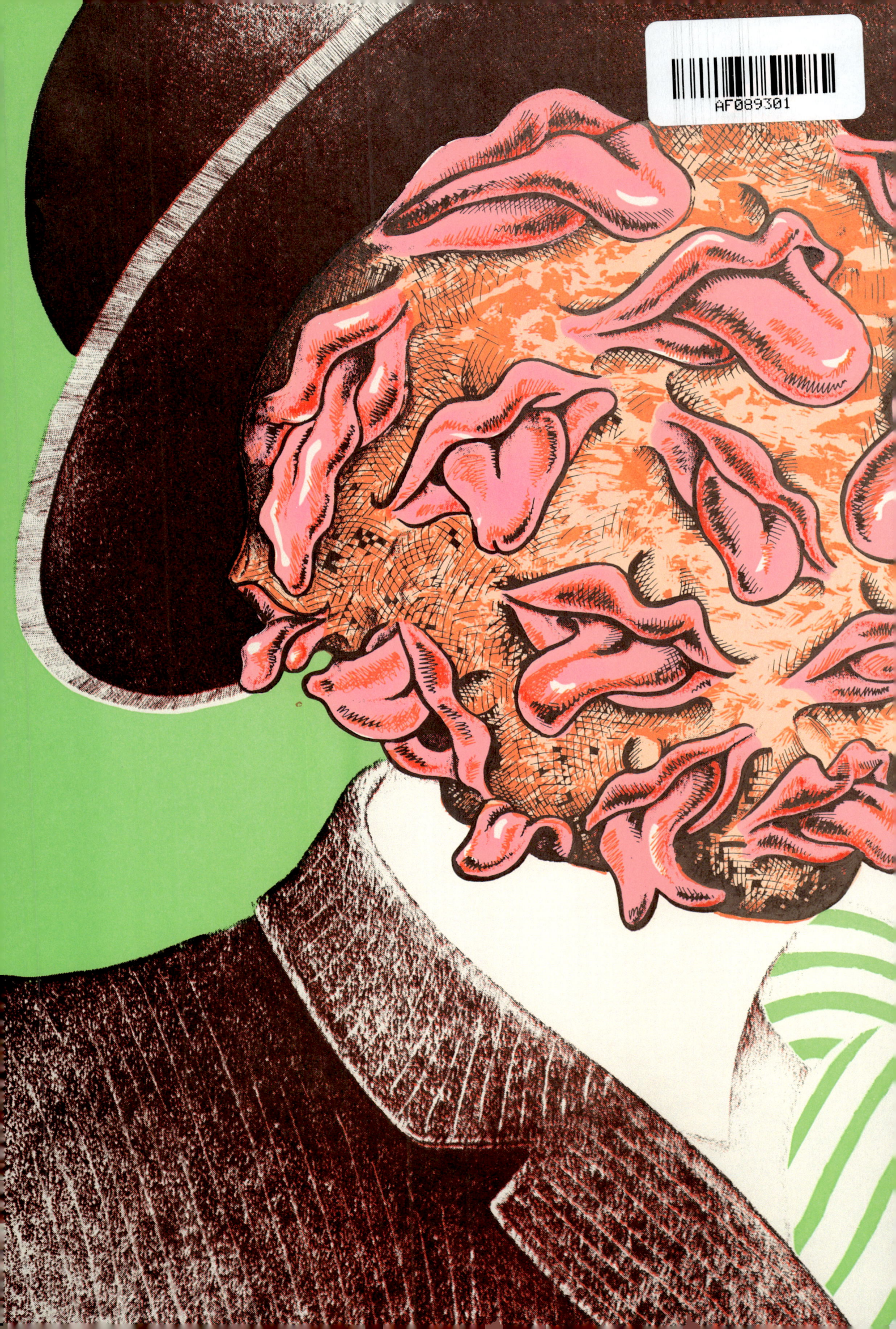

POSTER PADDI PRINT

Four Corners Books

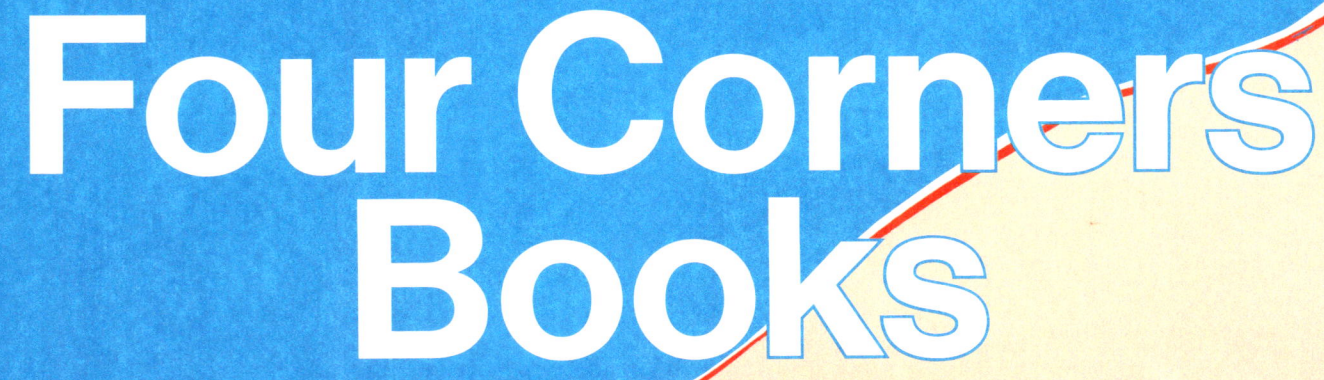

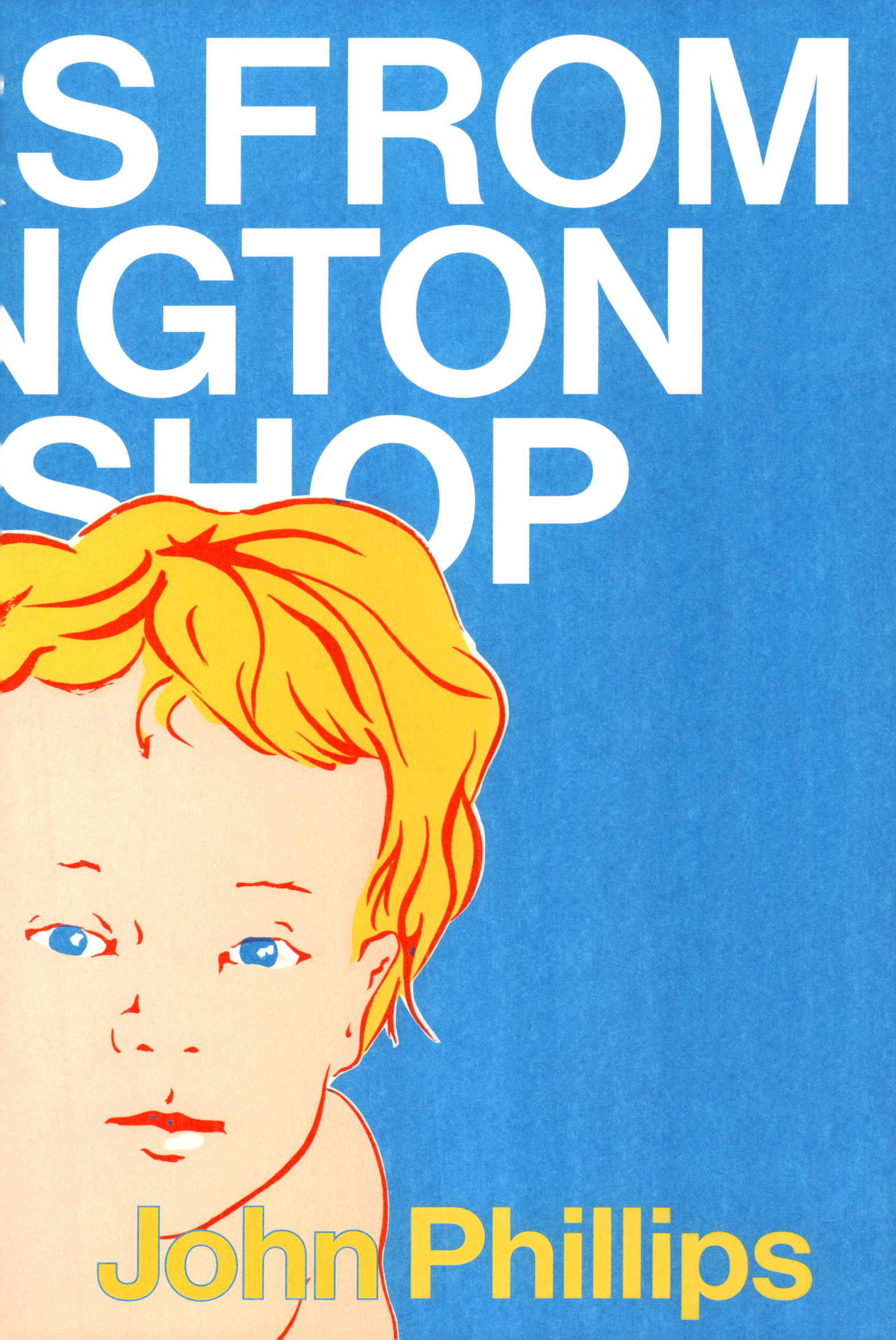

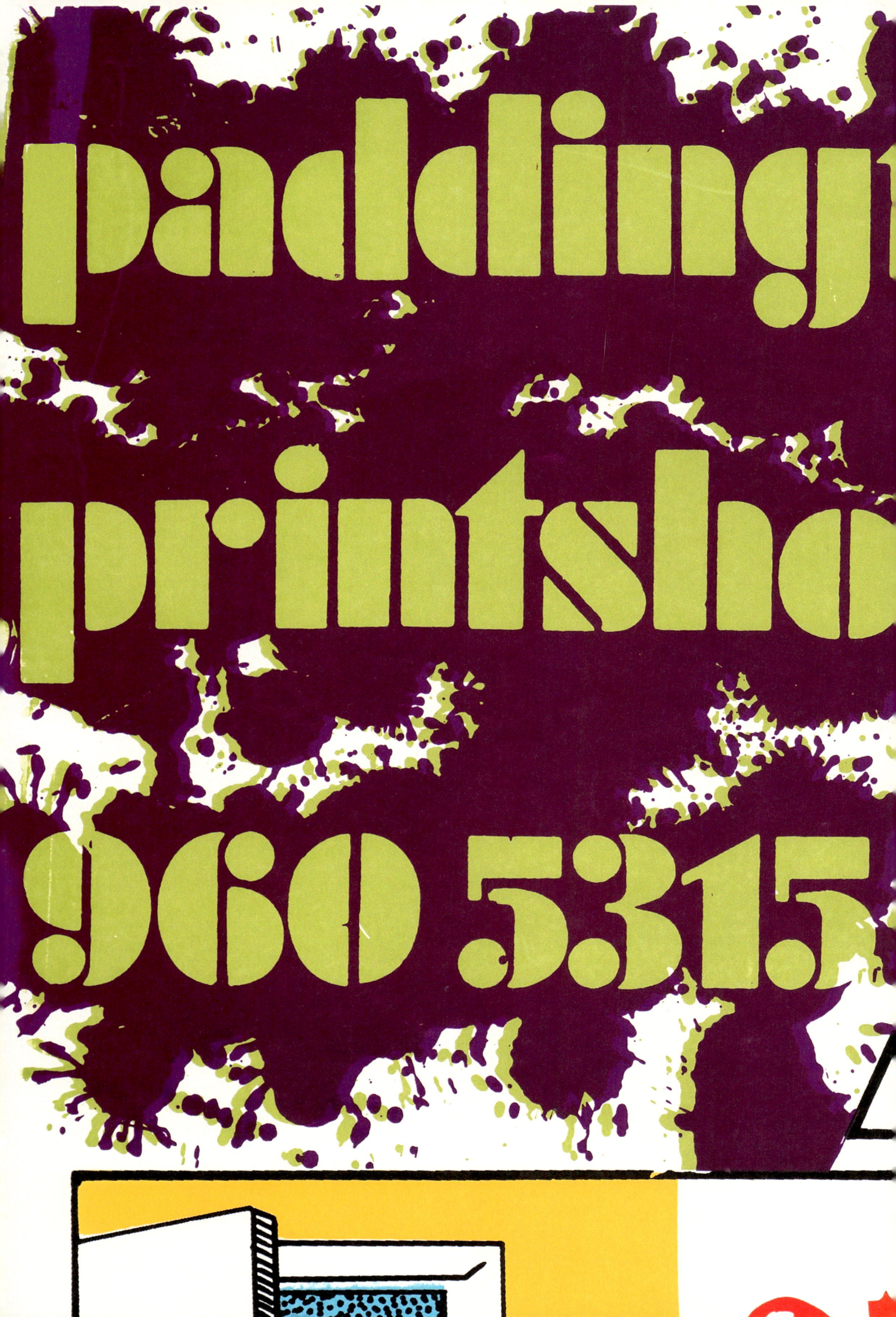

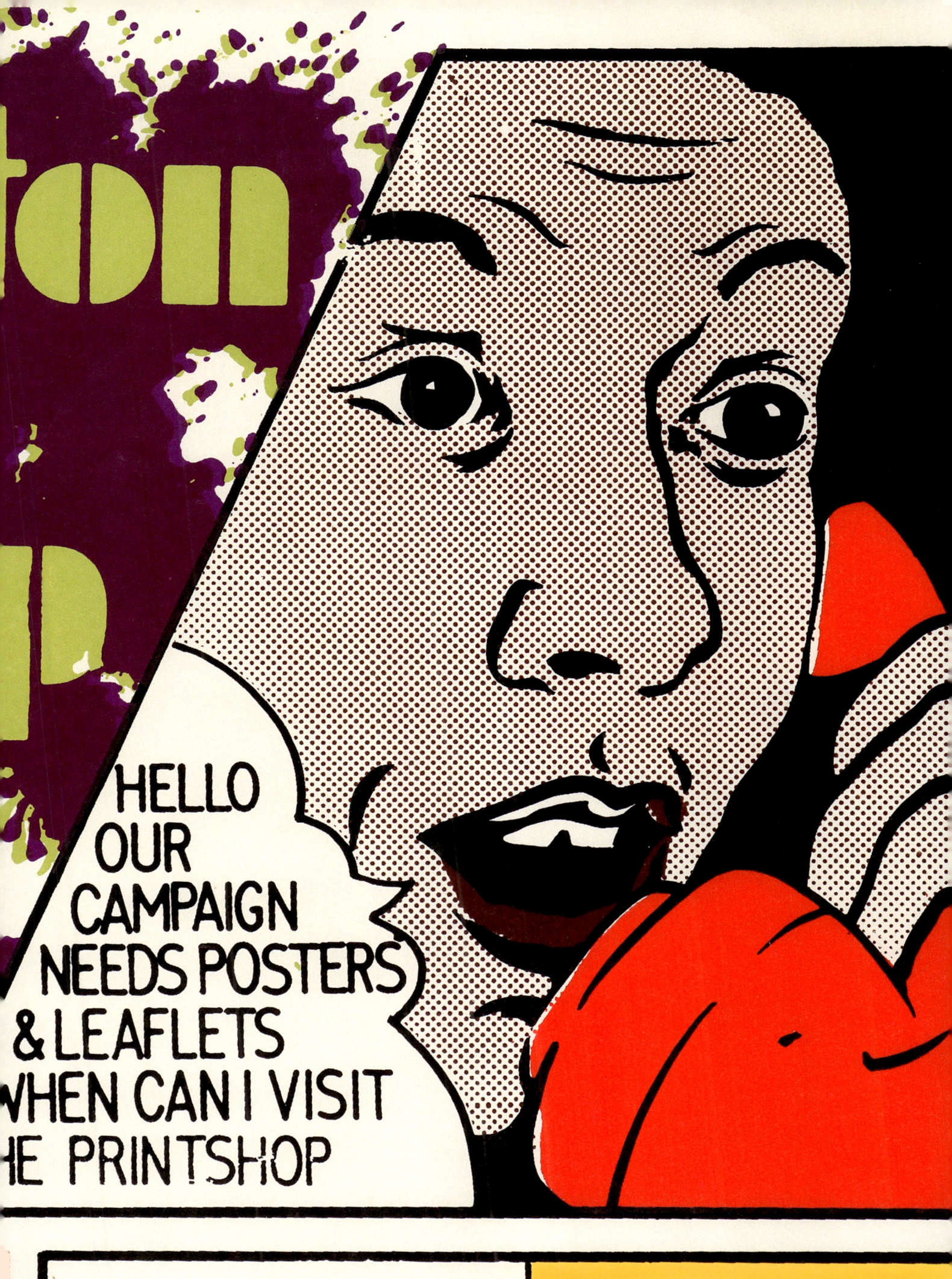

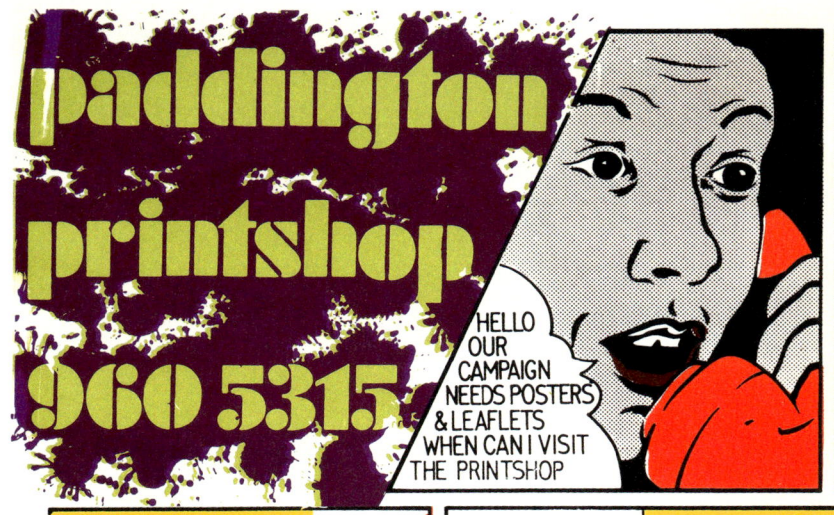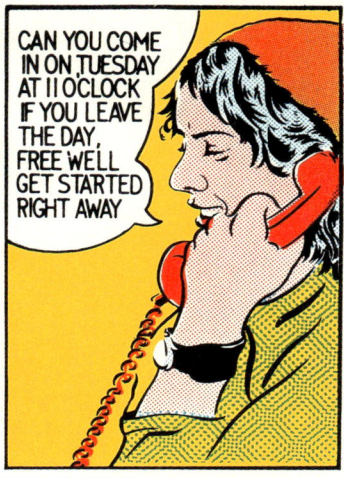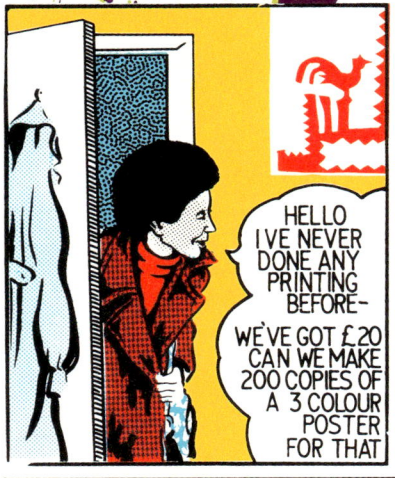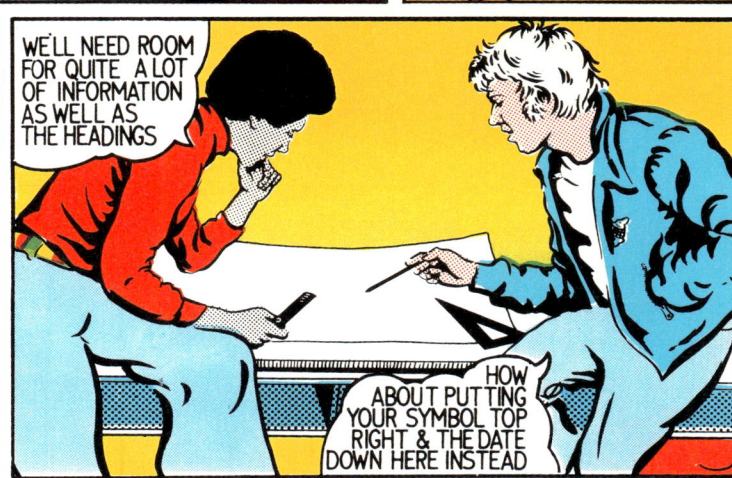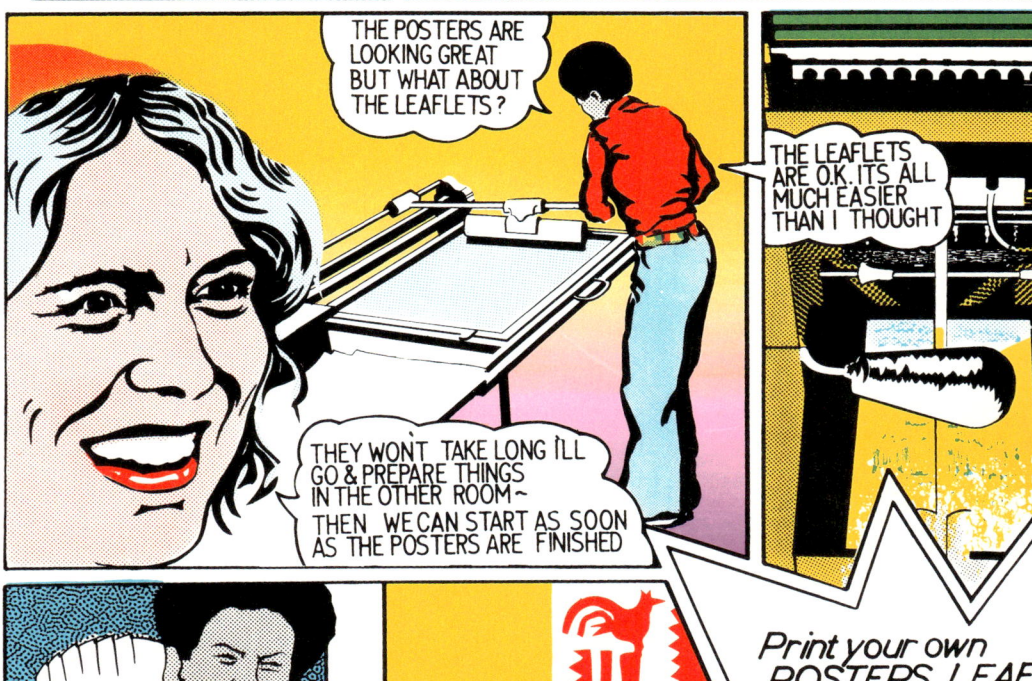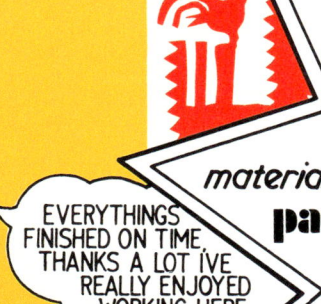

FOREWORD Andrzej Klimowski

The poster is a visual language with its own specific grammar and syntax. Its force depends on immediate, shorthand communication. It is both cerebral and sensuous because it has to activate the mind and seduce the eye. This kind of visual précis is difficult to pull off successfully; the poster designer has to devise a strategy to arrest the audience and then hold it long enough to give it the opportunity to engage in a mental dialogue with the visual message. It stirs the mind and forces the viewer to think, to take up a position, to ask questions: Do I agree with the message? Do I understand the premise? Have I ever thought about the subject before? Is my awareness of pressing matters, be they social, political, cultural or commercial, sharp enough? Thanks to the poster I can become enlightened, inspired or encouraged into action. The poster is certainly not a passive art form.

This is evident in the work produced by Paddington Printshop. Their aims and objectives were unambiguous, and what made their posters fresh was their engagement with the public: they had a clear and idealistic message. The lack of aesthetic subtlety and nuance becomes a strength. From today's perspective, they may appear naively sincere because of our constant use of irony and our conditioning by consumerist criteria. Posters now are predominantly commercial. Designers are preoccupied with lifestyle, hence the emphasis on aesthetics, elegance and sophistication.

The Paddington designers were solely interested in giving the local community a voice in fighting for their rights as citizens in a country that was biased towards private enrichment at the cost of the under privileged. The public housing situation was a particular question that needed addressing. Who would have imagined that poster design would have some say in the matter? Yet in the housing crisis of the North Kensington area, it did play a role, as John Phillips describes in his introduction, and was incredibly effective in redressing social disadvantages.

The poster makers adapted different styles to suit their messages; they referenced Pop Art, English vernacular comics like the Beano and echoed the stencilled posters of the Paris student riots of 1968. Despite these wide ranging influences, one could easily distinguish a Paddington Printshop poster by its brash irreverence and simplicity. I am tempted to say the posters were artless in that they lay emphasis on brutally honest communication, eschewing the niceties of aesthetic taste. They were certainly not eye candy. Nevertheless they did have their own specific visual attraction. The screen-printing technique employed by the designers and printers radiated with colour. Hand cut stencils combined with photographically transferred stencils allowed for a vital, dynamic use of composition analogous to punk rock. The spirit of freedom, idealism, immediacy and commitment was infectious and energising.

This collection of posters from the 1970s and 1980s provides us with an invaluable historical document. It should inspire and influence new generations of artists, designers and activists to invent their own graphic language, to communicate their beliefs and alert the public to the burning issues of the day.

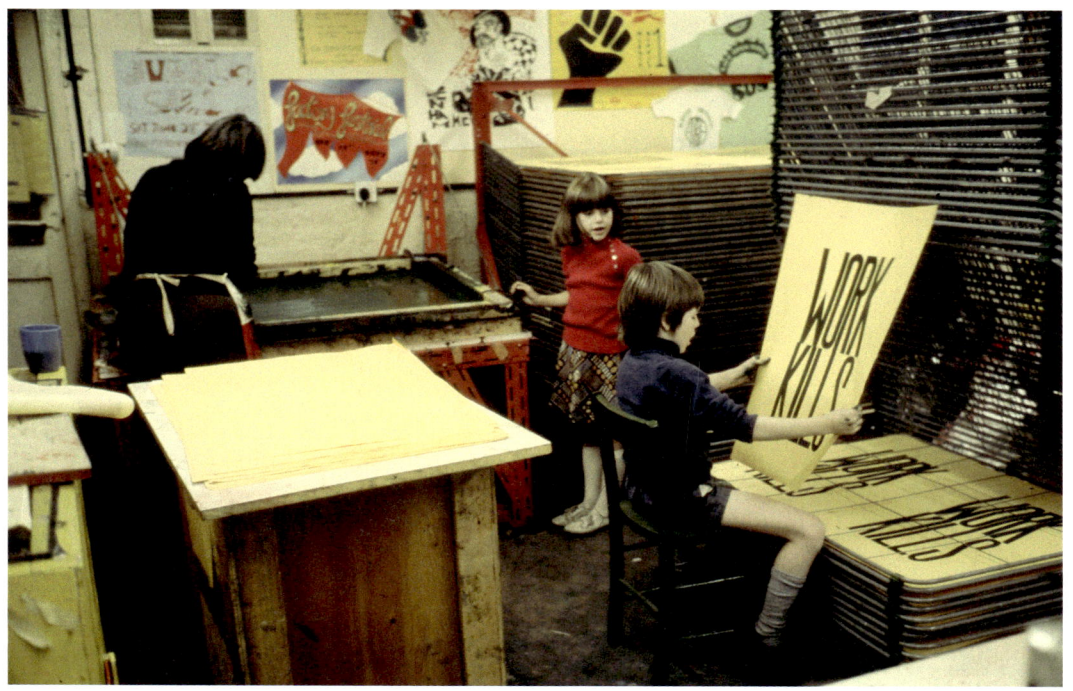
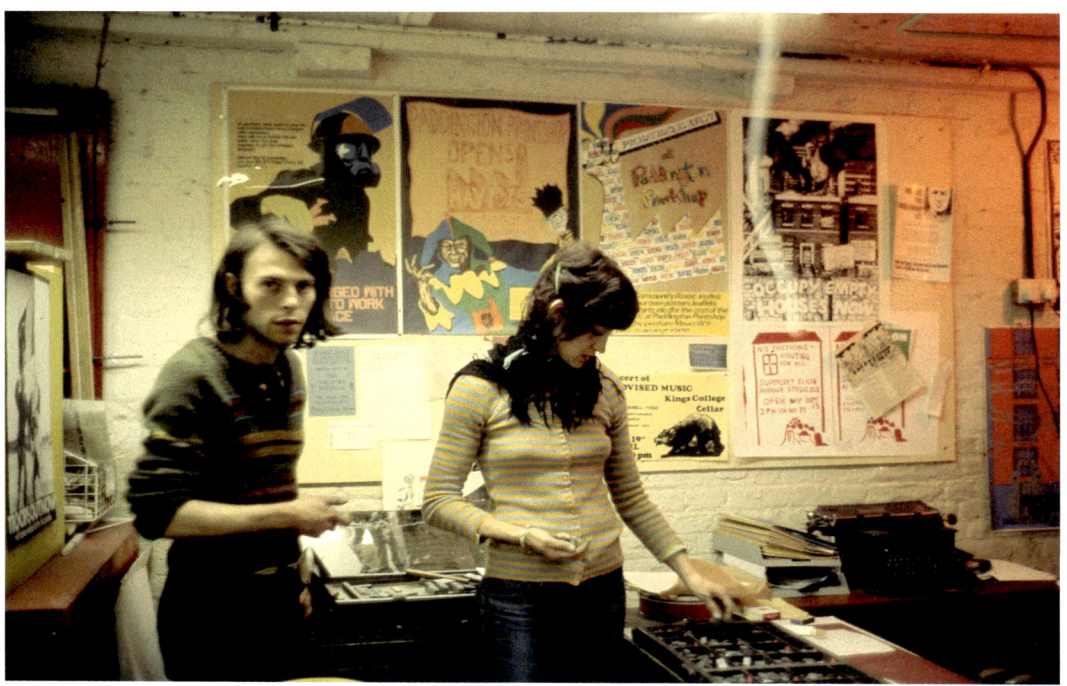
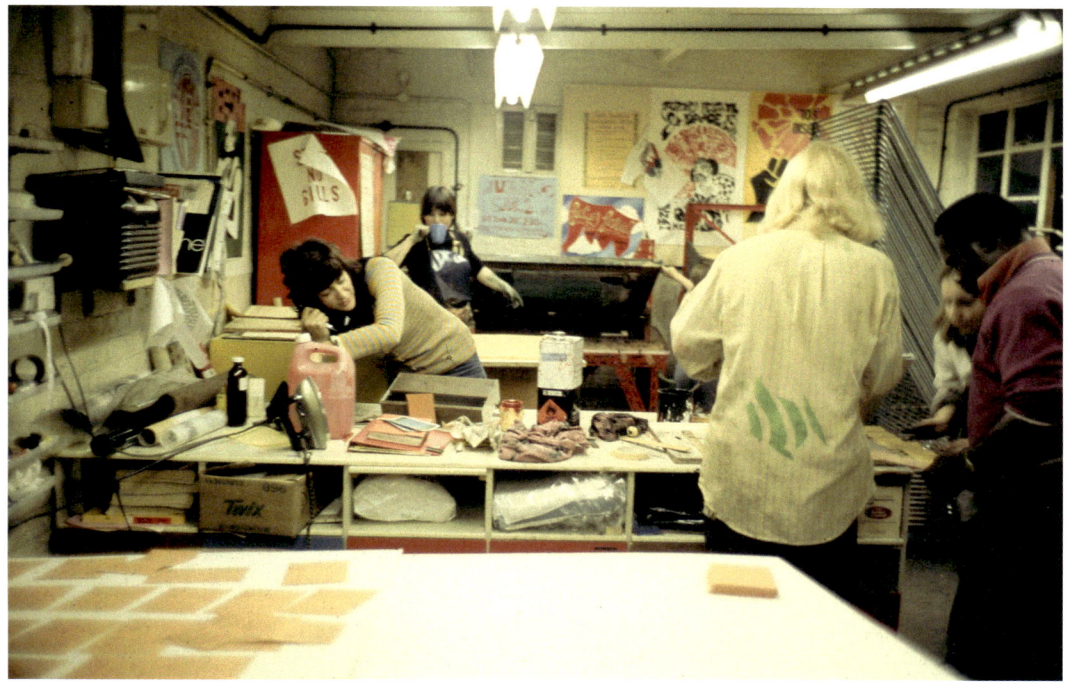

PADDINGTON PRINTSHOP   John Phillips

Paddington Printshop began, like many community-based projects, from a confluence of personal interests and local pressures. In 1972, after graduating from art school, I built some simple screen-print equipment, and from my kitchen table began to earn a freelance living. I knew little about printing and less about starting a business. But even so, the orders came in.

The clients were small theatres and grant-aided community organisations requiring posters. Over the next two years, this nascent resource attracted an ever-increasing stream of community and political activists. During 1974 this clientele was swollen by an influx of Chilean refugees. The kitchen graduated to printing posters with the artist/designer Edward Wright and painter Roberto Matta, and it was time to find a new home.

A local community centre offered a rent-free space to house the enterprise. I constructed the furniture and equipment from the debris of the 1974 Ideal Home Exhibition after tipping £5 each to two drivers responsible for removing the sets of this annual trade fair. Large wooden screens were stripped down, their laminated surfaces transformed into workbenches and screenprint equipment. Straight nails were recycled for their original purpose; bent ones were used to fine-tune the counterbalance weights.

When we arrived, Marylands Community Centre was a 17,000 sq. ft. abandoned factory. It had been given to the local community to run with the support of one full-time worker responsible for project development, plumbing, administration, youth work, fundraising, security and everything else thrown in his direction. He optimistically sold the heating system for scrap. Despite the cold, the centre, renamed The Factory flourished. Rum-fuelled domino competitions clattered through Sunday afternoons. The experimental theatre company, The People Show, moved in, painted the building, organised a surrealist kids disco and staged performances. Musicians, including Aswad, and Joe Strummer's pre-Clash band the 101ers, played regular gigs. Larry Forde and his band Sukuya built costumes for the 1975 Notting Hill Carnival. On August Bank Holiday Monday, the Factory gates opened to release a satire on every racist's stereotypical fantasy. Around 150 black men and women, having discarded the superfluous trimmings of decorum, paraded through the neighbourhood, bedecked in raffia skirts 'war paint' and brandishing spears. The whole ensemble was led by a king, crowned by a 'primitive' sculpture proudly displaying a sizable erect phallus.

And so we set out to contribute to local 'traditions'; to entertain, challenge and facilitate change.

A chance encounter with a recently-published booklet, *Community Arts Report: Arts Council of Great Britain* (1974), suggested a new opportunity for supporting the project through public grants. Paddington Printshop was among the first group of organisations supported by the Arts Council's new initiative. Our first funding application outlined the following aims: 'The Print Workshop has been formed on two basic principles: That it should teach people new and useful skills. That it should encourage them to use those skills in the artistic or visual interpretation of their beliefs.' The project was a joint enterprise with Pippa Smith, who gave up her teaching job to bring the social and educational skills that I lacked. Arts Council subsidy, and support from the community centre, covered the organisation's running costs and salaries. The groups who came to make posters, newsletters and leaflets contributed the cost of materials, and much of the labour.

North Paddington, the neighbourhood where we settled, lay on the northern fringe of Notting Hill, in west London. During the previous two decades a unique combination of deracination, poverty, activism, enterprise, scandal and celebrity, had granted the area notoriety. 'There was music in the cafes at night and revolution in the air'. Its contributions to the national landscape included, amongst much else: 1958 Race Riots, Rachmanism, the Profumo scandal, the British Black Panthers; the 60's underground movement with its music and magazines, Oz, Friendz, International Times, Hawkwind, T Rex, Pink Floyd. It was home to King Mob and members of the Angry Brigade. Performance was filmed, Bob Marley was busted, and Hendrix died there. It was the kind of place where a new kind of 'lifestyle' politics; blending community activism, civil rights and hedonism, flourished. Initially, our posters were, to a large extent, promotions for social gatherings – gigs and demonstrations, which went hand in hand with the creation of more permanent spaces. In 1976 the local council agreed to convert The Factory; install heating, working toilets, legal fire escapes and even a licensed bar, which replaced our 'improvised' system of selling raffle tickets, each of which 'won' a drink.

Following the conversion, Paddington Printshop opted for independence and The Factory emerged as one of the first black arts centres in the UK, subsequently called Yaa Asantewaa. Forty years on it is part of Carnival Village Trust.

We decided to become an educational charity; a formal structure that reflected what we perceived to be the educational values of the organisation, and which, as a not-for-profit, would, we hoped, facilitate our raising funds. The material sent in support of the application for charitable status described the Printshop's activities. One example explained how a couple had used the facilities to make their own wedding invitations. The Charity Commission highlighted this passage in its rejection letter. Education, we were informed, was a learning activity disengaged from practical application. The couple's wedding invitation, the letter informed us, was made in pursuit of a practical objective, and was therefore not educational. The Printshop became a Friendly Society. Its educational models were drawn from other sources: Ivan Illich's radical proposition, to replace schooling in childhood with lifelong learning networks; Paulo Freire's interweaving of literacy and politics; and the counter-culture models of free schools and universities.

Using the ground floor of a terraced house as a temporary base, we converted the basement of number one Elgin Avenue, and on moving in there left North Paddington Women's Centre as the new occupants of our temporary home.

Meanwhile, we helped Jamie McCullough create Meanwhile Gardens. The Gardens began, as Jamie subsequently recalled, 'with a piece of wasteland and a dream. The wasteland was by the canal in Paddington… The dream was that it didn't need to be like that'. With the intention of shaping land, Jamie, a sculptor, had recently learned to drive a JCB bulldozer. The council offered a temporary site and we worked together to form a charity, raise funds and engage a thirty-strong workforce to transform the space temporarily – hence the name, Meanwhile Gardens. We planted trees, created an open-air

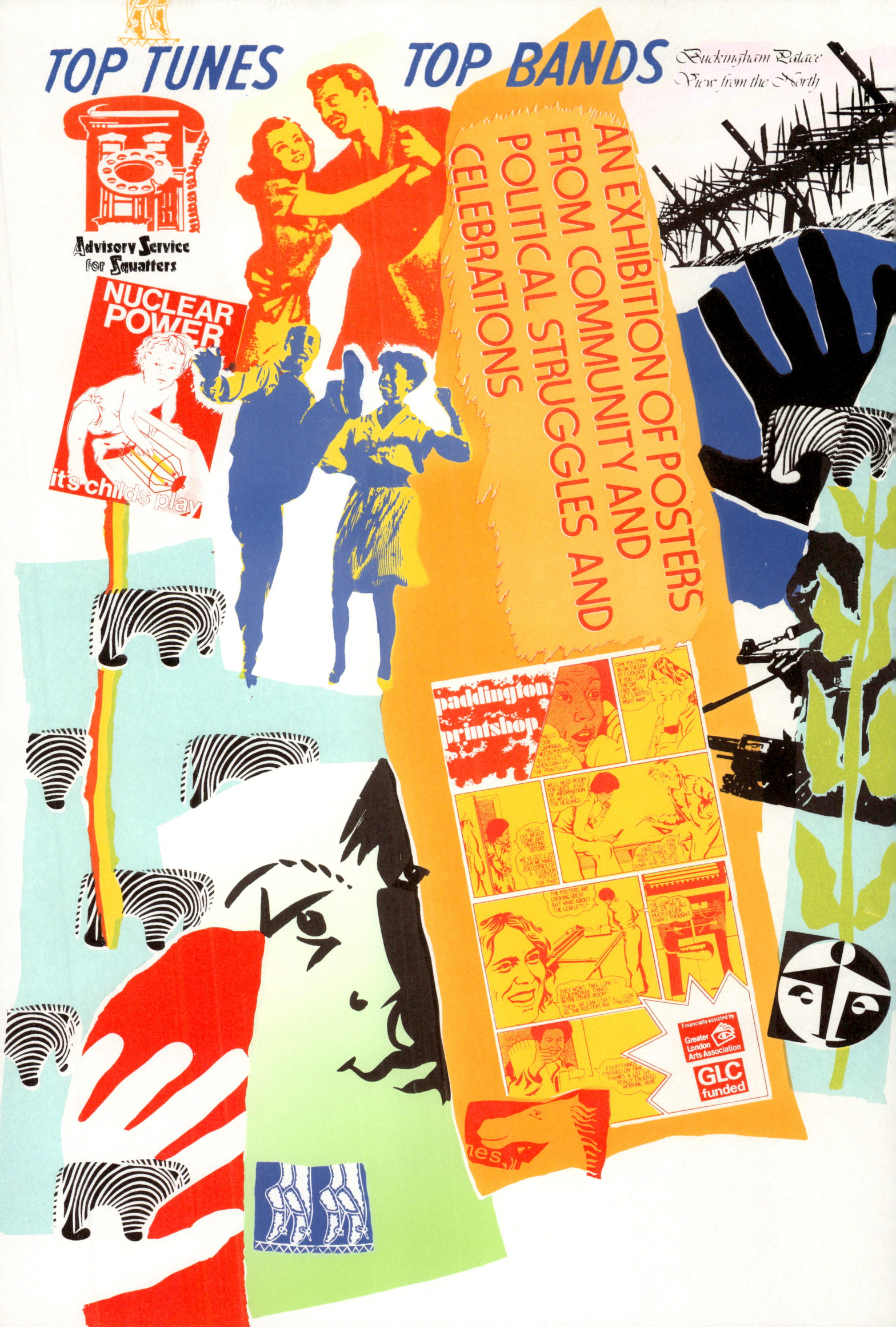

LOOKING...
FOR HELP WITH ARTWORK

GRAPHIC RESOURCE

PADDINGTON PRINTSHOP

1 ELGIN AVE, W.9.
EVERY WEDNESDAY 10~5
TEL: 286 1123 FOR DETAILS

theatre, constructed the first purpose-built skateboard park in the UK and made posters to promote the events we held there.

Following on from Meanwhile, and conscious that many local people had grown up in rural environments (in Spain, Portugal, Ireland, the Caribbean etc.) the Printshop initiated a rural project; Paddington Farm. We began by organising summer camps in the countryside for young people, and progressed to buying a fifty-acre farm near Glastonbury, with outbuildings converted for urban visitors, and produce sold back in the Paddington neighbourhood. Paddington Arts, a youth project offering performance and video training for local young people was a further offshoot from the farm.

Other important advice and neighbourhood centres were established in the area including one at 510 Harrow Road, which became the base for many community and pressure groups that regularly engaged the Printshop's services.

Undoubtedly, housing was the most significant issue that the community faced. Many streets were lined with corrugated iron, many properties boarded-up, many people were homeless, or living in overcrowded conditions, and much profit could be made from speculation. Even the associations responsible for addressing social housing needs joined the frenzy. They bought properties and left them empty, because the moment a tenant moved in a property's value fell.

To highlight this scandal, we worked with disgruntled officials and board members from these dissolute trusts. The insiders supplied addresses of their association's unoccupied 'investments' to teams of volunteers who painted large red crosses on the doors and windows, along with posters proclaiming these properties 'Another Empty Home'. Subsequently, the 'whistle-blowers' raised the matter of these 'desecrations' internally to push for a change in policy. From a local initiative, this grew into a national campaign.

Locally, a number of anarchic initiatives sprang up. Writer Heathcote Williams established the Rough Tough Cream Puff Estate Agency, which 'jemmied-open' properties and published a regular bulletin advertising their availability for squatters: '36 St Lukes Road, would suit astronomer due to lack of roof.' The agency claimed to have housed over 3,000 people. In 1977, Heathcote was appointed the Republic of Frestonia's ambassador to the UK, following the initiative by a group of squatters on Freston Road to secede from the UK in response to the council's attempts to convict them. With the motto Sumus Una Familia (we are all one family), the 1.8 acre landmass of Frestonia issued its own passports and postage stamps, established its own national theatre, art gallery and cinema, and applied for membership of the UN.

From across London, the Advisory Service for Squatters came to make posters promoting their advice and legal support services, and from the offices above us, Campaign Against a Criminal Trespass Law, the Campaign to Legalise Cannabis, the drug advisory service Release, and the armed forces rights group At Ease came downstairs to make publicity.

The largest, and most high-profile housing campaign the Printshop was involved with began in 1984. Before the introduction of the National Tenants Right-to-Buy Scheme, Westminster city council decided to sell an entire council estate to the private sector. The Printshop happened to be located on this estate, which comprised approximately 1,000 housing units. A tenants' delegation arrived at our door. Could we make a poster suggesting that this was a bad idea? We did! During the next four years, the Printshop produced thousands of postcards and billboard-sized posters supporting the tenants' cause. Successive development companies shied away from a scheme which was so vehemently opposed by the residents. The council ceased to undertake repairs, but the campaigners persisted.

When the residents finally won the right to buy and manage their own estate, it was valued at minus £17 million, due to lack of maintenance. The Walterton and Elgin Action Group became a model for resident control. Within ten years it became a capital asset worth hundreds of millions of pounds. Research now indicates that the health, job and education prospects of tenants are better than comparable occupants of social housing. But the story did not end there. The campaign went on to identify possible misuse of public funds in the pursuit of political gain. A council-wide policy, called Building Stable Communities, had pursued the objective of strategically selling social housing stock to the private sector in the belief that home owners would be more likely to vote Conservative. The public auditors identified misuse of public funds expenditure to be £47 million. The leader of the council, and close associate of Margaret Thatcher, Dame Shirley Porter, left the country in the wake of this massive scandal.

Within three years of the Arts Council's initial support for Community Arts in 1975, the sector had grown into an eclectic movement, supported at national and local level. Amid the festivals, murals and inflatable sculptures, printshops, many based on the Paddington model, were established throughout the UK. Political change, from 1979, saw decreased infrastructural support for all things community, and a commensurate decrease in the demand for community-based poster and print resources. By the end of the 1980s, the majority of community-based printshops across the UK had closed, and in 1991, Paddington Printshop formally closed and transferred its assets to a newly formed charity – the London Print Workshop (subsequently londonprintstudio). The new organisation moved to larger premises, provided support services to artists and continues to support socially engaged art projects in the local community. In the years of operation, much has changed, and much remains the same.

Page 6
PADDINGTON PRINTSHOP PUBLICITY, 1977, John Phillips

Page 8
Making posters at the Printshop, c. 1975. Centre photo shows John Phillips and Diney Bierski.

Page 11
PADDINGTON PRINTSHOP EXHIBITION, 1985, John Phillips

Page 12
PADDINGTON PRINTSHOP, c. 1981, Anne Dundon

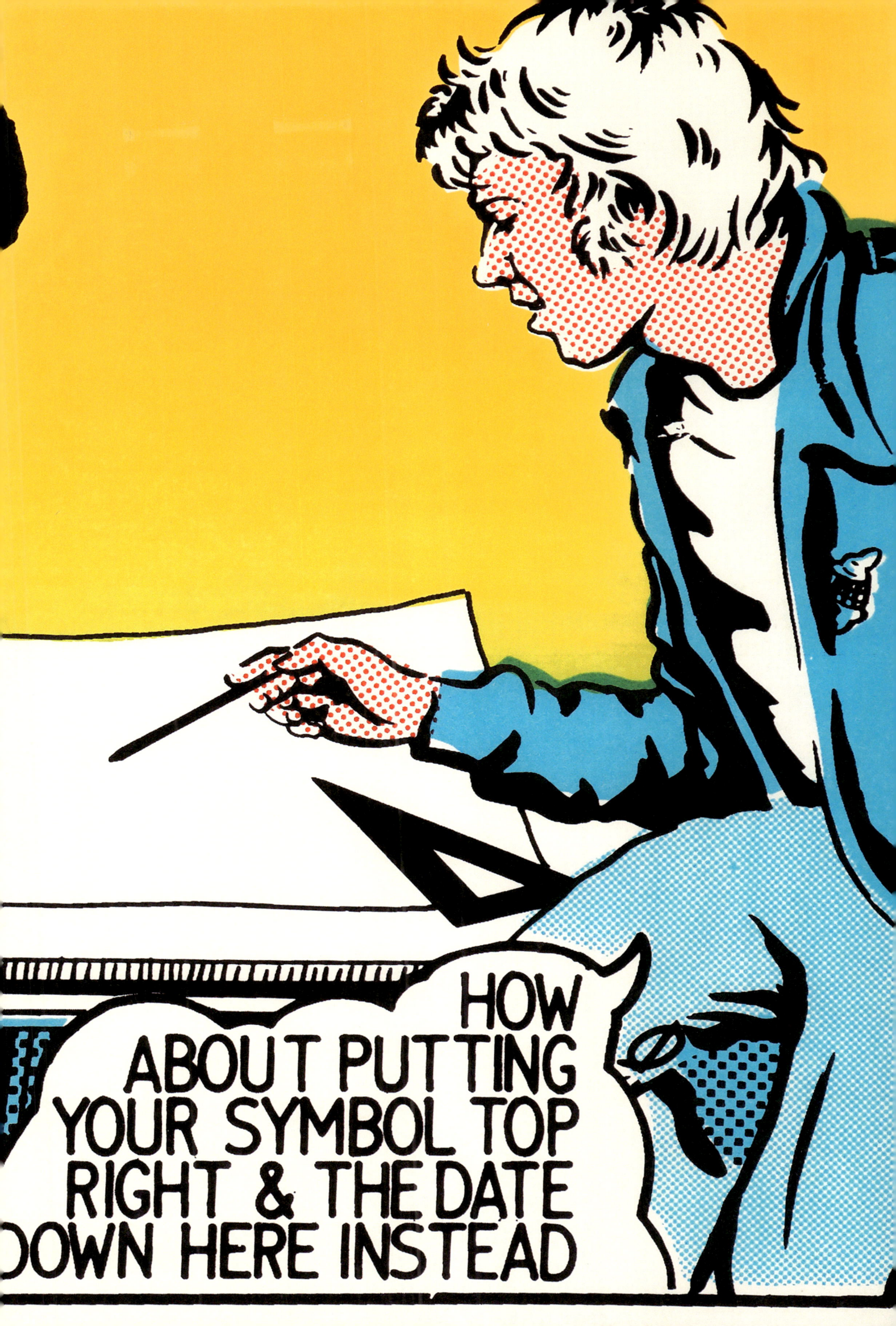

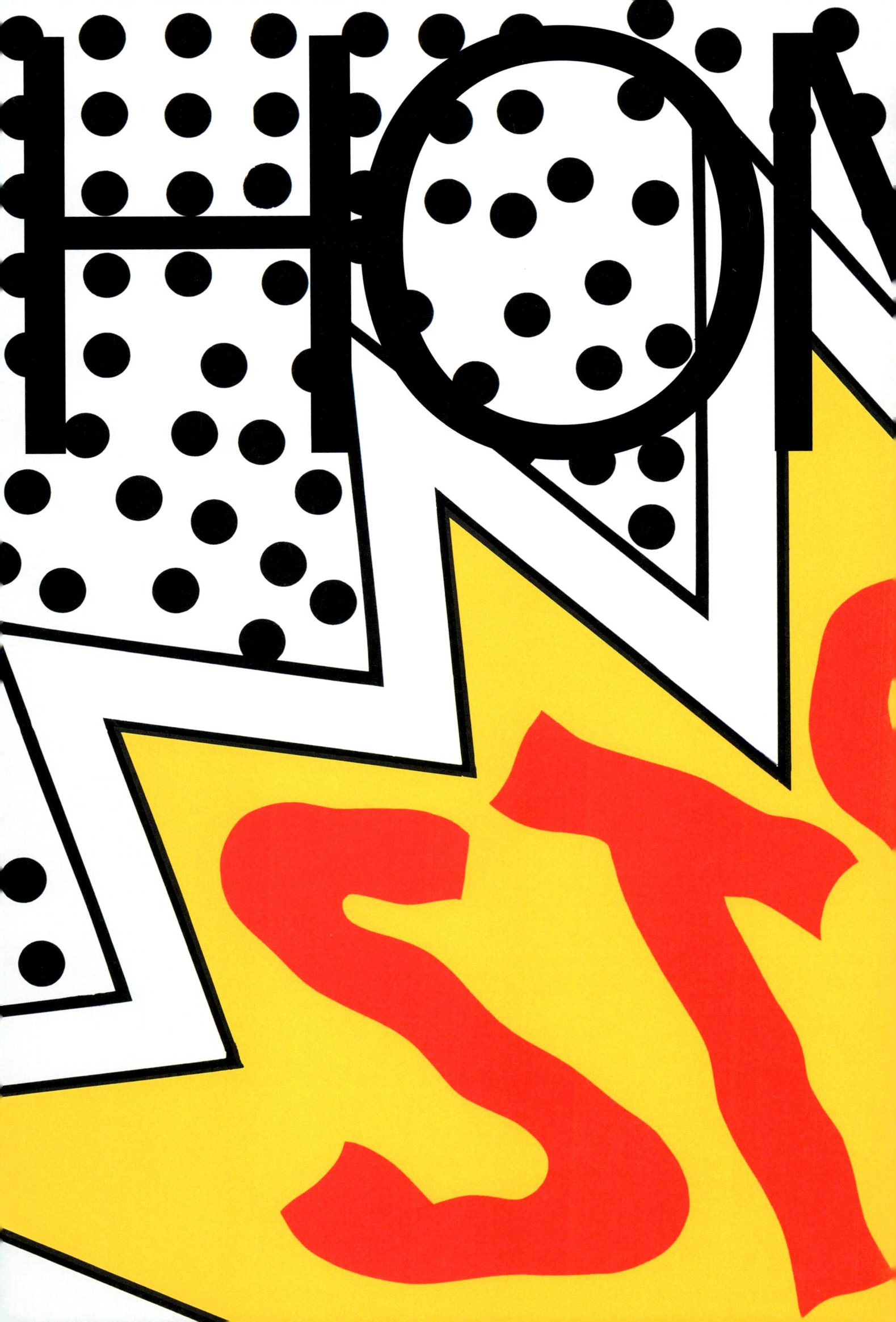

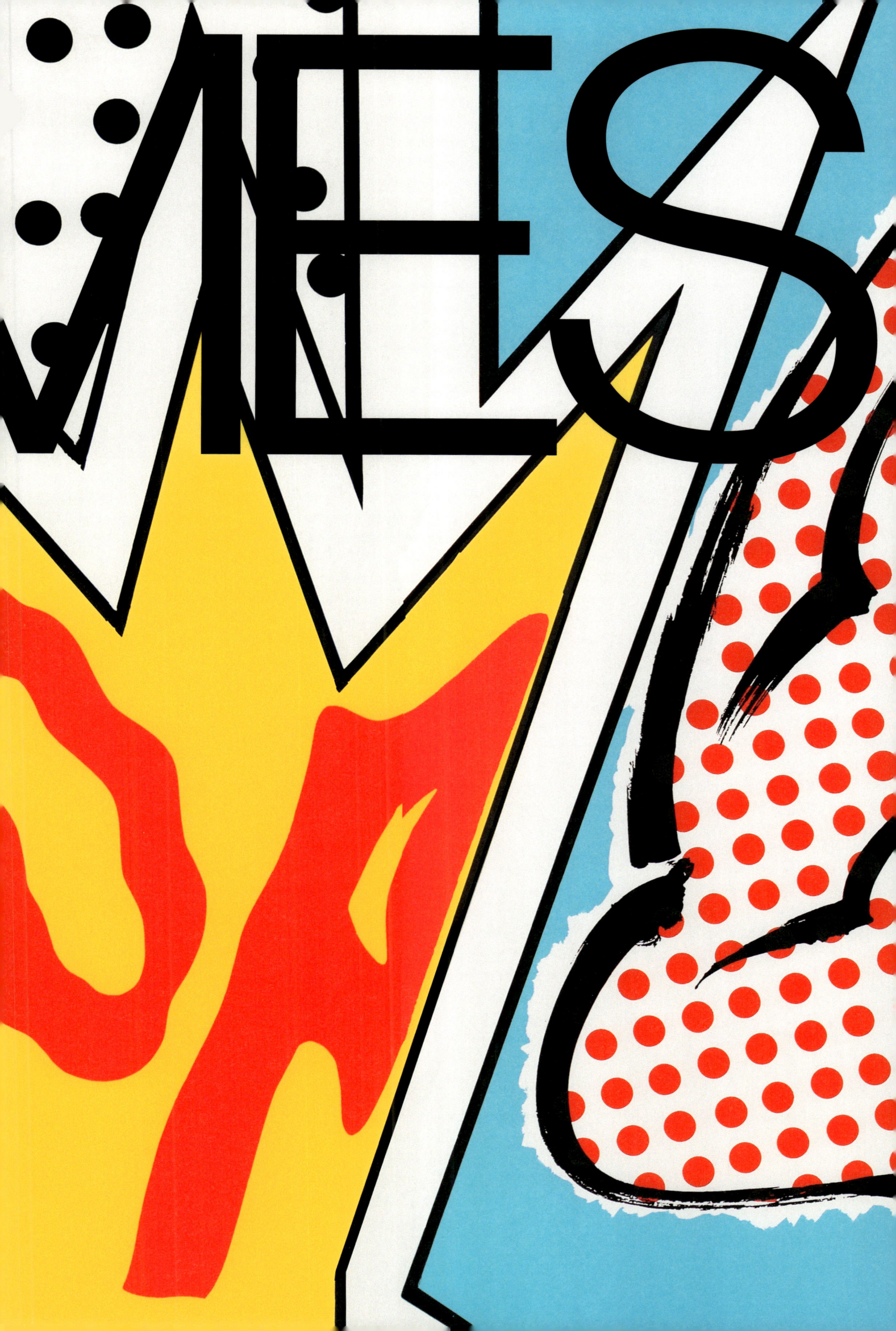

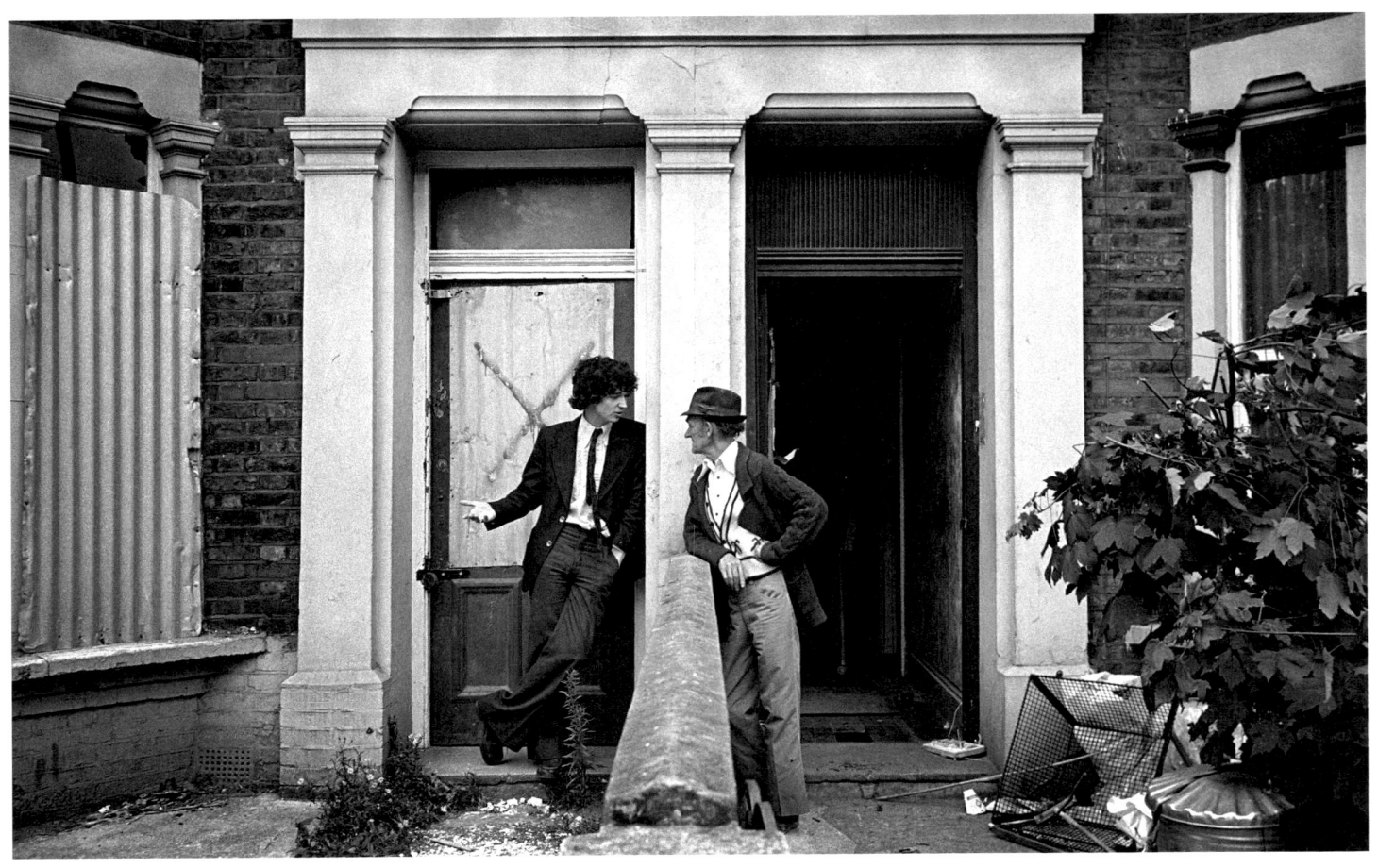

Above
A squatter and a workman talking outside a house in Bravington Road in 1977. Photo by Philip Wolmuth.

Opposite
OCCUPY EMPTY HOUSES NOW,
1976, Anonymous

Next pages
NO EVICTIONS – HOUSING FOR ALL,
c.1975, Anonymous

Housing was the single most important issue in the area, which hosted a very low proportion of owner occupiers. The majority of the population was housed in either social housing or low standard private rental. Property speculation had additionally led to a disproportionate percentage of boarded up properties, which were subsequently squatted.

Tenants associations, dominated by the longer established white community, and united by a common landlord, mobilized around common issues, while more recently arrived migrants were frequently exploited by the private sector. The squatting community was *majoritarily* young, highly educated, regionally networked, and attuned to using posters for both campaigns and advertising fundraising benefits. Groups of squats within neighbourhoods promoted alternative lifestyles, featuring communal facilities and gardens.

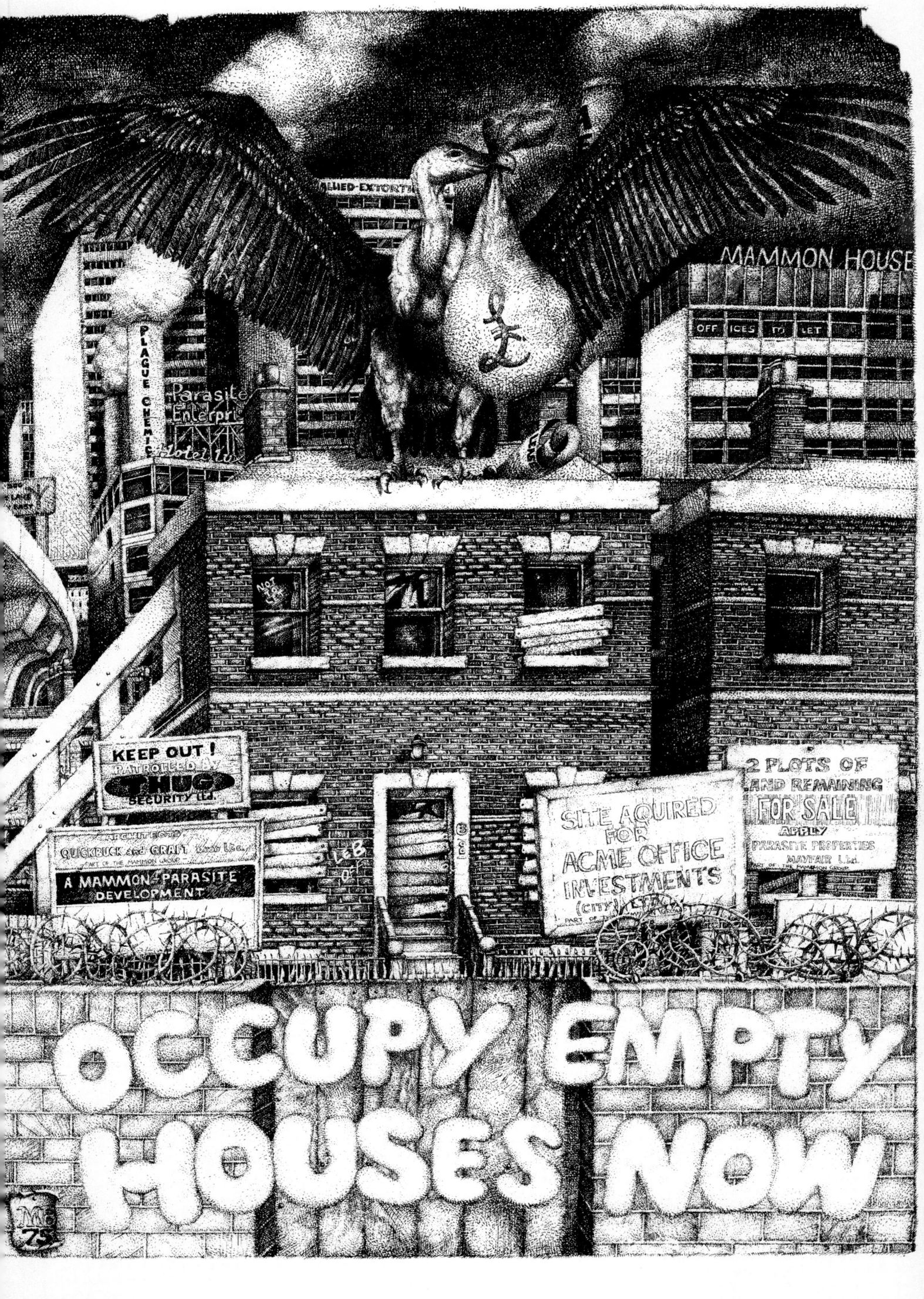

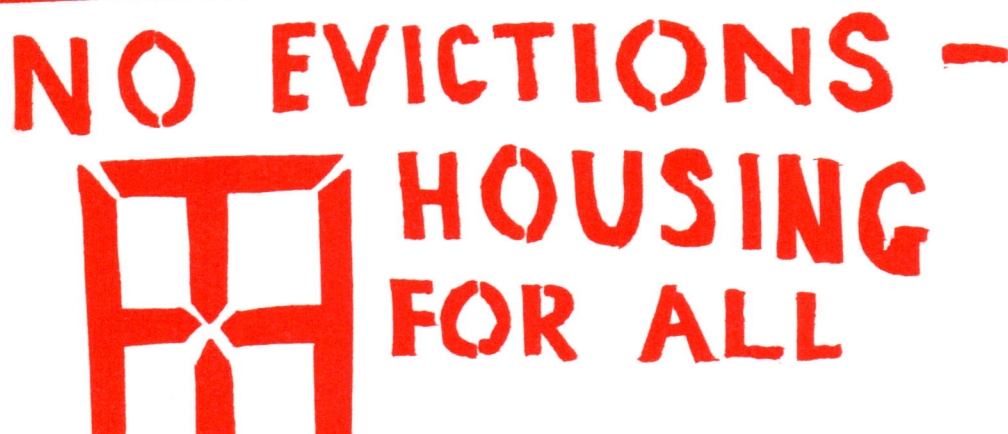

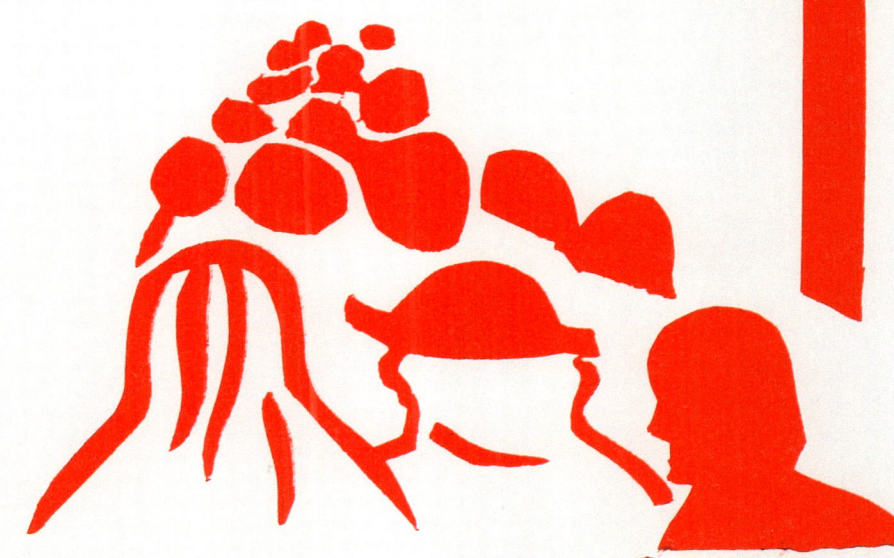

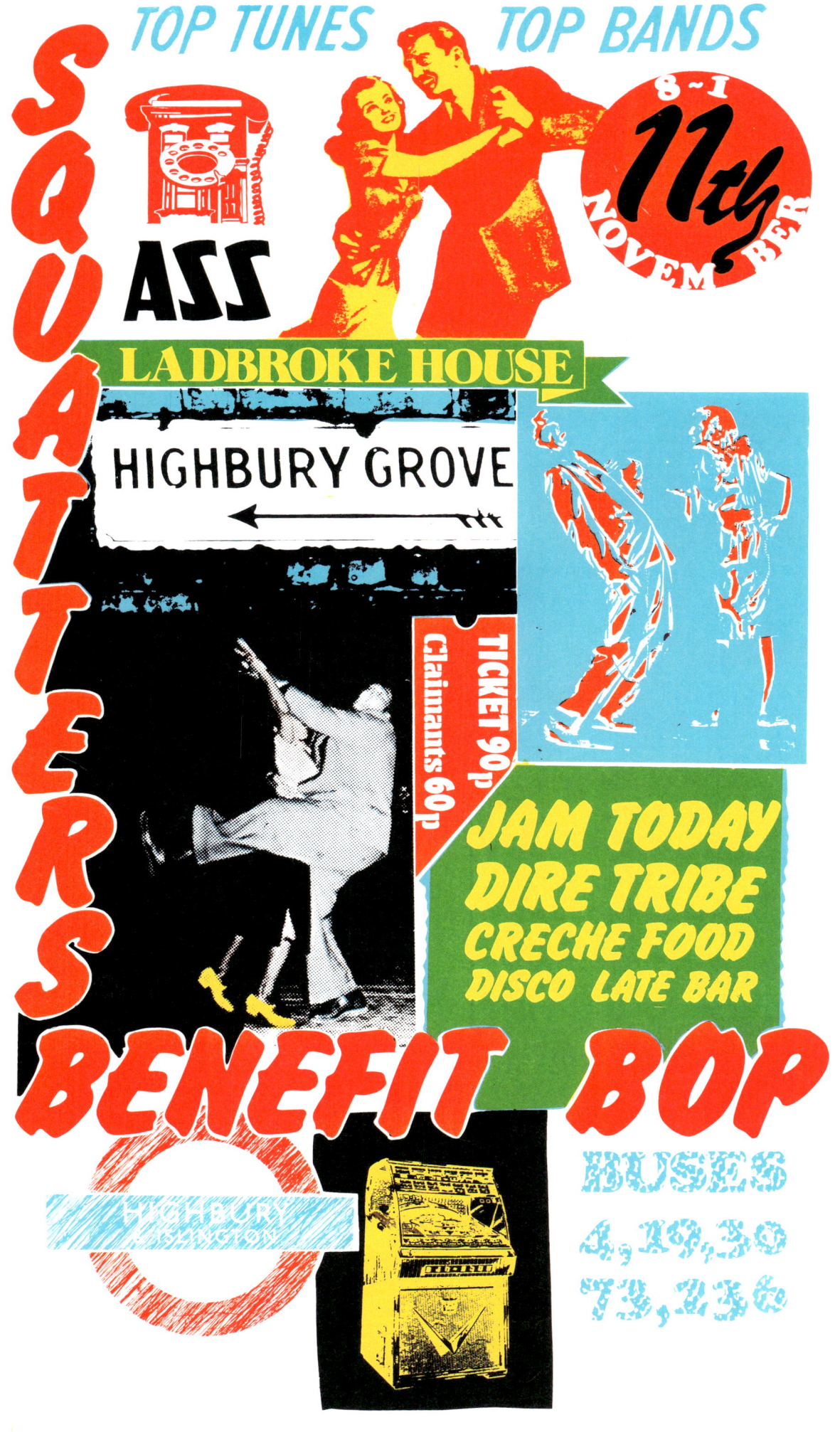

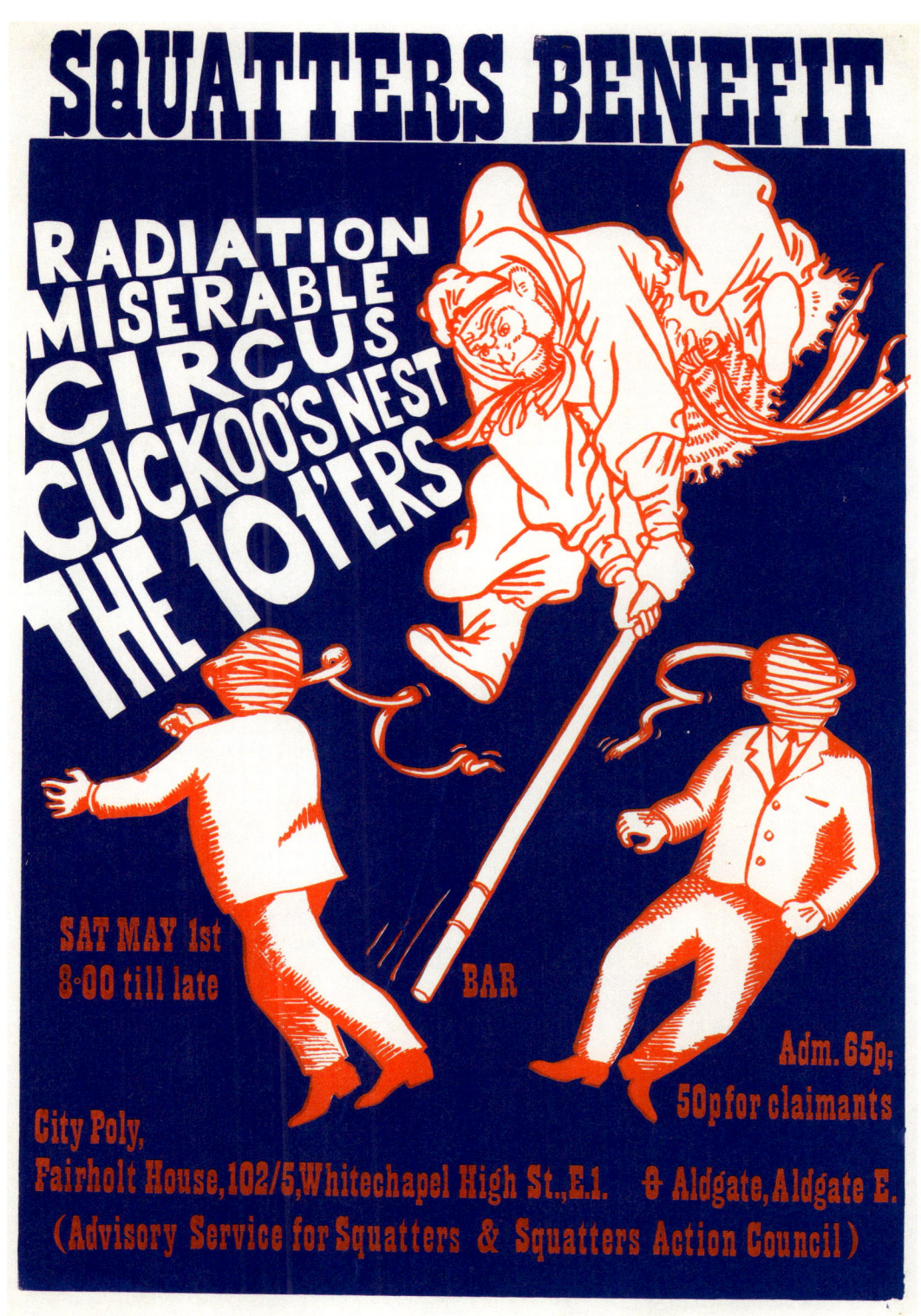

Opposite
SQUATTER'S BENEFIT BOP,
1978, John Phillips

Above
SQUATTER'S BENEFIT,
1976, Brian Deighton

Next pages
SQUATTER'S CONFERENCE,
1977, John Phillips and Brian Deighton

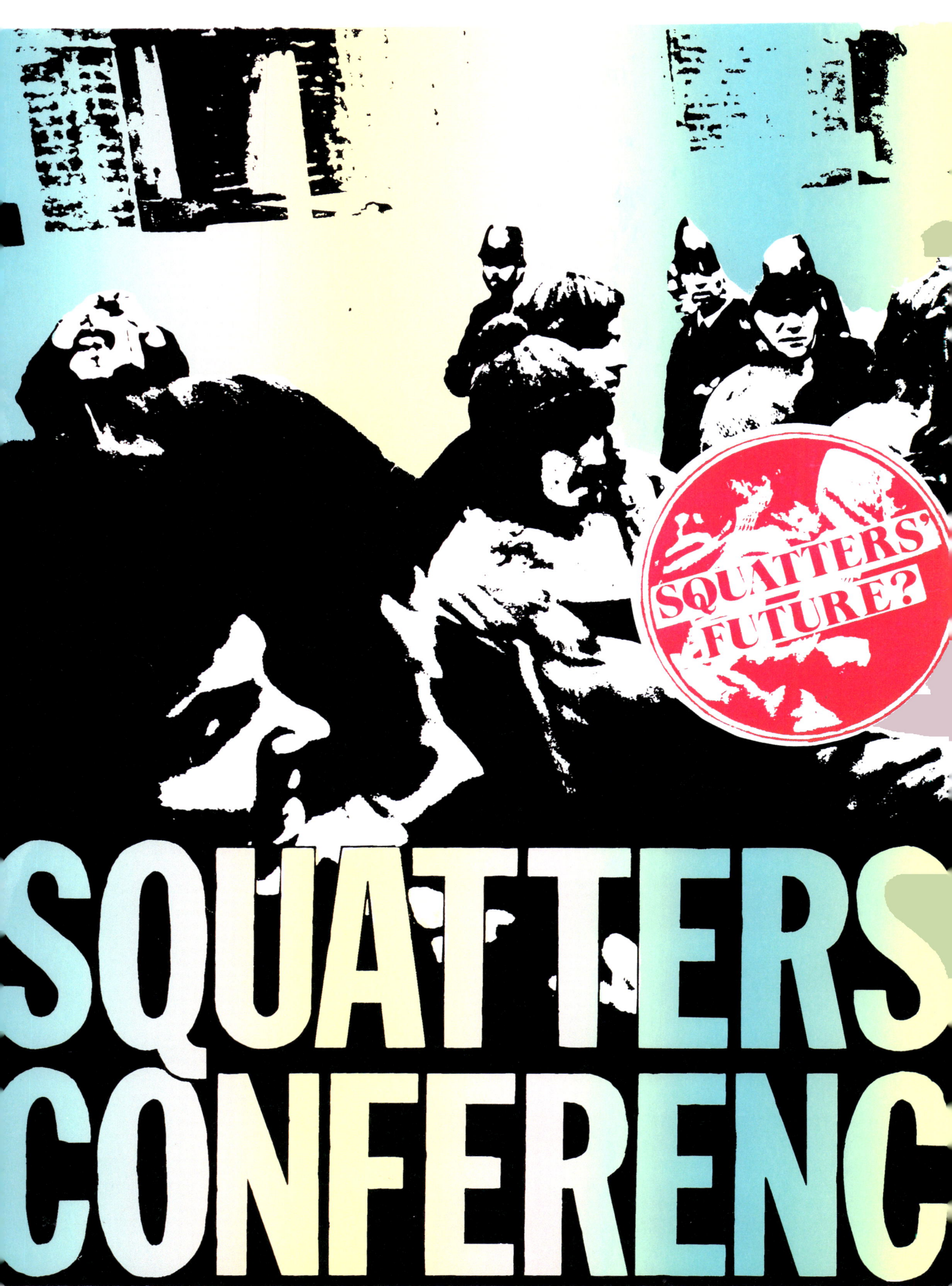

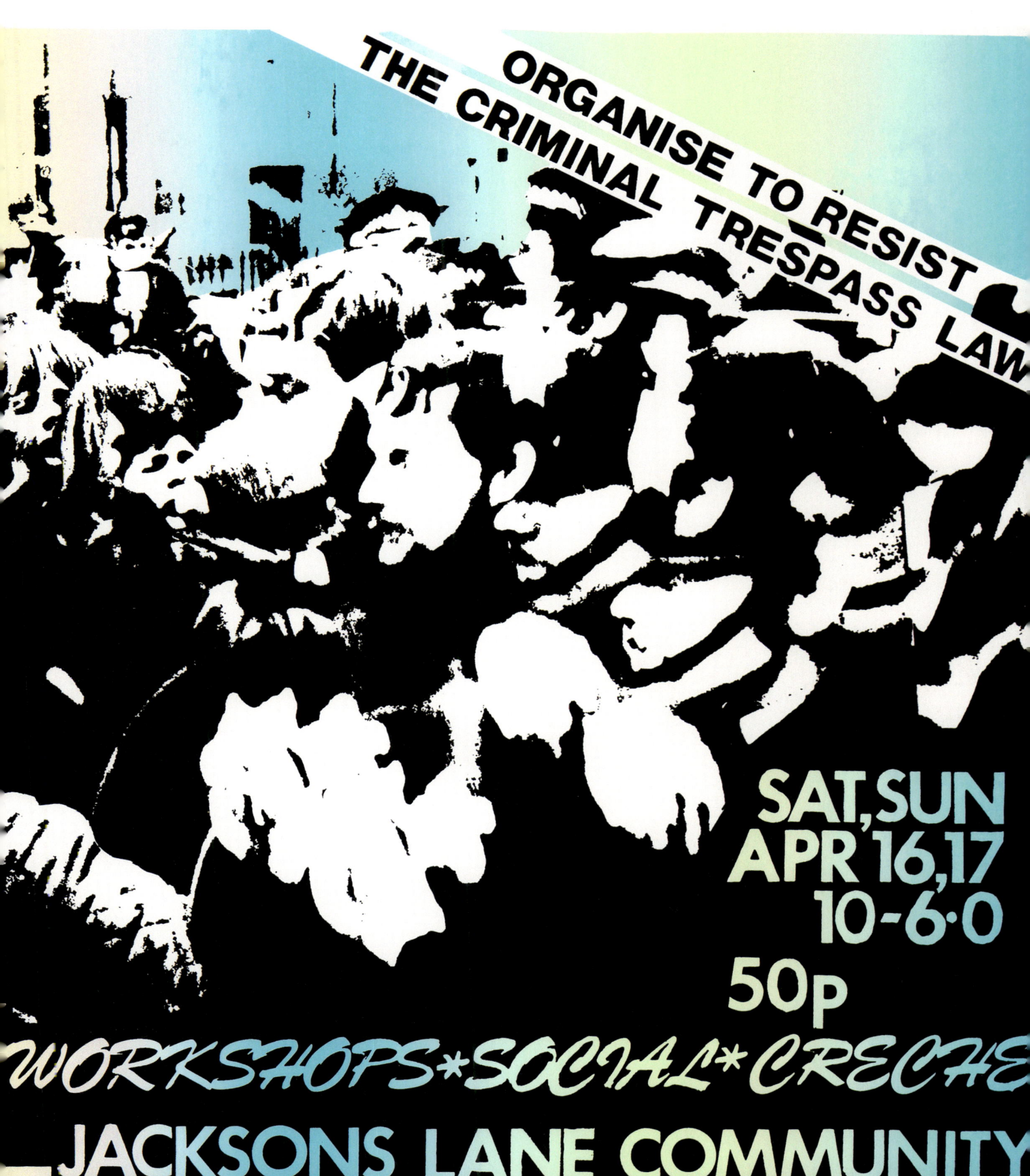

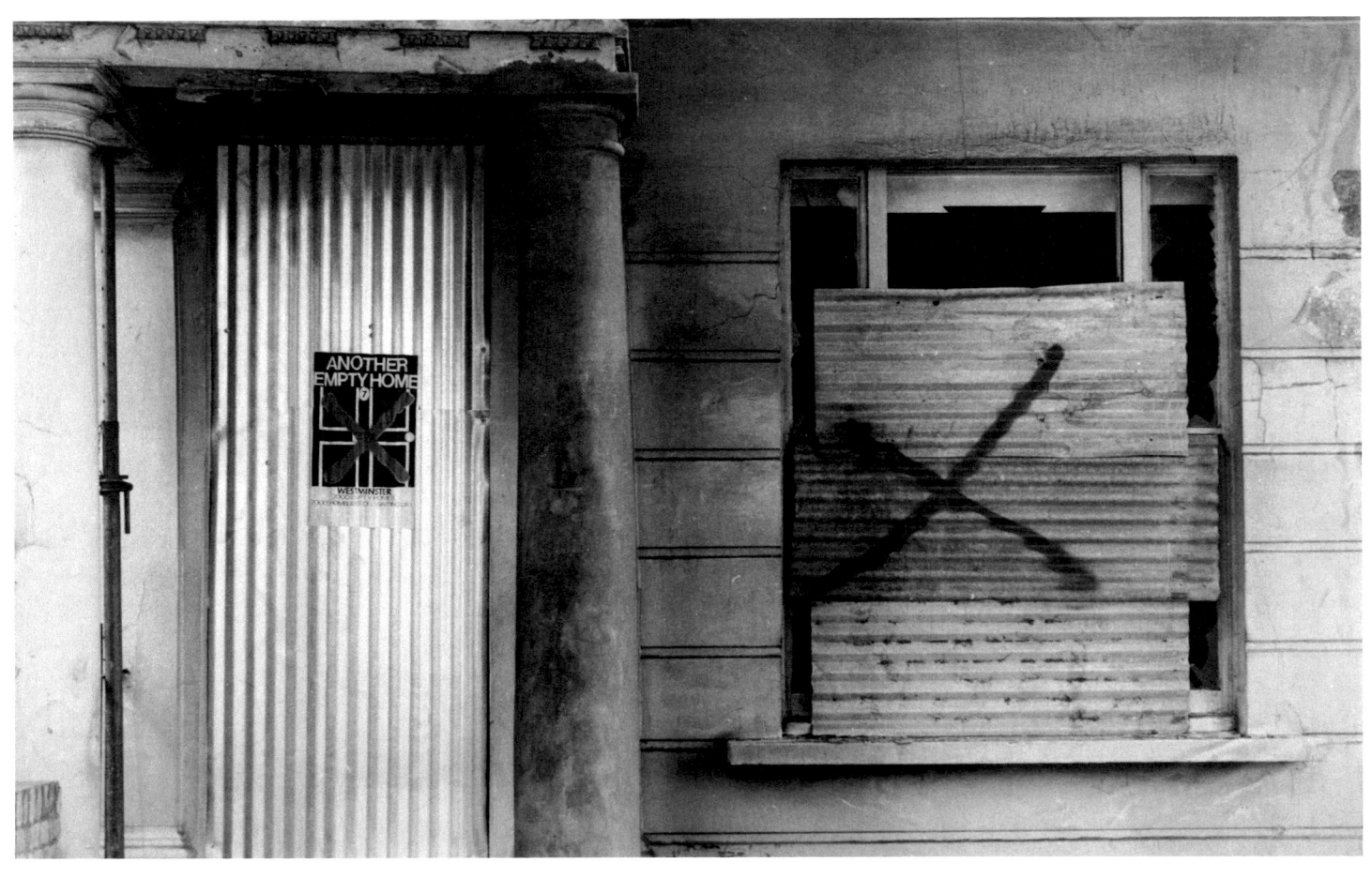

Next pages

ANOTHER EMPTY HOME,
1976, Pippa Smith

STILL EMPTY, 1976, Pippa Smith

Started locally in Paddington and the district of Westminster, this practice of marking empty houses with red crosses became a national campaign.

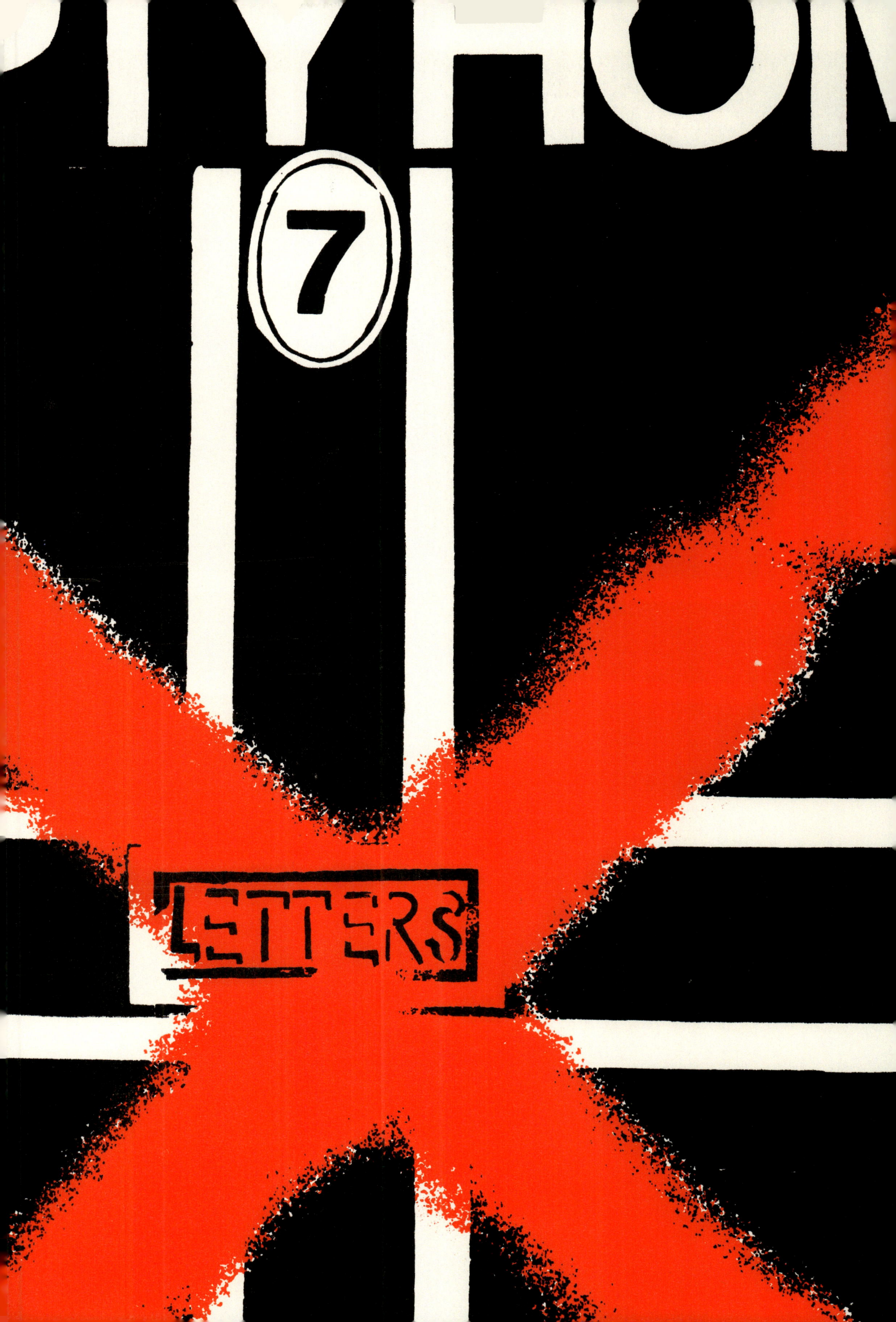

STILL EMPTY!

STILL EMPTY!
STILL EMPTY!
STILL EMPTY!
STILL EMPTY!
STILL EMPTY!
STILL EMPTY!

FRESTON ROAD, 1977, Anonymous

In 1977, when the GLC threatened to evict them, squatters living in the Freston Road area held a referendum, and declared the area as an independent country: The Free and Independent Republic of Frestonia. This lasted well into the next decade, when many Frestonians set up a housing co-operative.

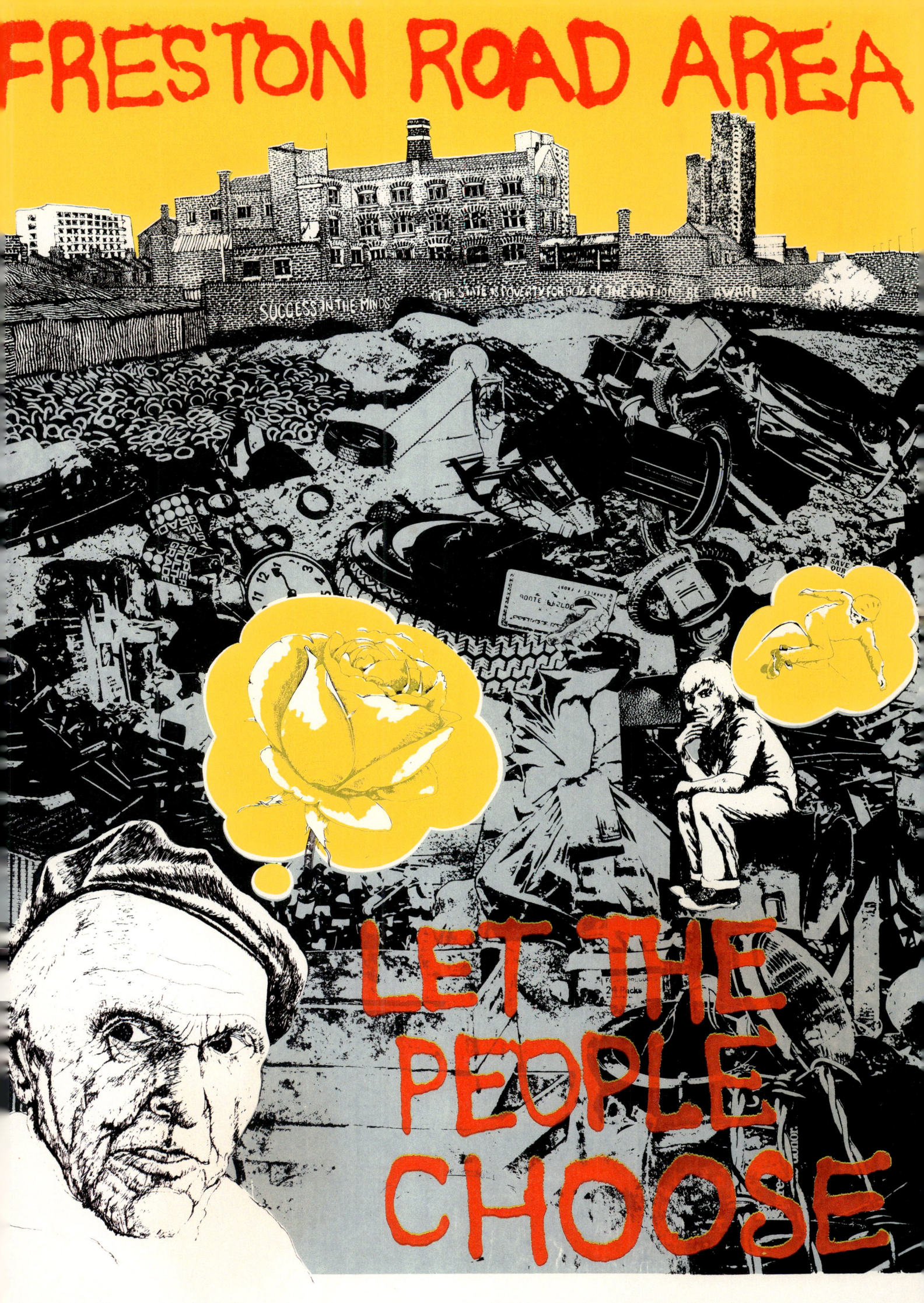

ADVISORY SERVICE FOR SQUATTERS,
1979, John Phillips

This provided legal advice to squatters and homeless people, and offered an estate agent services for newly acquirable properties.

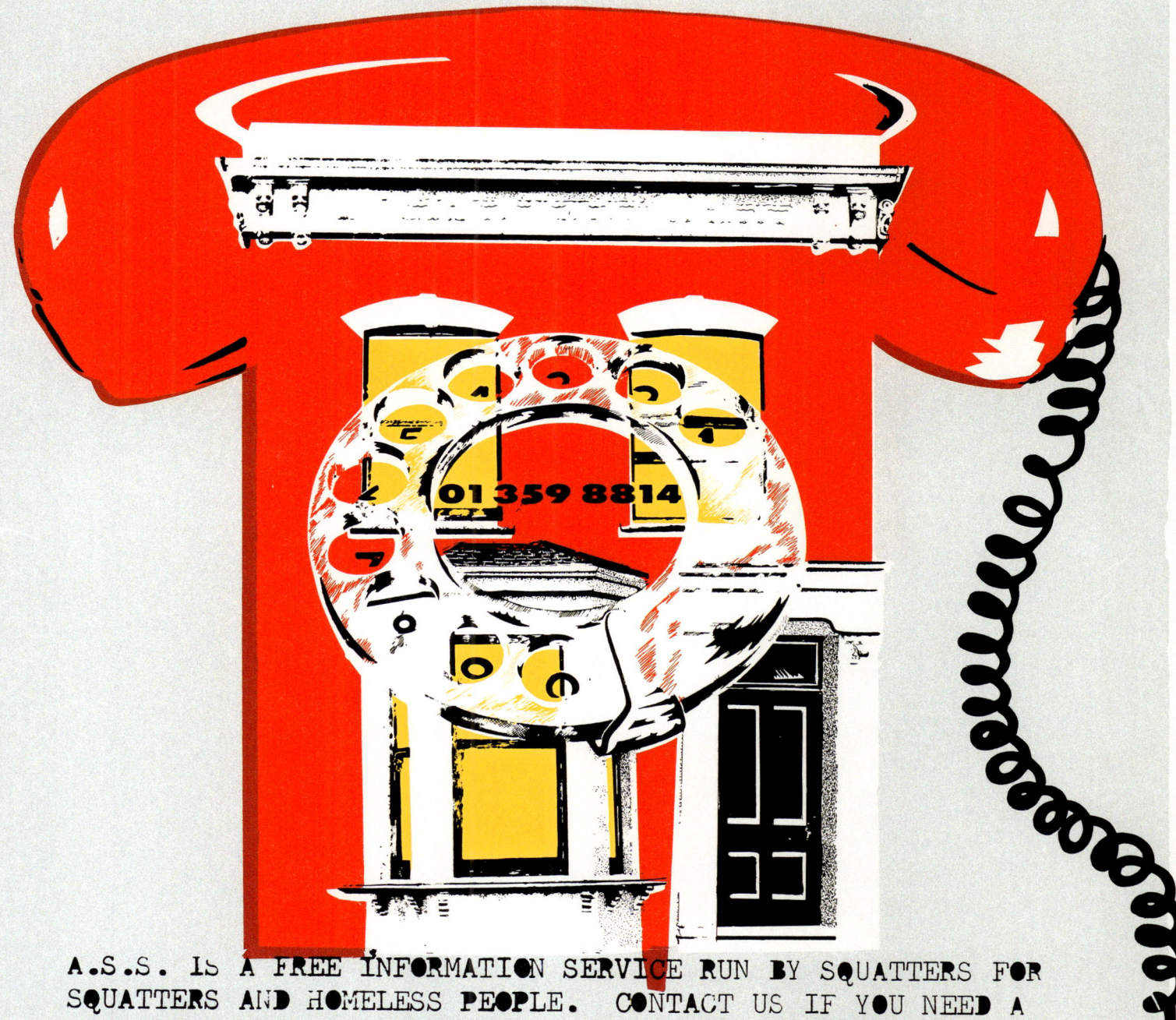

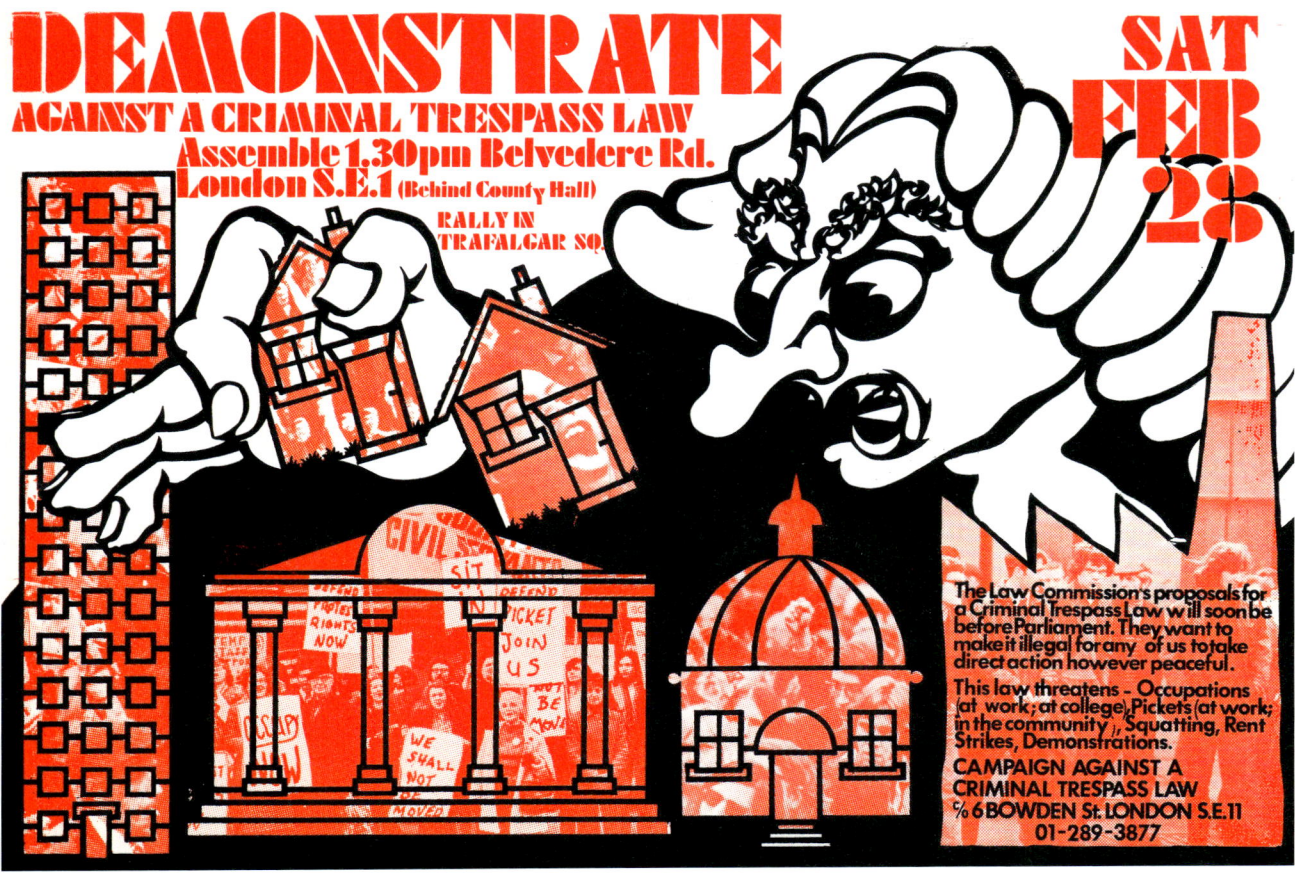

Above
DEMONSTRATE AGAINST
A CRIMINAL TRESPASS LAW,
1976, John Phillips

Opposite
JOIN THE CAMPAIGN AGAINST
A CRIMINAL TRESPASS LAW,
1976, John Phillips

Next pages
BENEFIT BOP, 1978, John Phillips

The national Campaign Against a Criminal Trespass Law opposed the introduction of legislation making squatting or occupations a criminal, as opposed to a civil, offence. This meant that anyone squatting an empty property would be breaking the law and could be imprisoned.

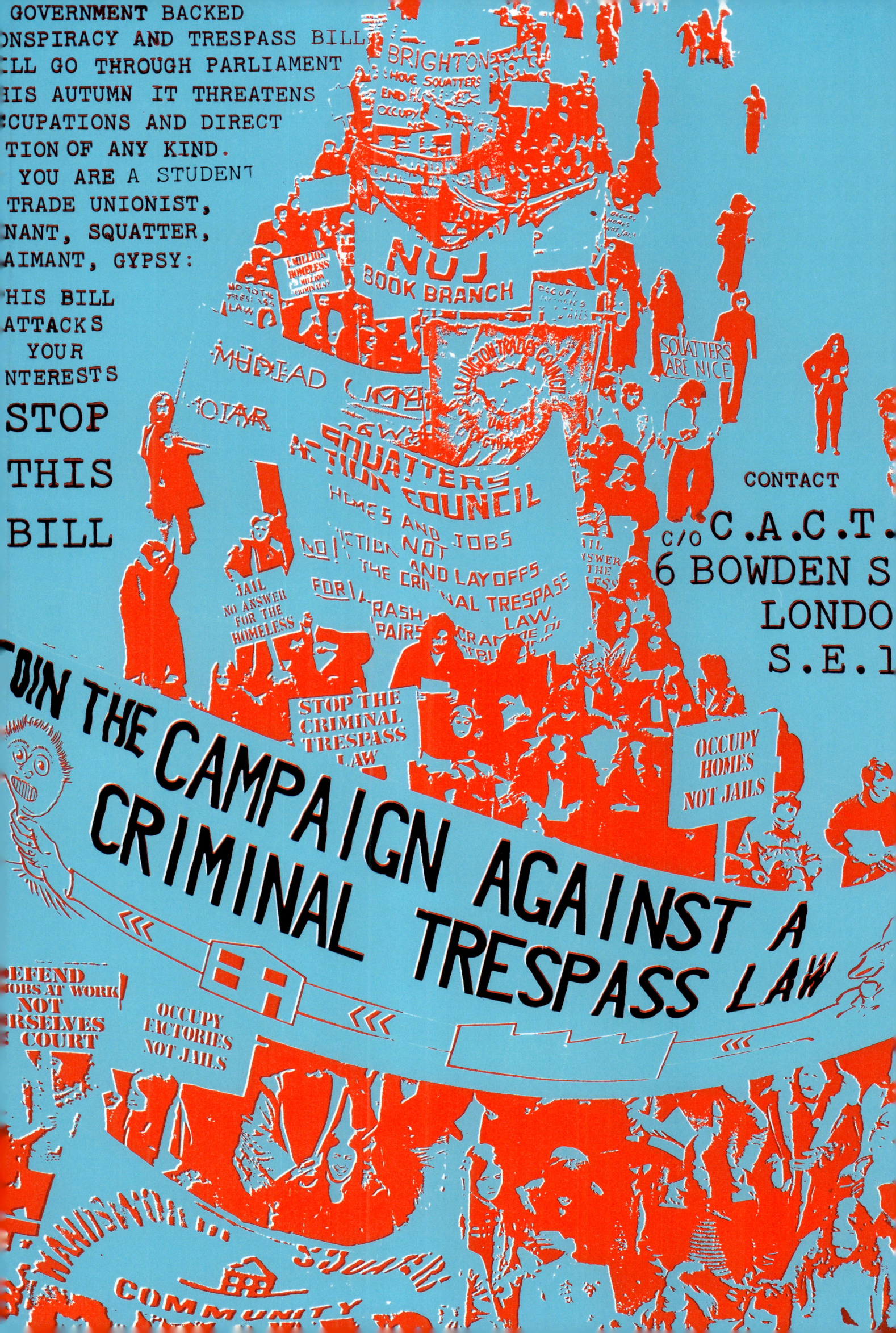

campaign against a criminal trespass law

c/o 35 Wellington St., London WC2 01-289 3877

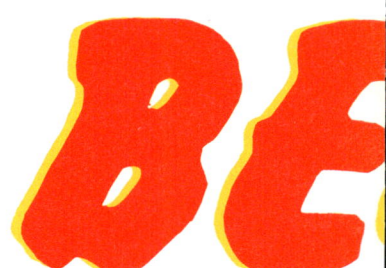

Behind the growing exploitation of the 'law and order' theme by all the main political parties, and the recent calls for increased police powers, lies a process in which the machinery of law (Parliament, police and the courts) is increasingly being used to restrict the ability of our movement to picket, to strike, to demonstrate or to occupy in defence of its interests.

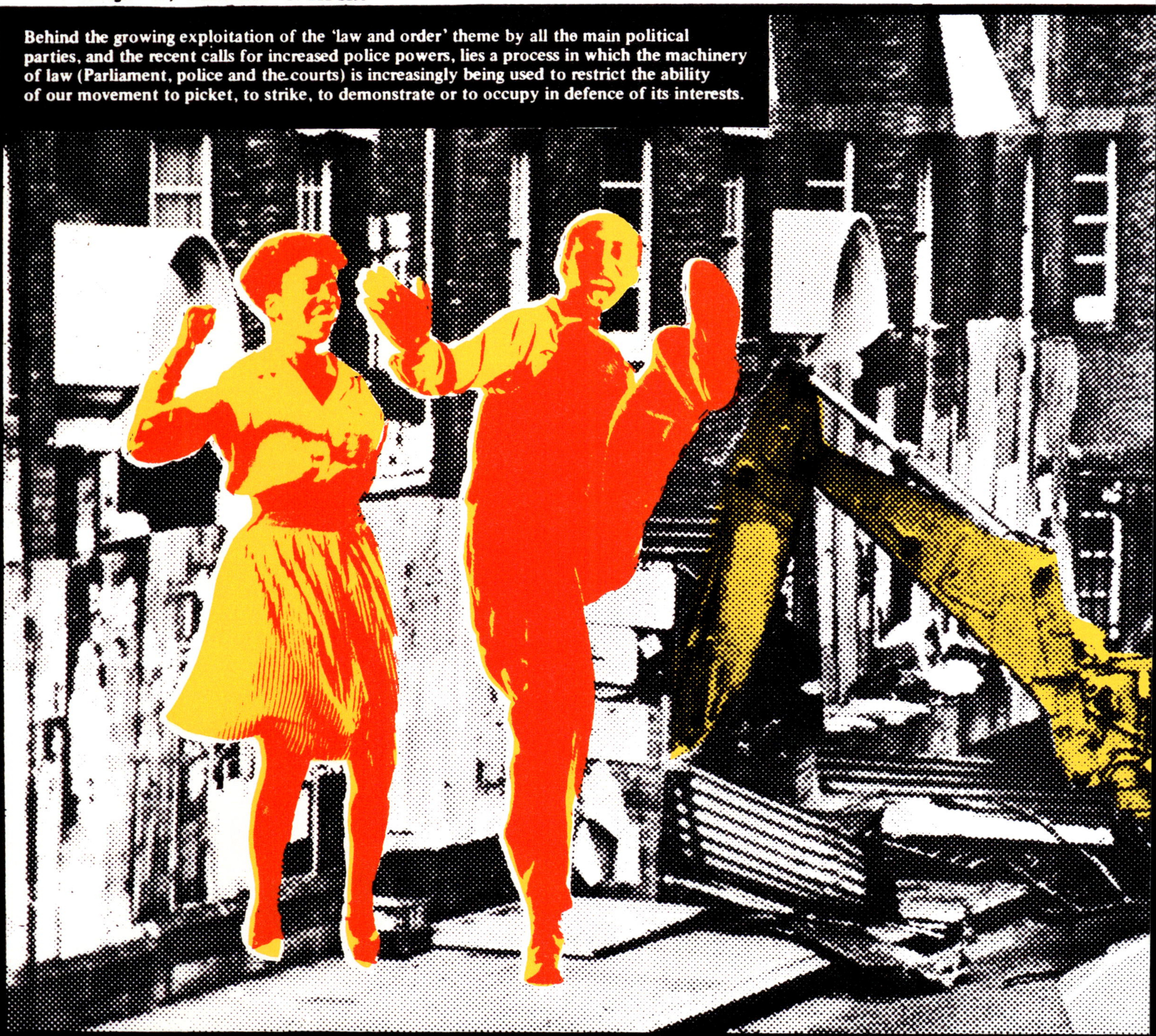

NATIONAL CONFERENCE
'Occupations, Criminal Trespass and the use of the Law'

SATURDAY NOVEMBER 11th 1978
CONWAY HALL, RED LION SQUARE, LONDON WC1

10.00am - 6.30pm Conference fee: £2.00 (claimants, OAPs etc. : £1.00)

THE RESISTE DISCO - FOO

SATURDAY
CONWAY HALL, R
Neares

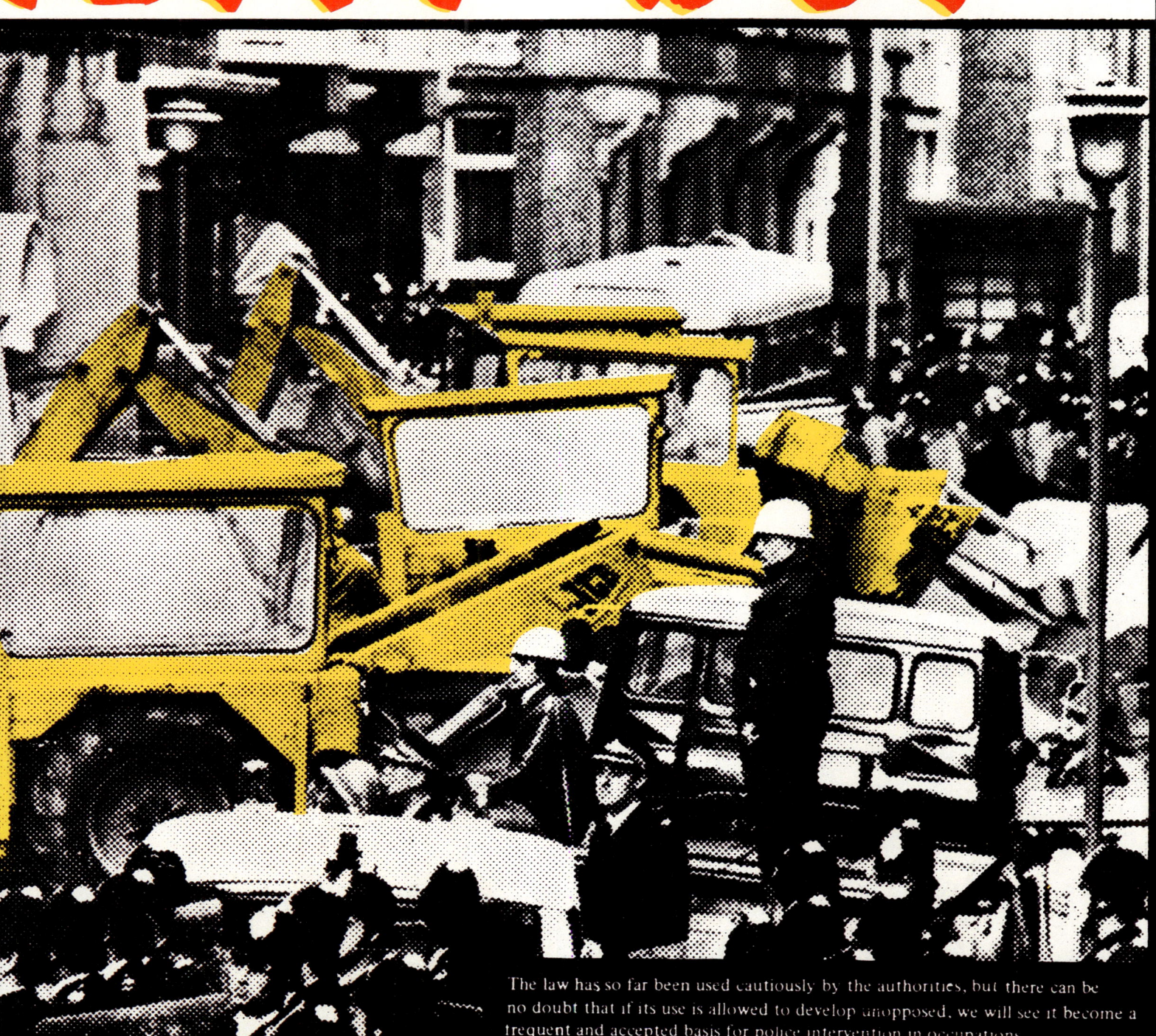

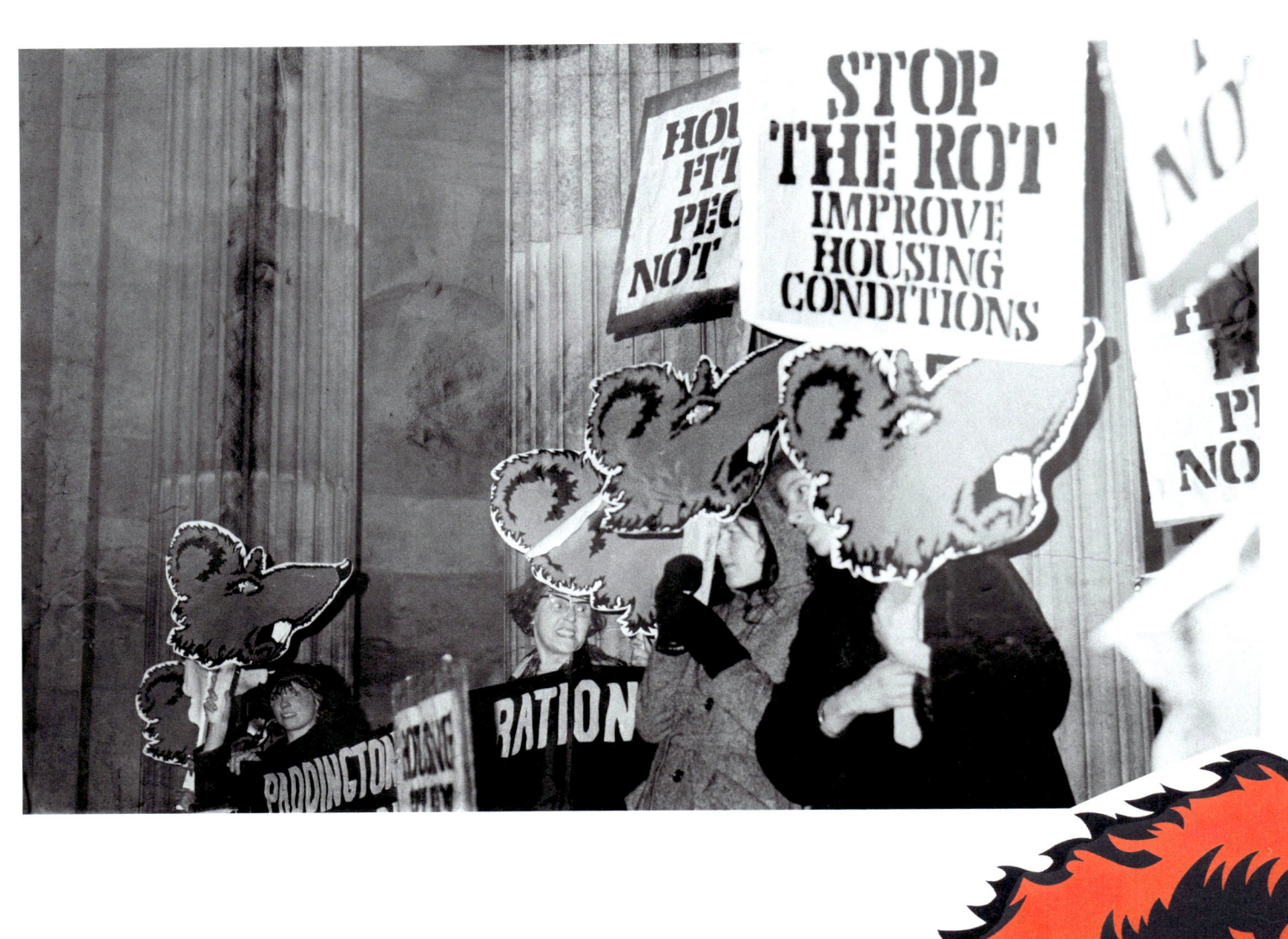

RAT MASK, 1975, John Phillips

With high concentrations of poorly maintained multi-occupancy properties in the local private rented sector, local activists campaigned for local council intervention under the slogan 'Housing Fit for People not Rats'. The rat heads we made were worn by demonstrators outside Westminster Council House on 1 December, 1975. Photo by John Phillips.

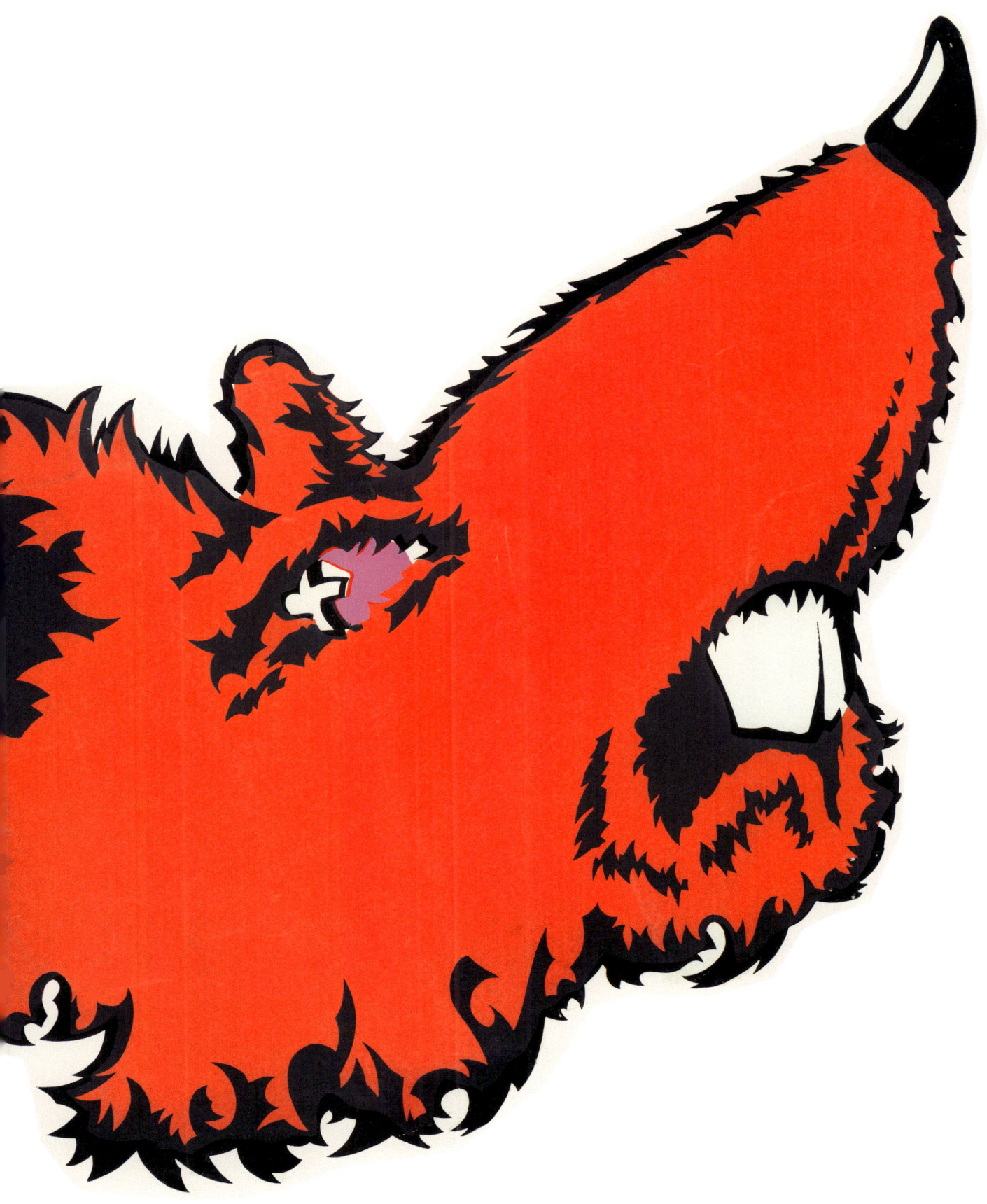

Opposite
MONEY TALKS, 1987, John Phillips

These posters (opposite and on the following pages) were created for a successful council tenants campaign, which began in 1986 when Westminster City Council proposed the sale of 1,000 social housing units to the private sector. It ended six years later when the tenants-controlled Walterton and Elgin Housing Association, having fought off an array of developers, won the right to take possession of their whole estate, supported by a bursary of £16 million to refurbish the properties. The organisation became a model of tenant-controlled social housing.

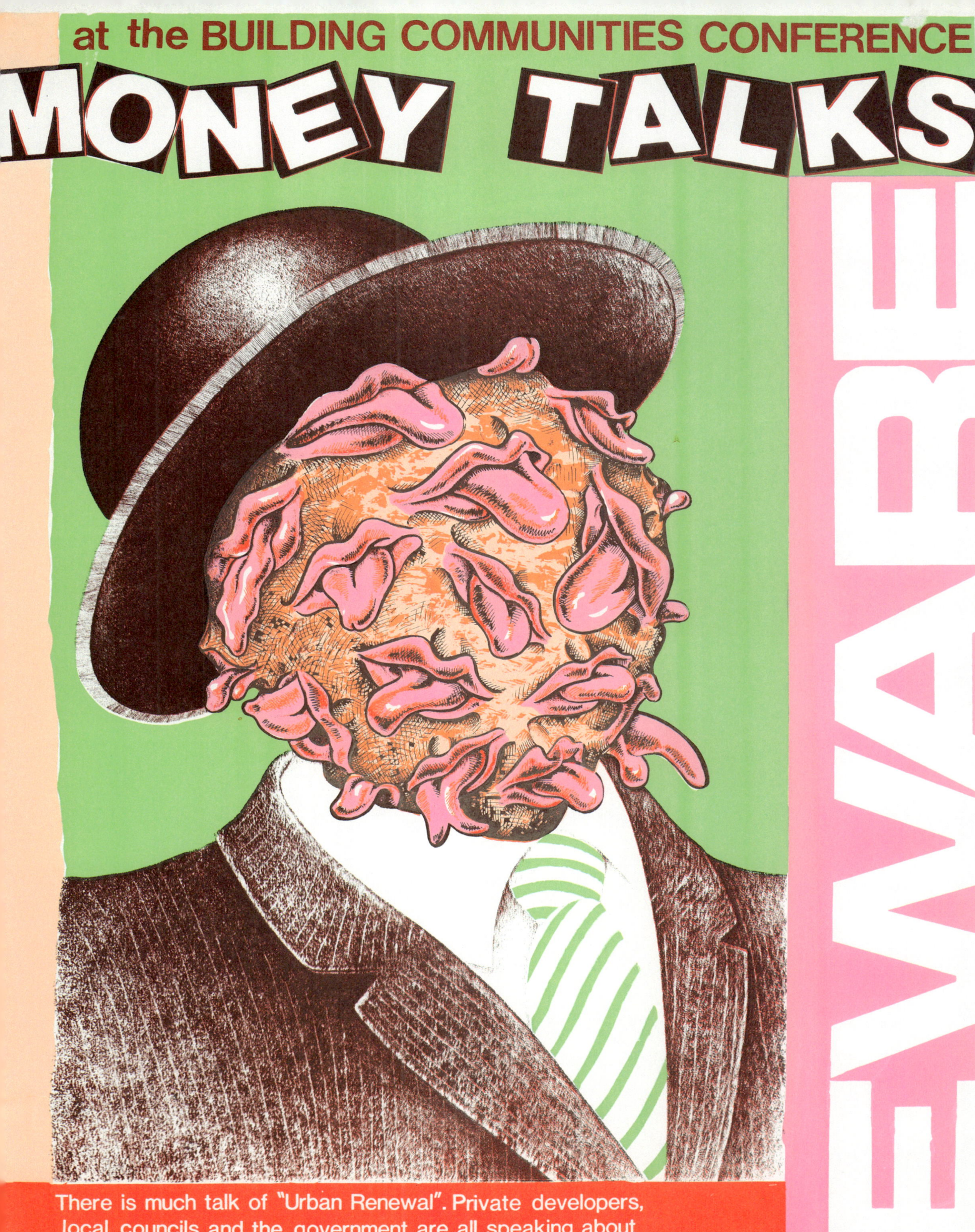

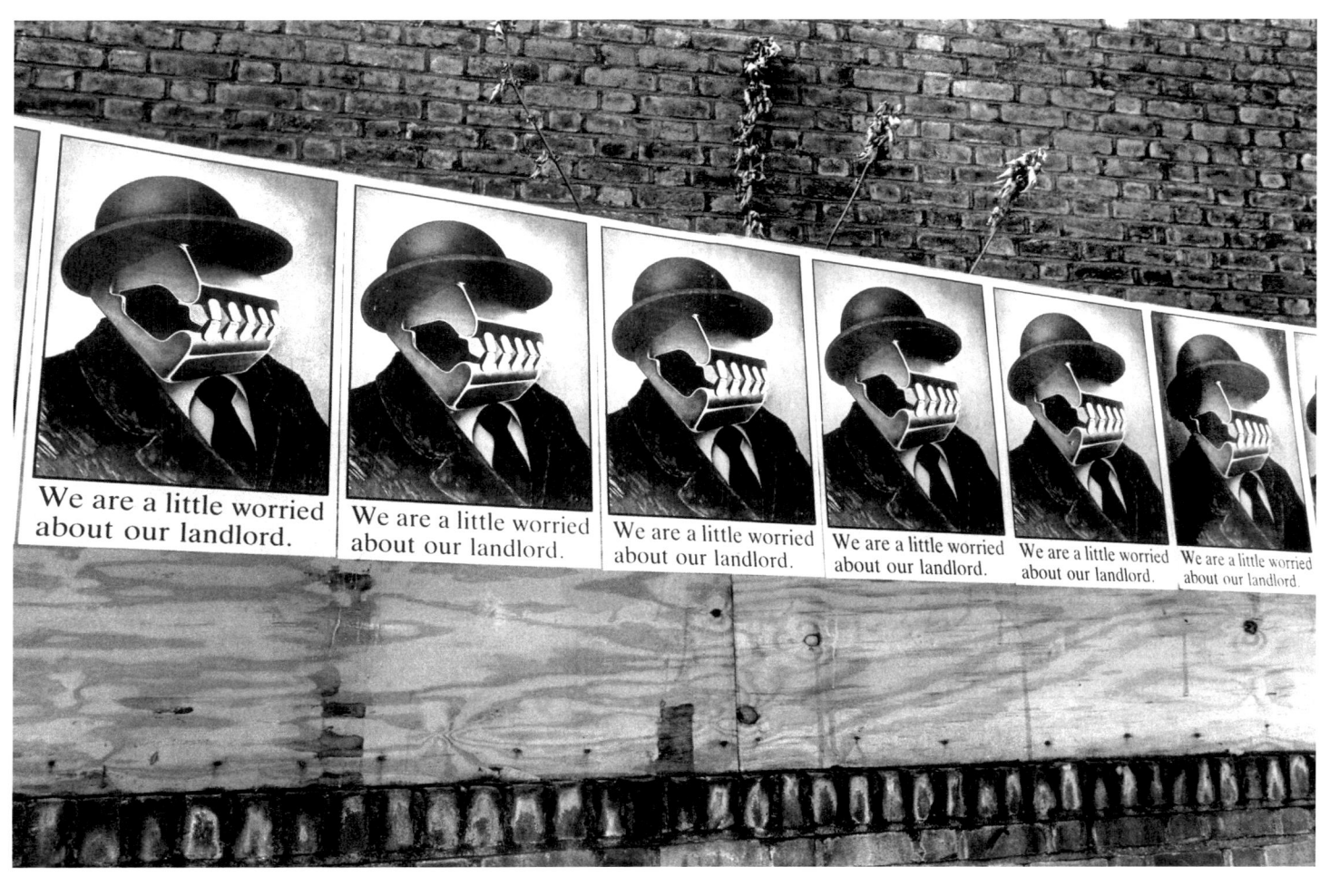

Above
Walterton and Elgin Action Group posters on the Walterton Estate.
Photo by Philip Wolmuth.

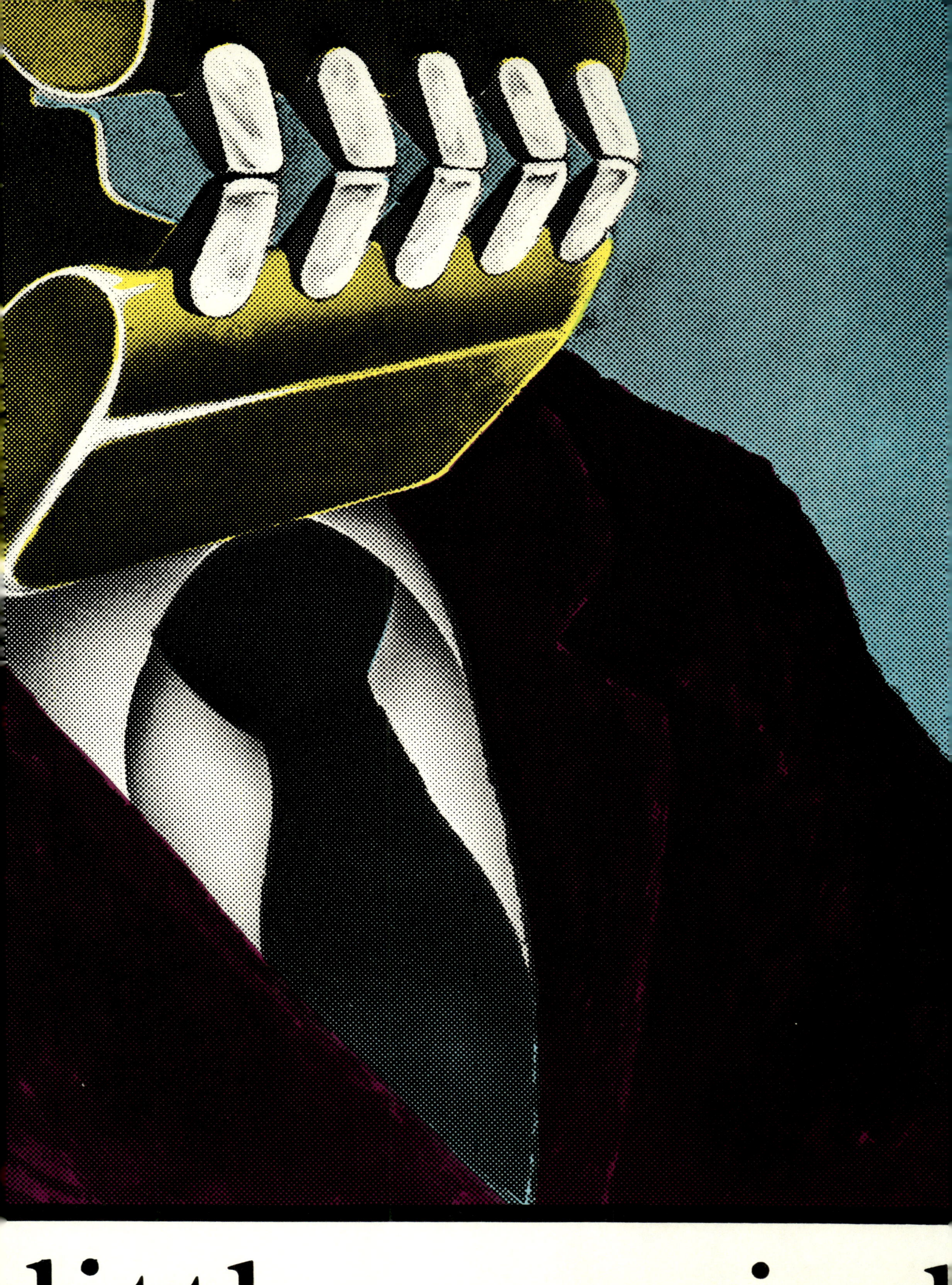

Opposite
LANDLORD, 1986, John Phillips

Next pages
WHY ARE THESE MEN SMILING?,
1987, John Phillips

WE WILL STOP WESTMINSTER
COUNCIL, 1988, John Phillips

ON AVERAGE HOUSING CONDITIONS
IN WESTMINSTER ARE THE BEST
IN THE COUNTRY, 1988, John Phillips

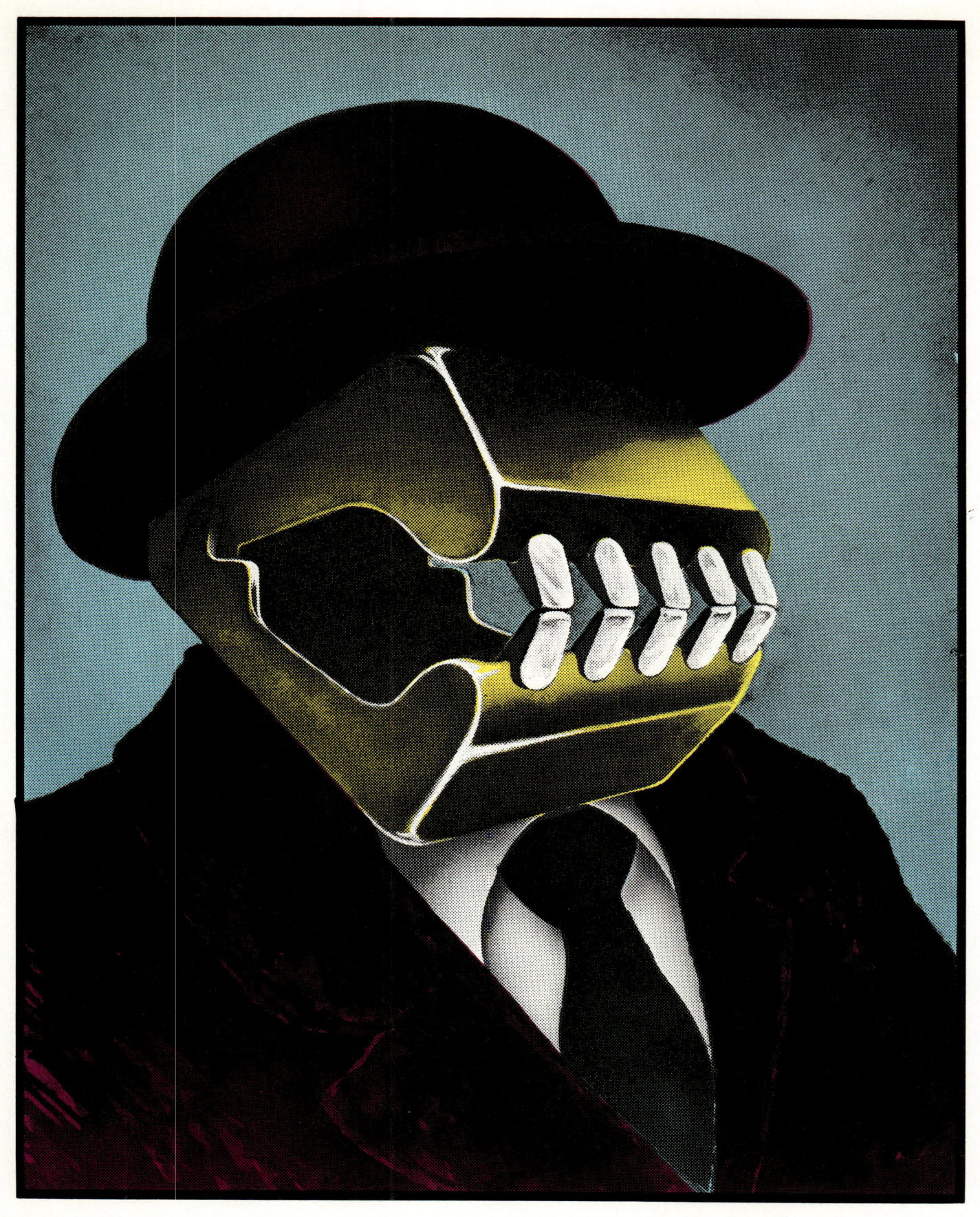

We are a little worried about our landlord.

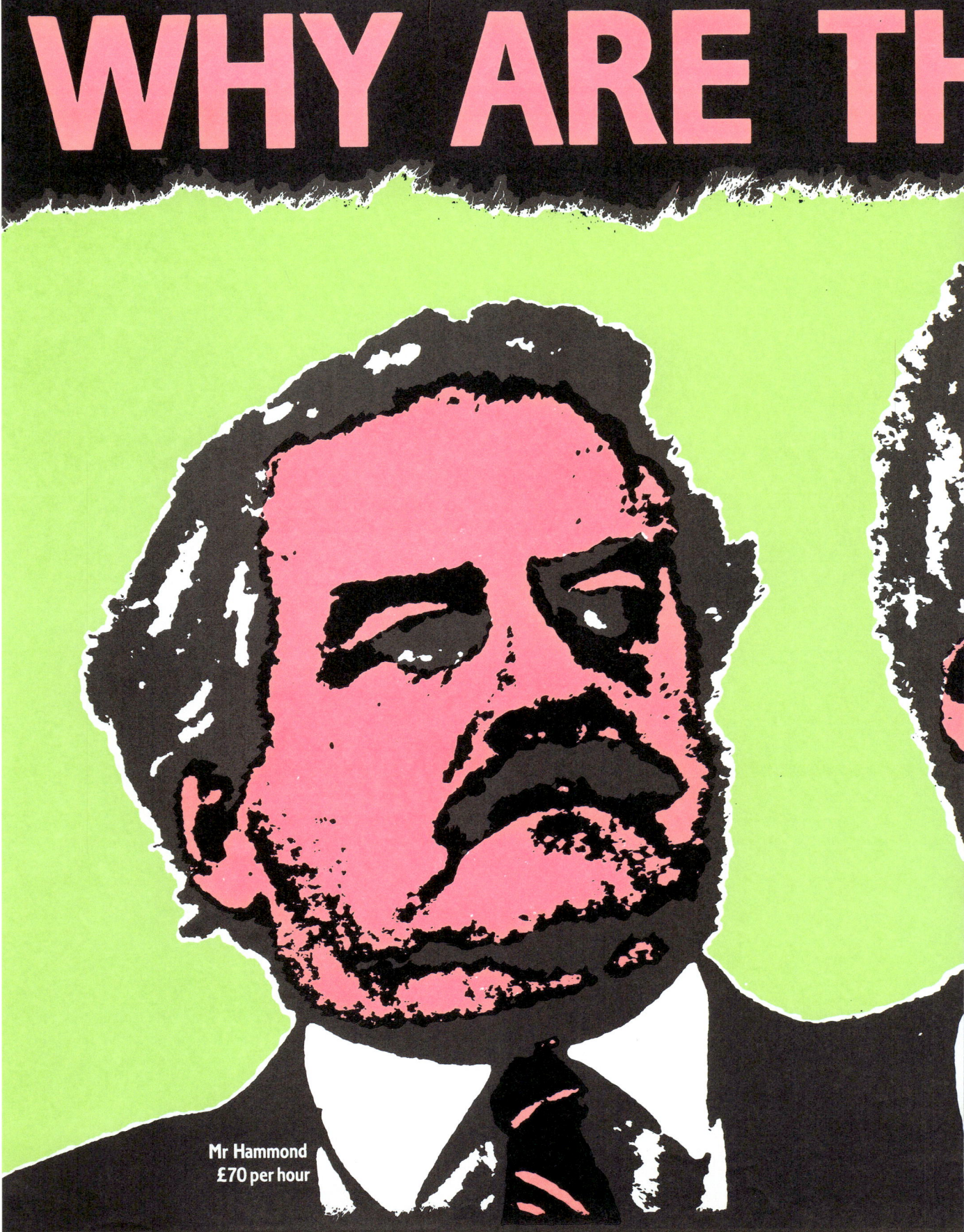

WHY ARE TH

Mr Hammond
£70 per hour

Westminster City Council is trying to sell homes on the Walterto
and Elgin Estates to private developers. Because it has cut bac
on so many staff in the Housing Department it has decided to hir
private consultants to advise on and manage deals with developer

The hourly rate which the Council is paying for workers in two o
these companies, Project Management International (P.M.I.), an
Oppenheimers (solicitors), is printed here. P.M.I. expect t
receive £1 million for five years work on the scheme. Neithe
P.M.I. nor Oppenheimers will be involved in carrying out an
repairs. They will only be selling homes.

If you would like further infor
can ring any of these gentlemen

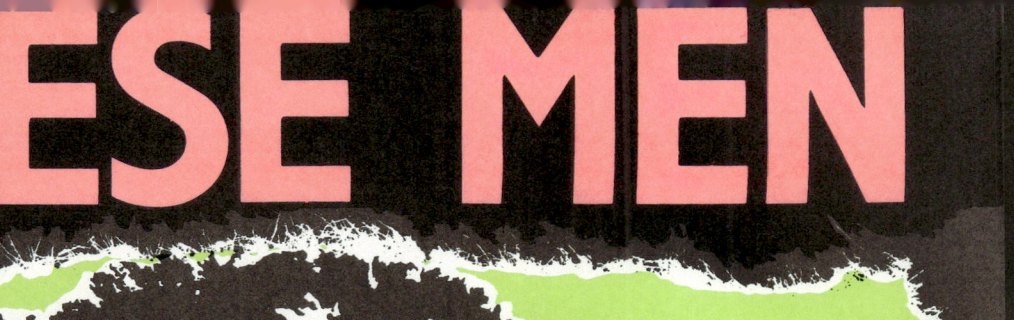

ESE MEN ... SMILING?

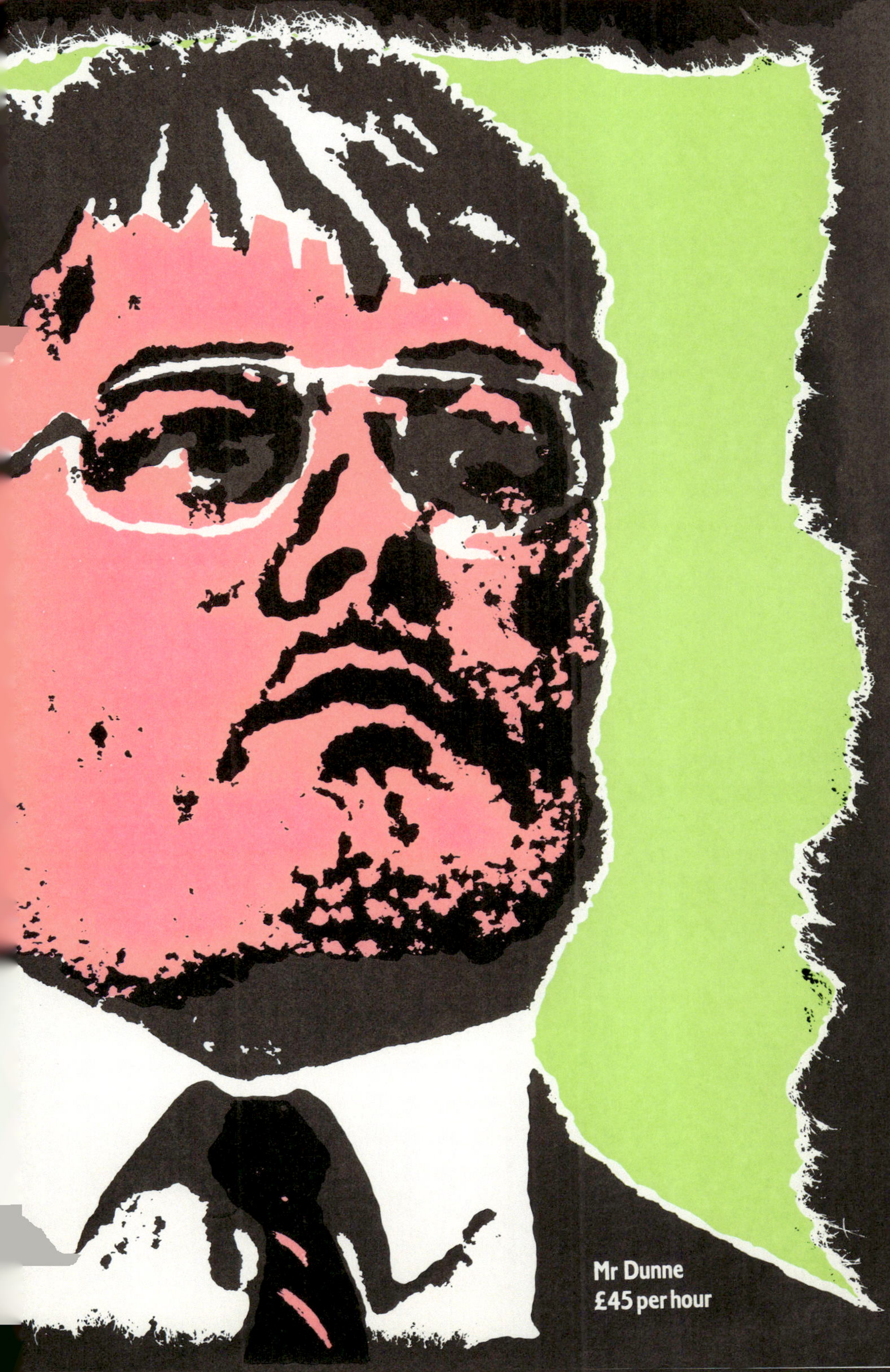

Mr Dunne
£45 per hour

```
Project Management International Tel. 897 1121
Michael Dunne
     Project Manager  ............  £45.per hour.
F.A. Hammond
     Senior Partner   ............  £70.per hour.

Oppenheimers (Solicitors)          Tel.628 9611
Martin King
     Legal Assistant  .......  £90/125.per hour.
Lord Nathan
     Senior Partner   ...........  £140.per hour.
```

ion about this, you
the above numbers.

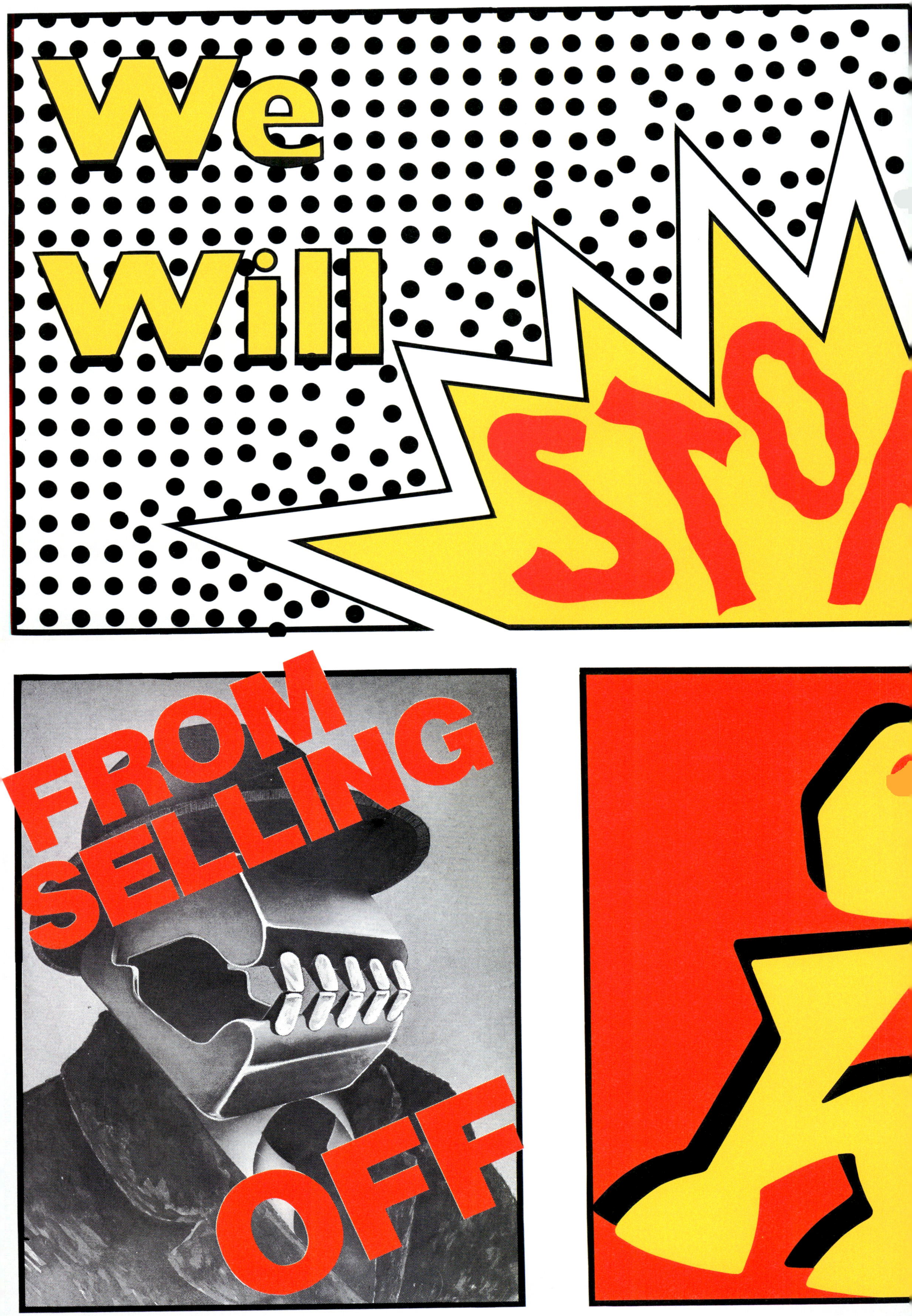

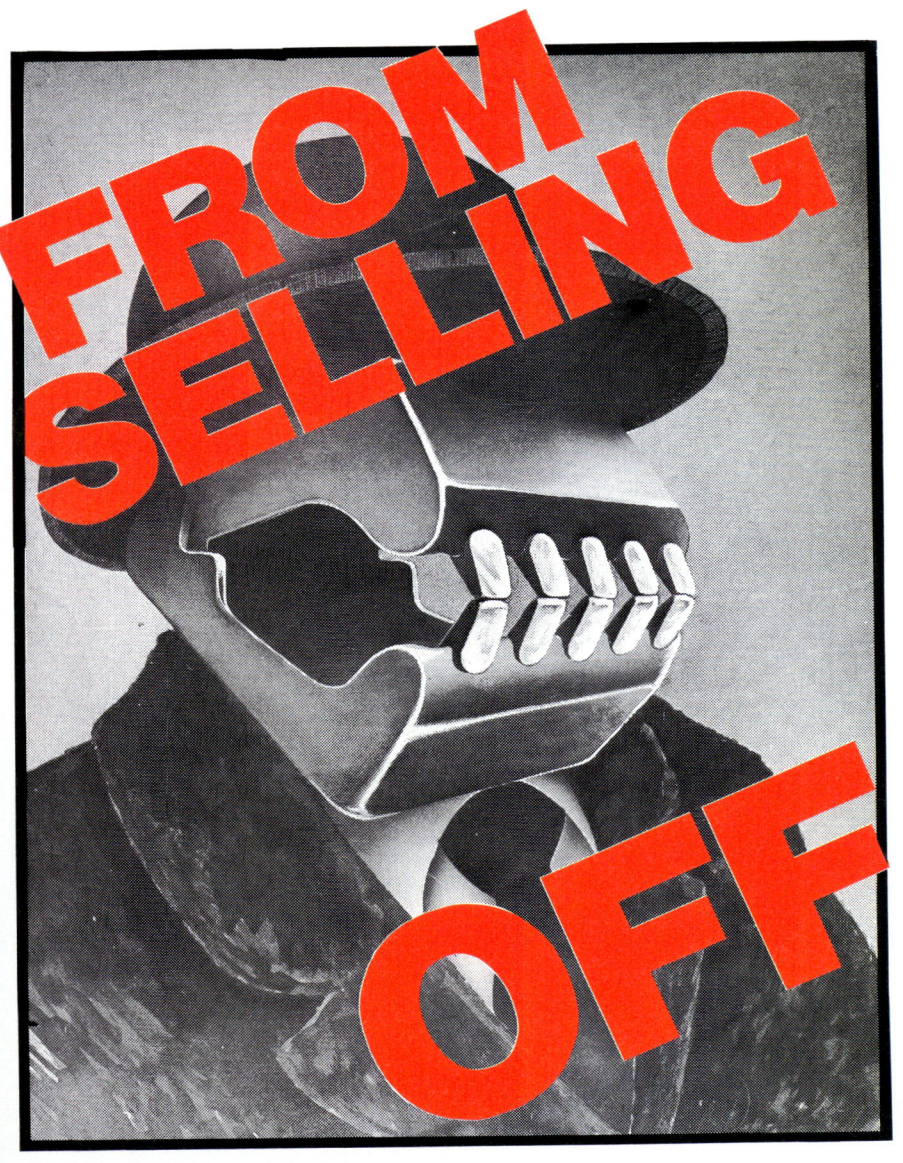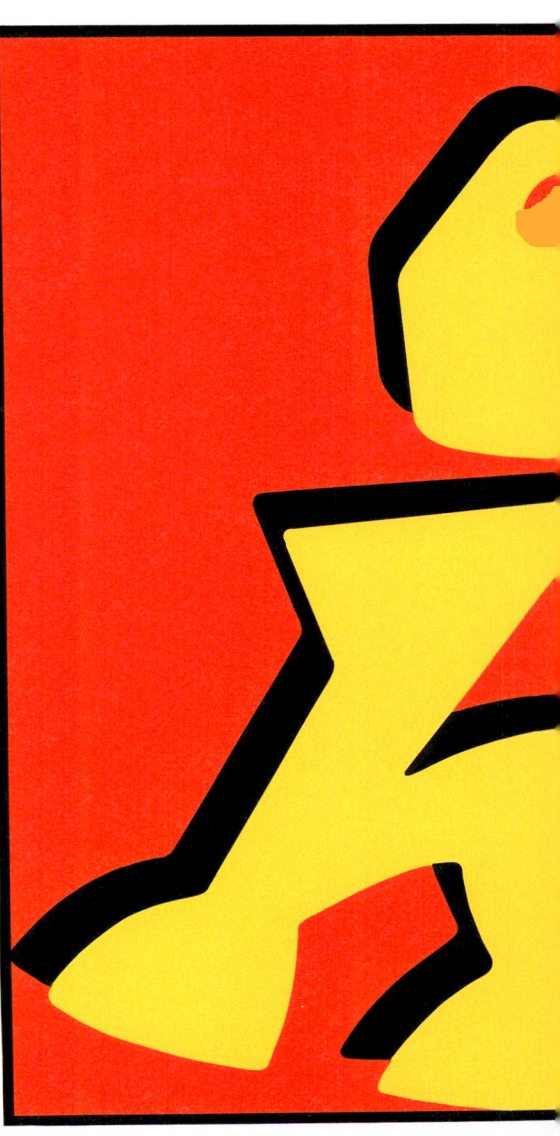

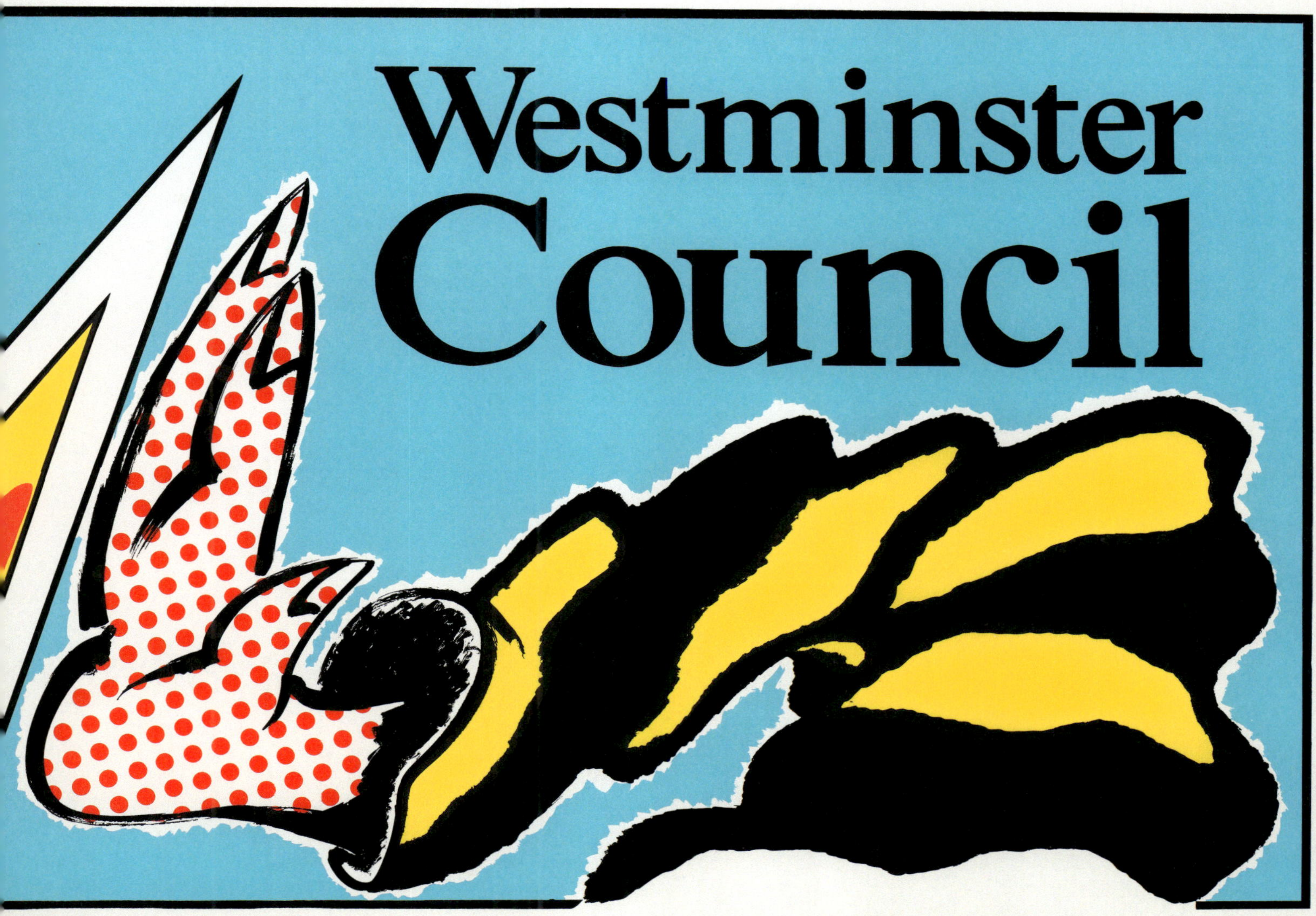

Westminster Council

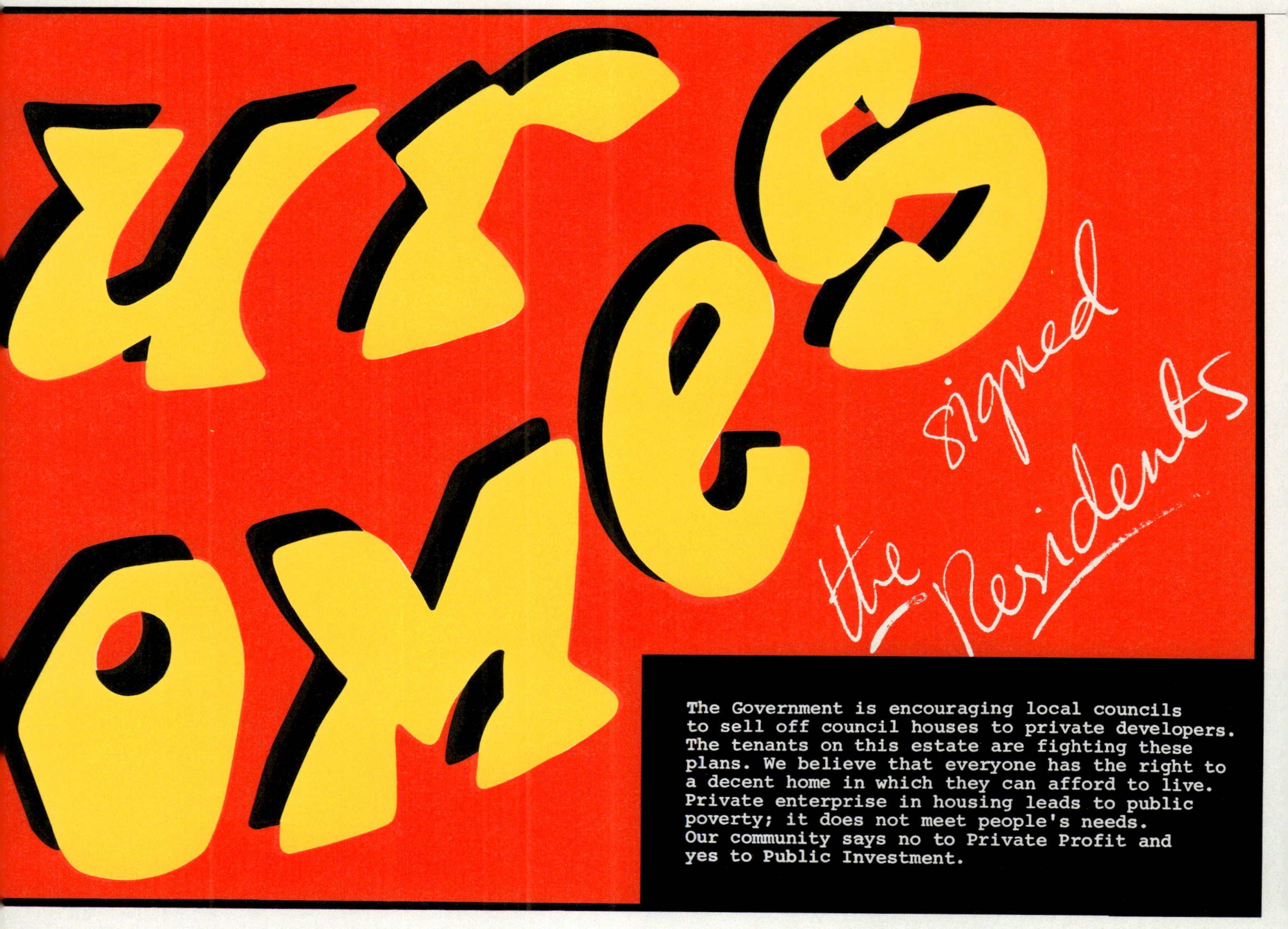

signed the Residents

The Government is encouraging local councils to sell off council houses to private developers. The tenants on this estate are fighting these plans. We believe that everyone has the right to a decent home in which they can afford to live. Private enterprise in housing leads to public poverty; it does not meet people's needs. Our community says no to Private Profit and yes to Public Investment.

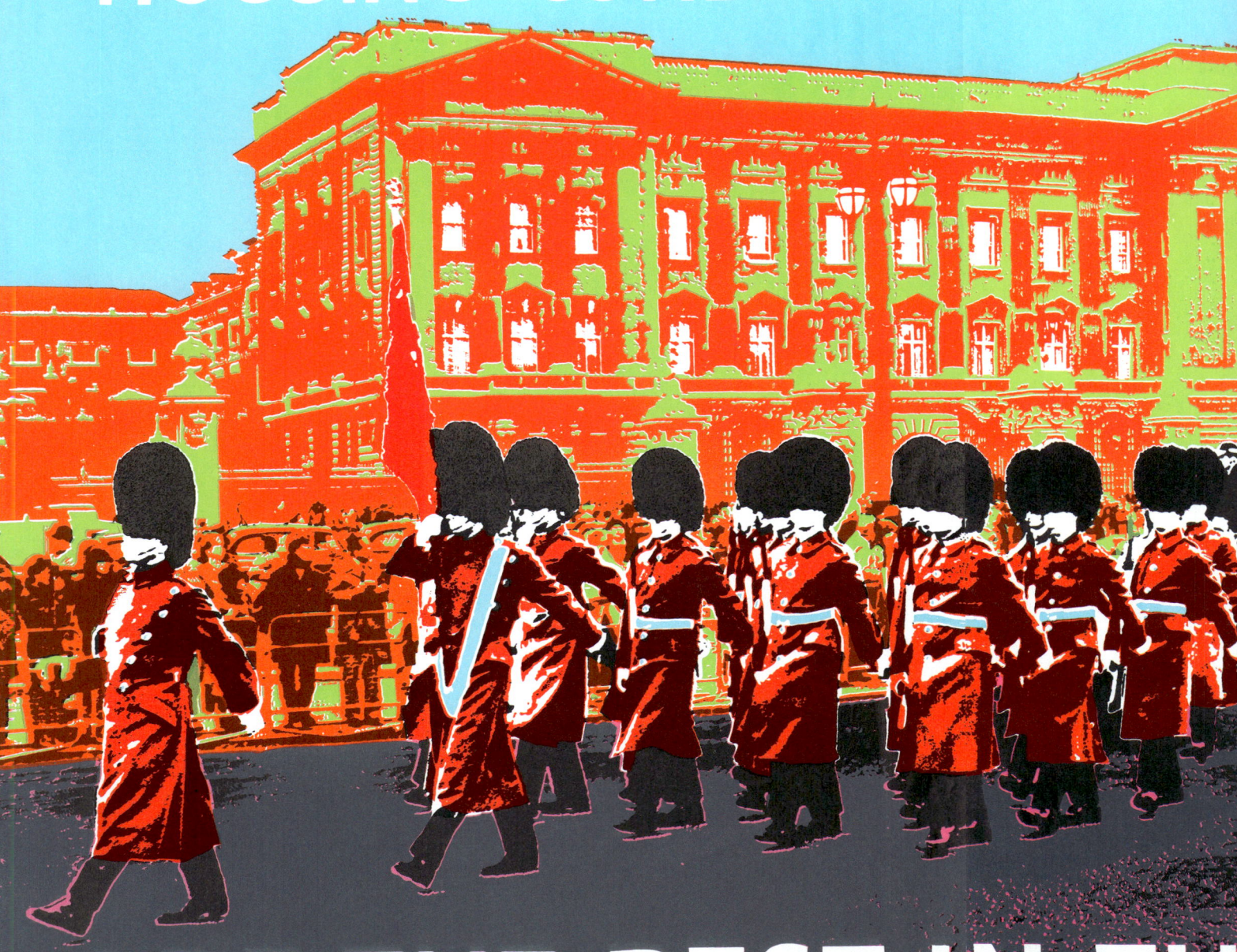

ON AVERAGE
HOUSING CONDITIONS IN W
ARE THE BEST IN TH

The City of Westminster is the richest borough in the country. The Windsors live here. One of their 466 properties in the borough is pictured above. Last year (85/86), the Crown paid £67 million to the City Council in rates.
The Government is housed here. Last year it paid the Council £12½ million in rates.
Westminster is the centre of commerce. Last year commercial ratepayers paid the Council £344 million.
Yet the borough's wealth is not confined to a handful of individuals and institutions. Many rich people live here. 3000 even have their second homes here.
Westminster has the highest rateable value in the country.

Many poor people live here, some in the worst housing conditions to be found in the country.

12,000 households live in one room, 2000 homes have no bath, and 6000 households are not self-contained and are forced to share toilet facilities. 42% of council housing stock is in need of renovation. The Council pays for over 500 families to live in overcrowded bed and breakfast hostels.
Many have no homes at all. In the streets of the city today more people sleep rough than did in the days of Dickens.

A city possessing such an abundance of wealth could remedy these appalling conditions, but the Council is not prepared to do so.

Westminster City Co
embarked on a progr
off its homes to de
property speculator
This worsens condit
and the city's poor
greater wealth for

There is an alterna
It is possible for
minster to live in

THERE ARE 9341 HOUS
COUNCIL'S WAITING L

THERE ARE 9000 EMPT
WHICH HAVE STOOD EM

The Council owns ov
these empty propert
are in the hands of
lords and housing a

ESTMINSTER

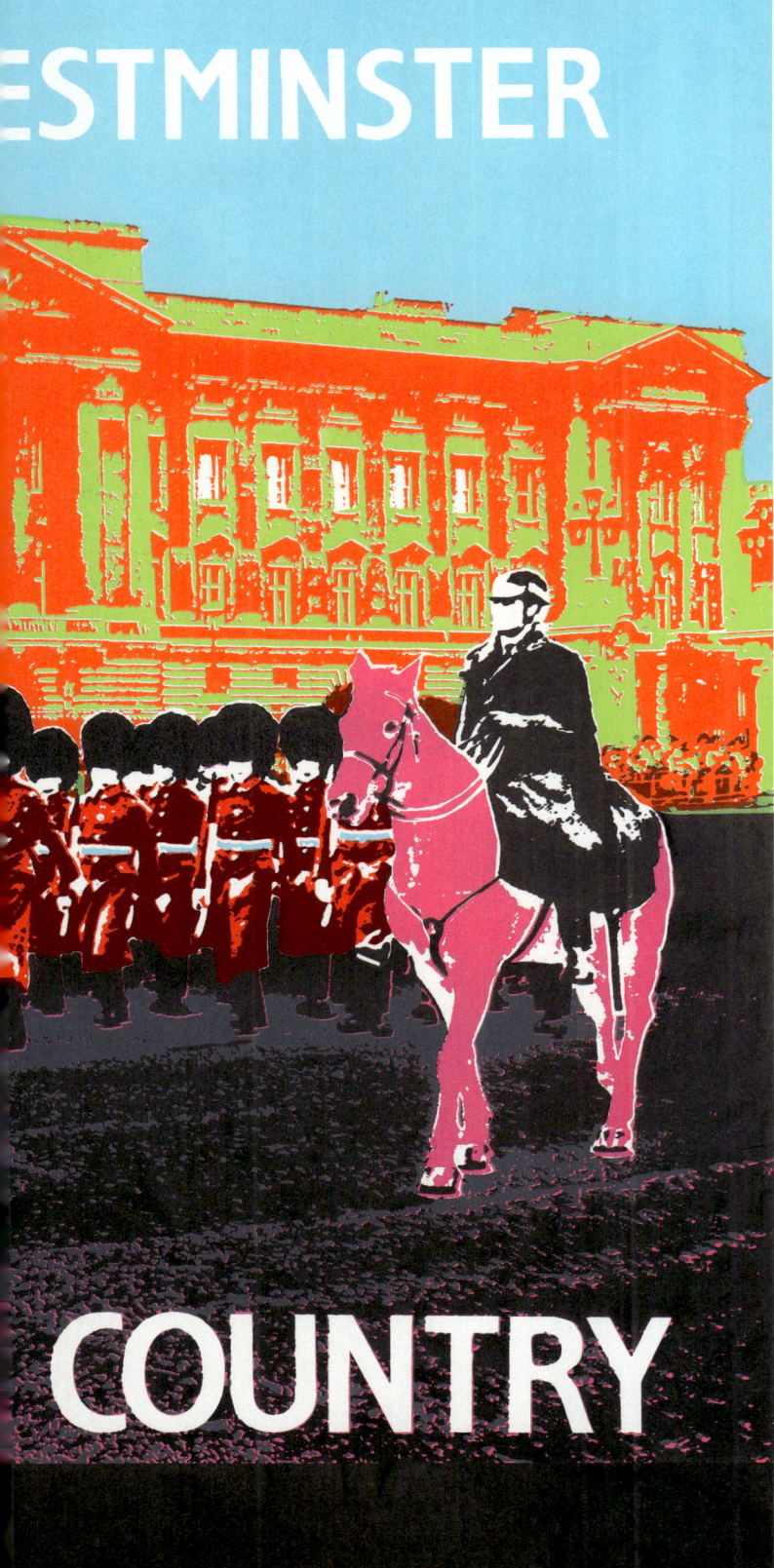

COUNTRY

s	According to the Government's own
selling	figures, the average cost in central
and	London of building a new family home
	is £7000 per year. The cost of buying
tenants	existing stock is £5500 per year.
ovides	The average cost of keeping a family
's rich.	in bed and breakfast accommodation is
	£10,950 per year.
ution.	The annual cost to the Council of
in West-	providing one new family home is half
ousing.	the cost of keeping the same family
	in bed and breakfast.
N THE	If the Council spent on a public
	housing programme the £67 million
	which it receives each year in rates
MANY OF	from the Crown, it could house every-
YEARS.	one on the waiting list within the
	next five years.
of	If the Council also spent the £41
rest	million which it has received from the
land-	sale of council properties it could
ons.	solve the housing crisis even sooner.

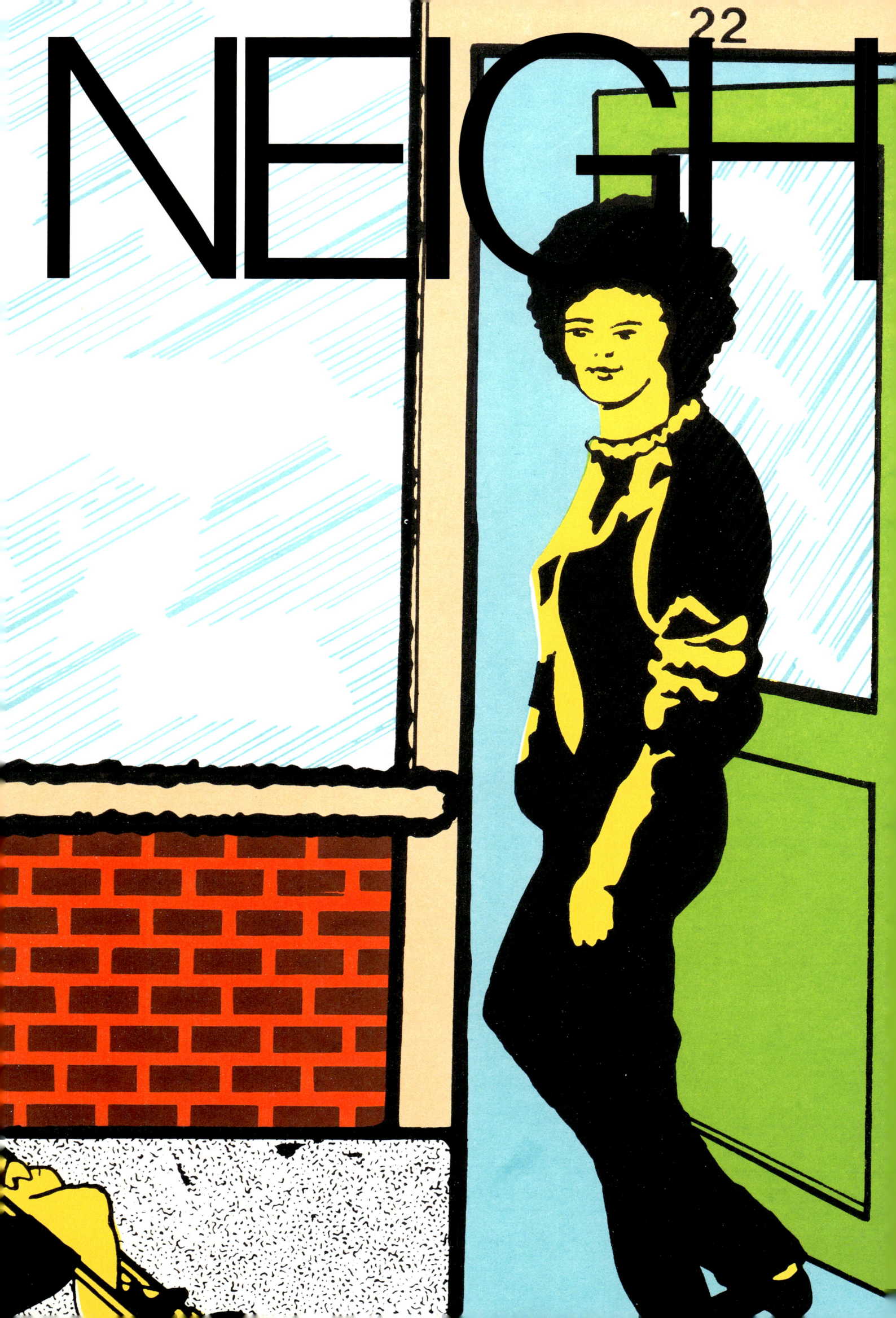

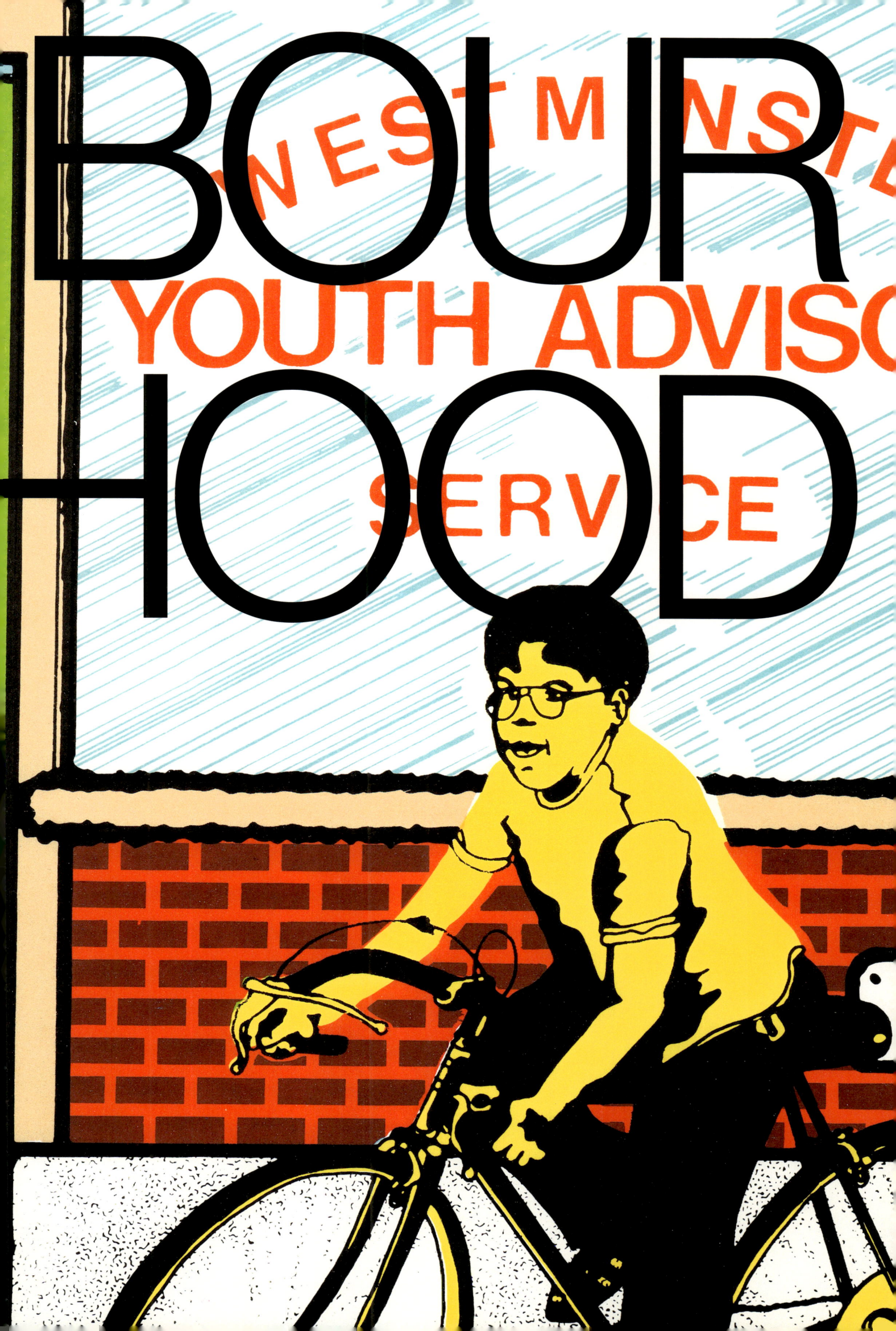

Opposite
PADDINGTON PRINTSHOP OPENS
MAY 1ST, 1975, John Phillips

In 1974, a disused 17,000 square foot taxi-meter factory, situated in Chippenham Mews, W9 and owned by Westminster City Council, was leased to Marylands Community Association on a peppercorn rent. The Association leased a room to the newly-formed Paddington Printshop and the building was renamed The Factory. During its initial phase of semi-dereliction, 1974 to 1976, The Factory hosted numerous fringe theatre groups including: CAST (Cartoon Archetypical Slogan Theatre), Pip Simmons, Red Ladder, and The People Show alongside Larry Forde's carnival band, Sukuya.

Benefits and events regularly featured Joe Strummer in his earlier incarnation as 'Woody', lead singer in the local squatters band the 101ers, and the local reggae band Aswad.

Following conversion in 1977, The Factory supported emerging new areas of performance including Mustapha Matura's and Charlie Hanson's Black Theatre Co-operative and Tony Allen's and Alexei Sayle's Alternative Cabaret. The Factory also hosted numerous benefit events for local organisations and campaigns including Rock Against Racism and North Paddington Women's Project. It has since changed its name to the Yaa Asantewaa Arts Centre, focused on African Caribbean arts. Today it is part of the umbrella organisation Carnival Village.

Next pages

PRINTING IS EASY, 1976,
John Phillips

STARRING THE PEOPLE SHOW, 1976,
John Phillips

ROCK 'N' ROLL NIGHT, 1979,
Brian Deighton

TEA AND ROCK CAKES, 1974,
John Phillips

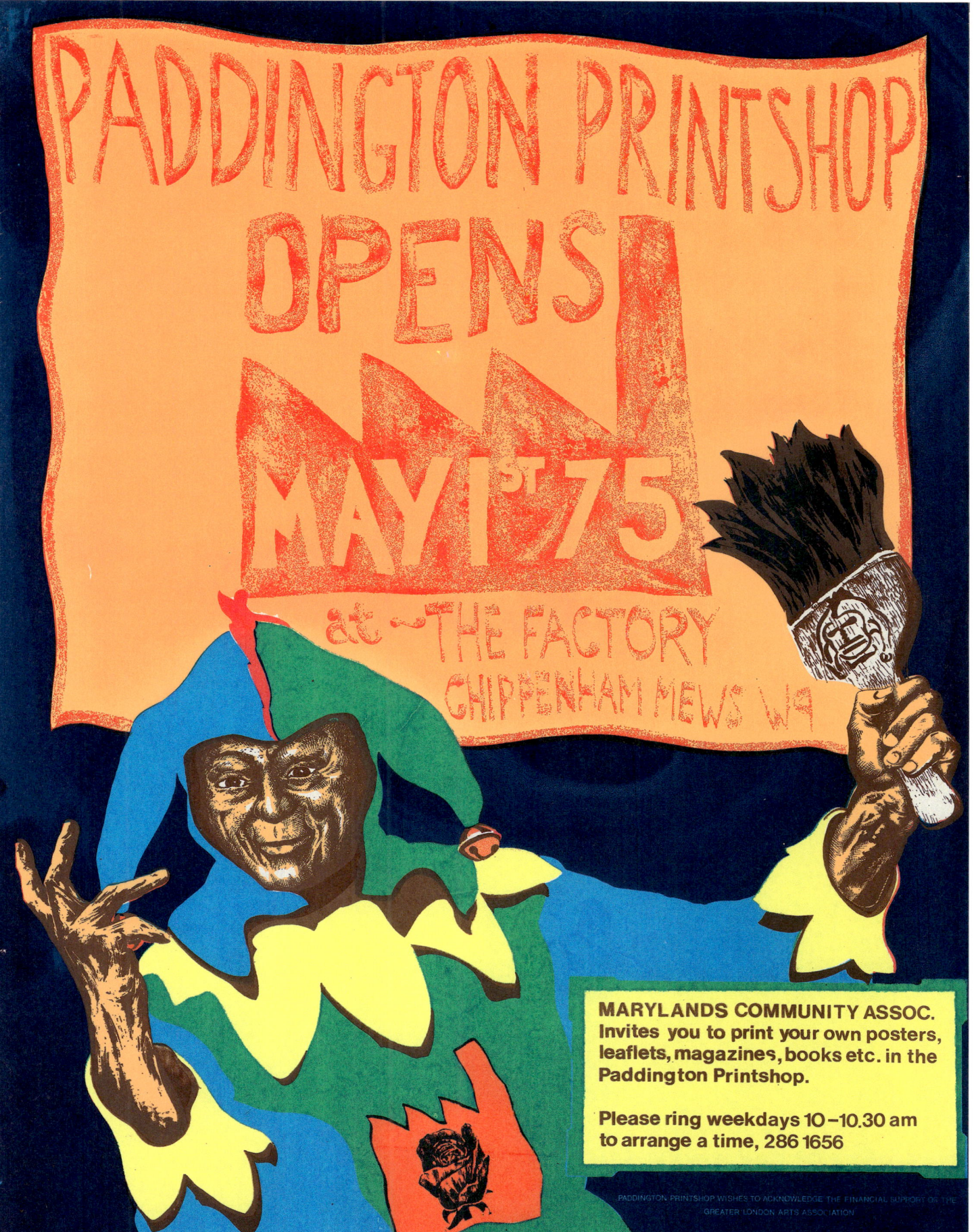

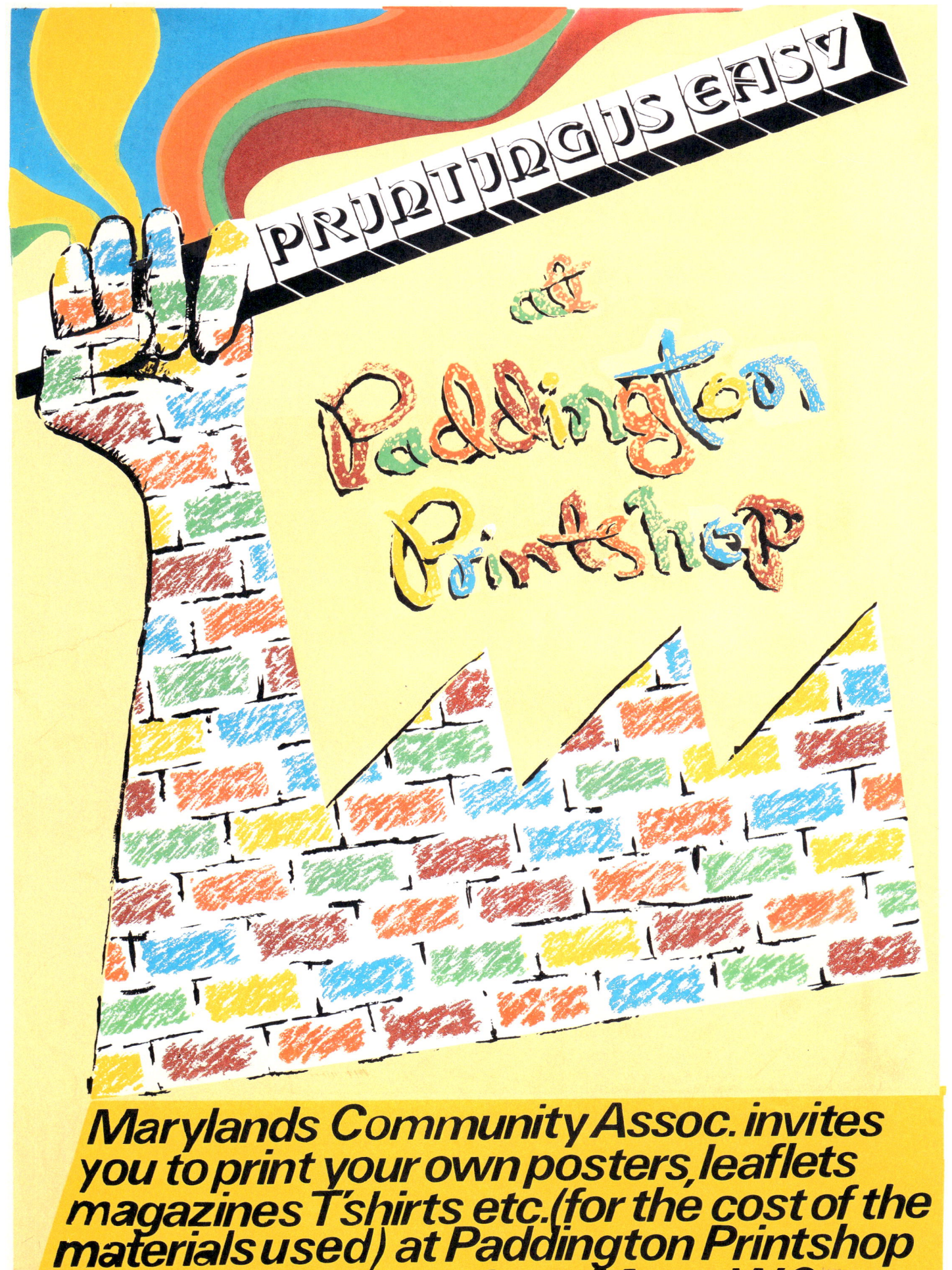

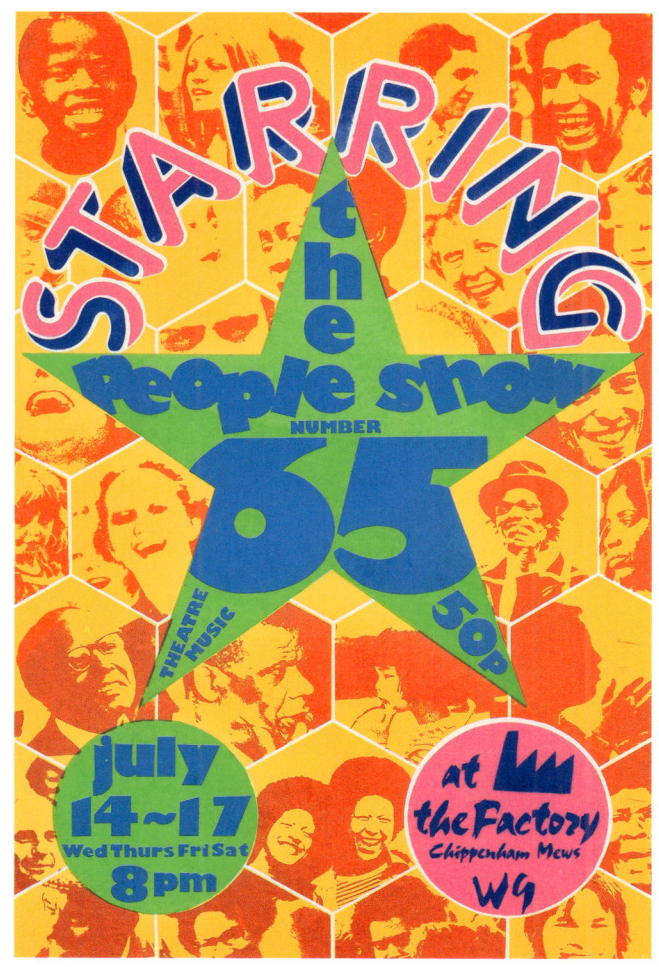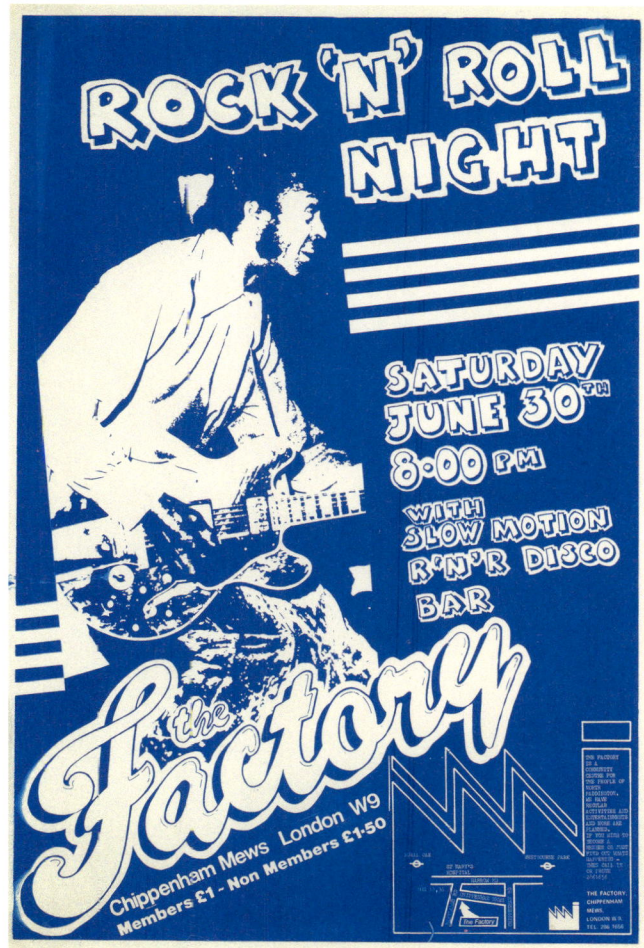

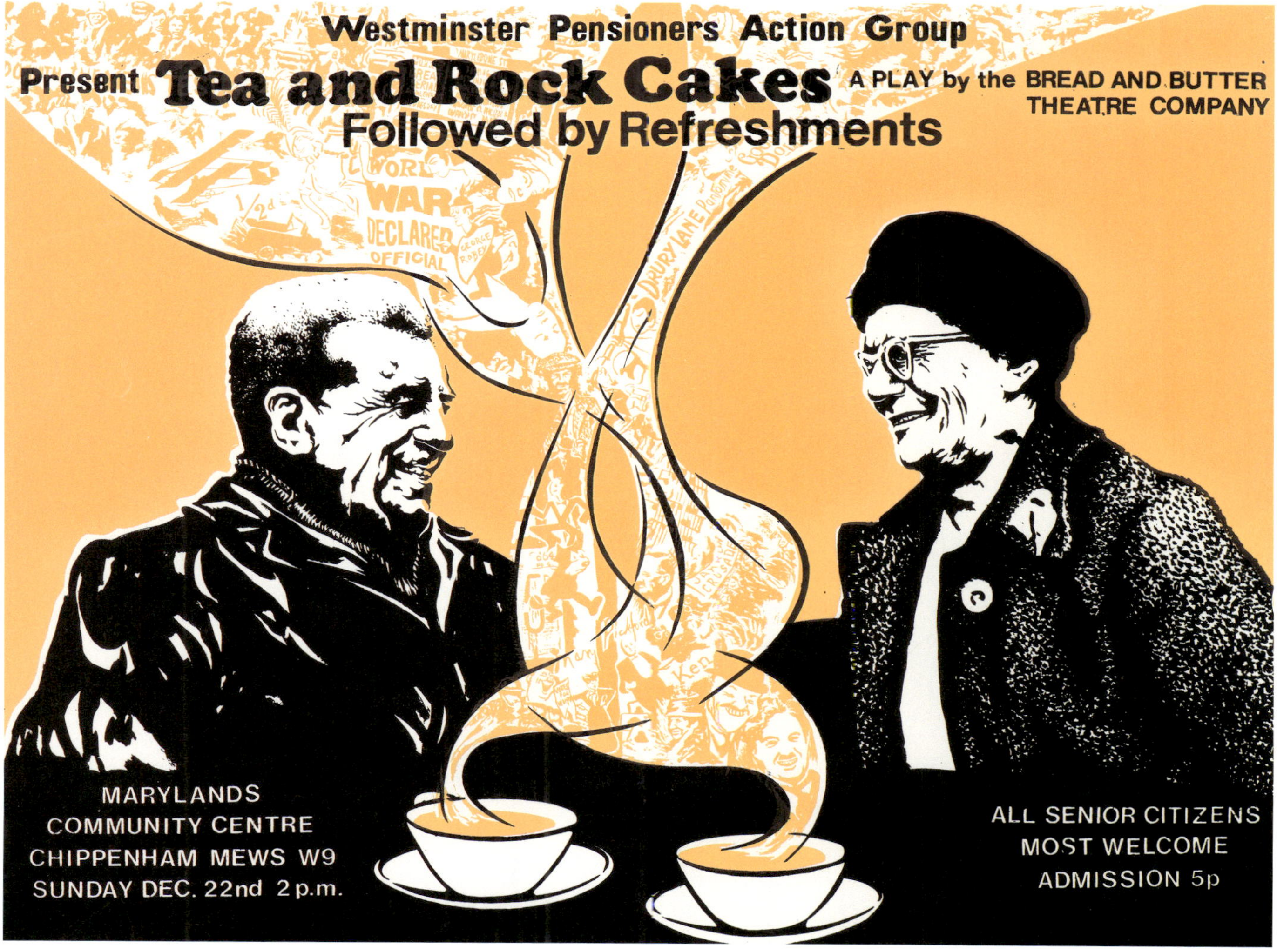

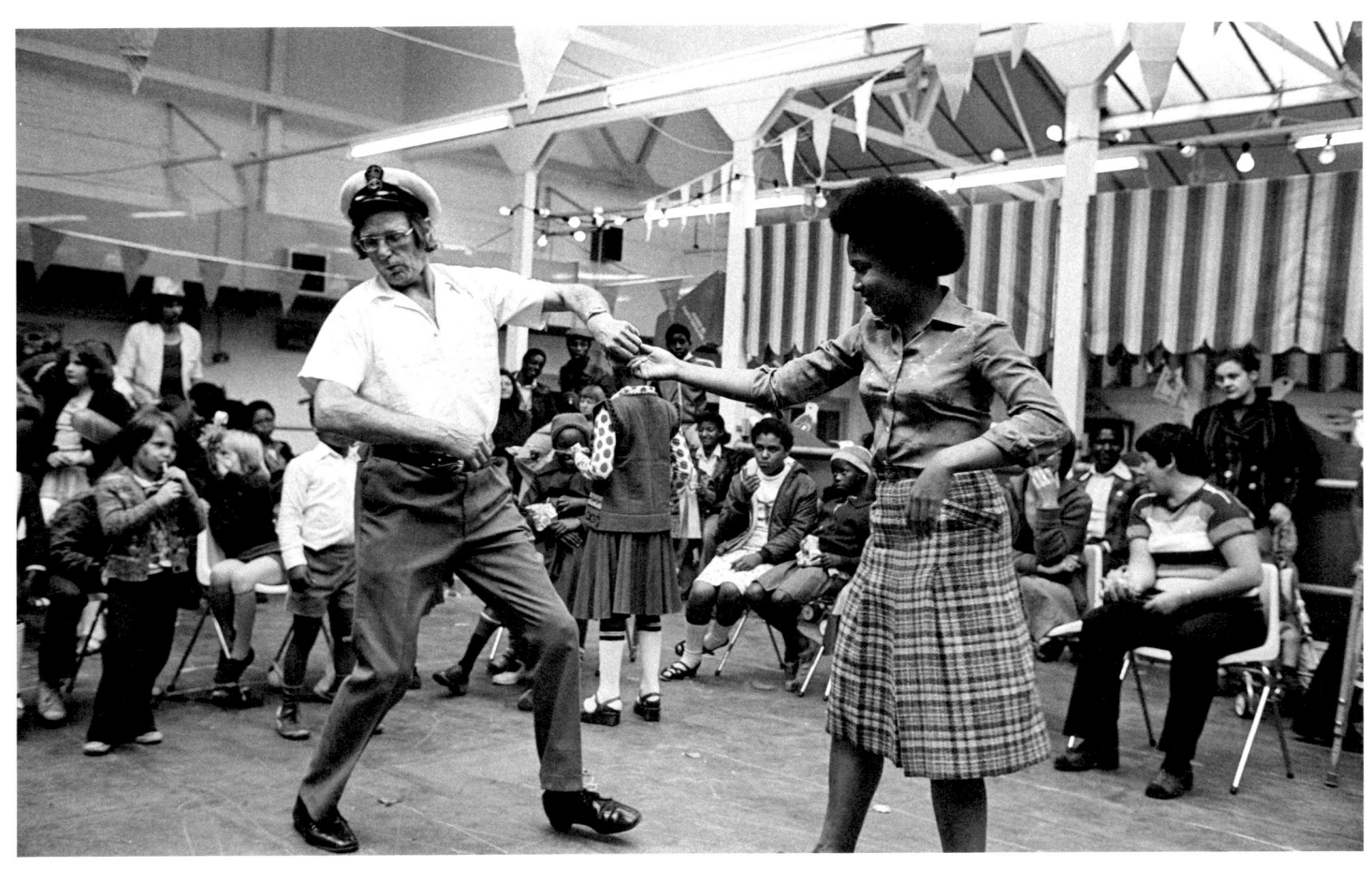

Above
Paddington-by-the-Sea community festival at The Factory, 1978.
Photo by Philip Wolmuth.

Opposite
FESTIVAL DANCE, 1978, John Phillips

Next pages
WELCOME HOME JACKO, 1977,
Mark Minton

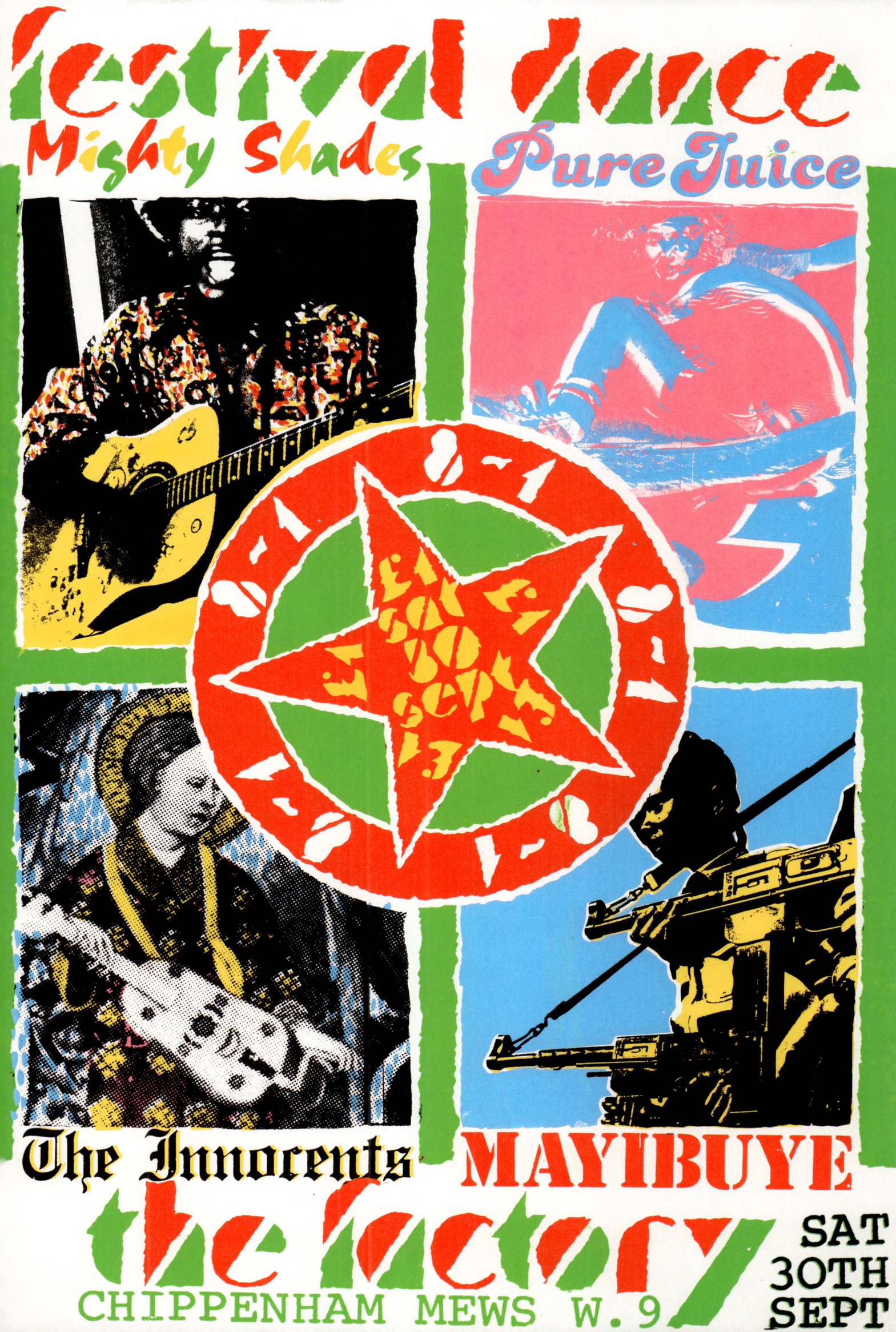

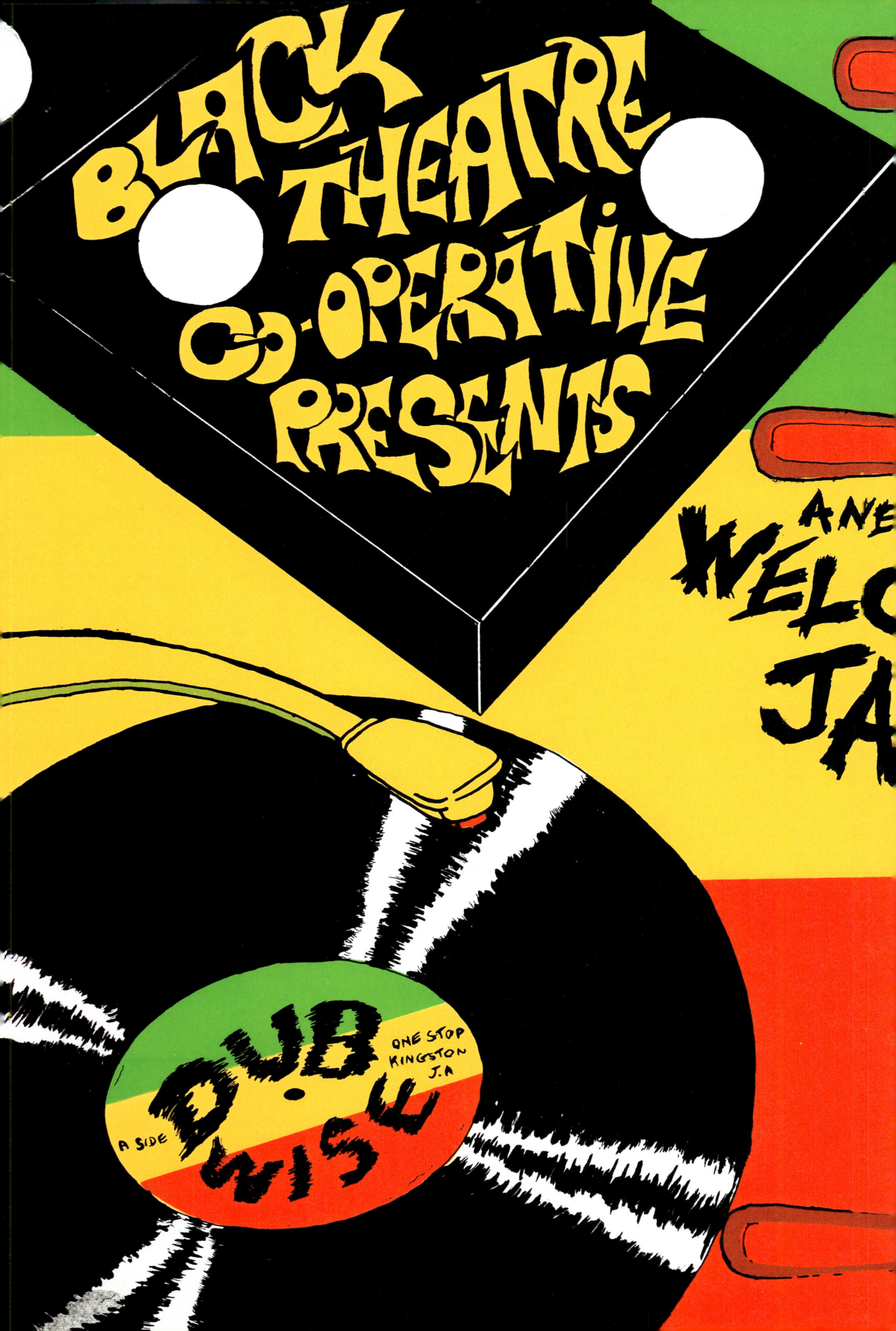

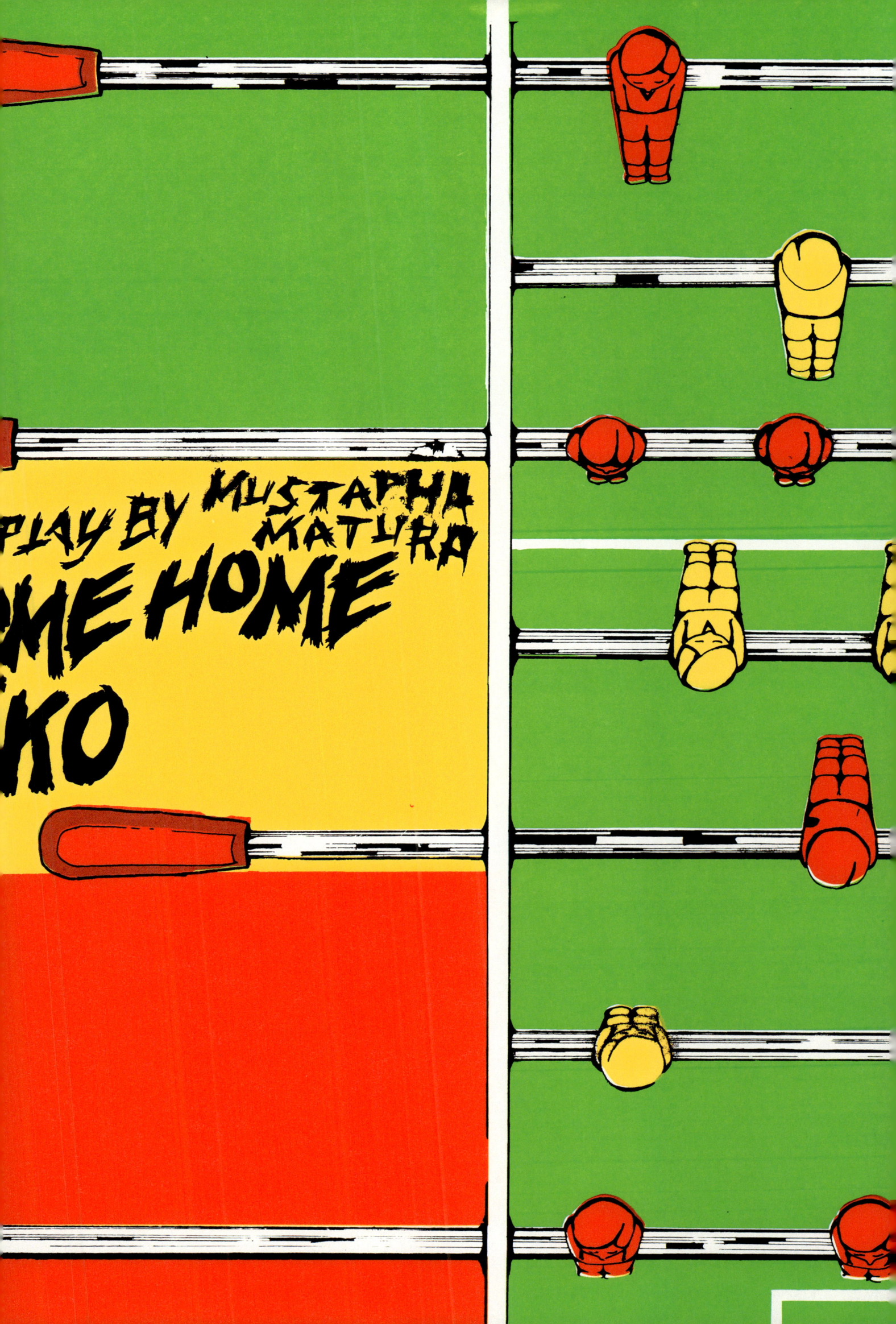

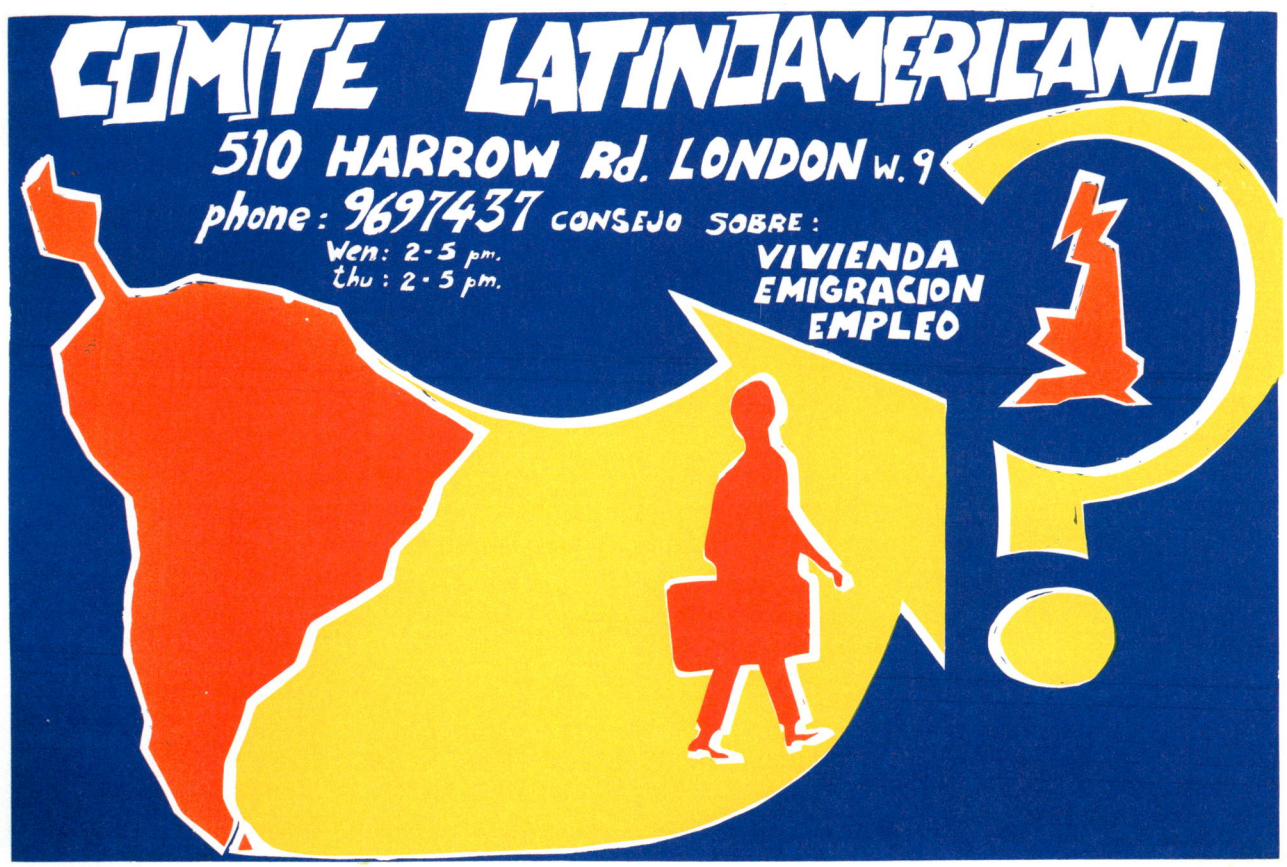

Above
COMITÉ LATINAMERICANO,
c. 1976, Jay Talbot

Opposite
510 CENTRE BENEFIT,
1978, John Phillips

510 Centre (1975–1987) was a neighbourhood centre, focused on community development work, supported by the local council. Its programmes sought to assist and empower local people, many of whom were among the poorest and most marginalised members of society. The centre housed numerous ad-hoc groups and associations including tenants and claimants associations, cultural groups and organisations such as Comité Latinamericano, which offered advice and support to South American migrants.

CENTRE BENEFIT DANCE

15th JULY **7·30 to 11·30**

BAR — DISCO — FOLK MUSIC

THE MAGNETS
ROUGH THEATRE

£1 → 60p claimants

AT THE FACTORY
CHIPPENHAM MEWS W9

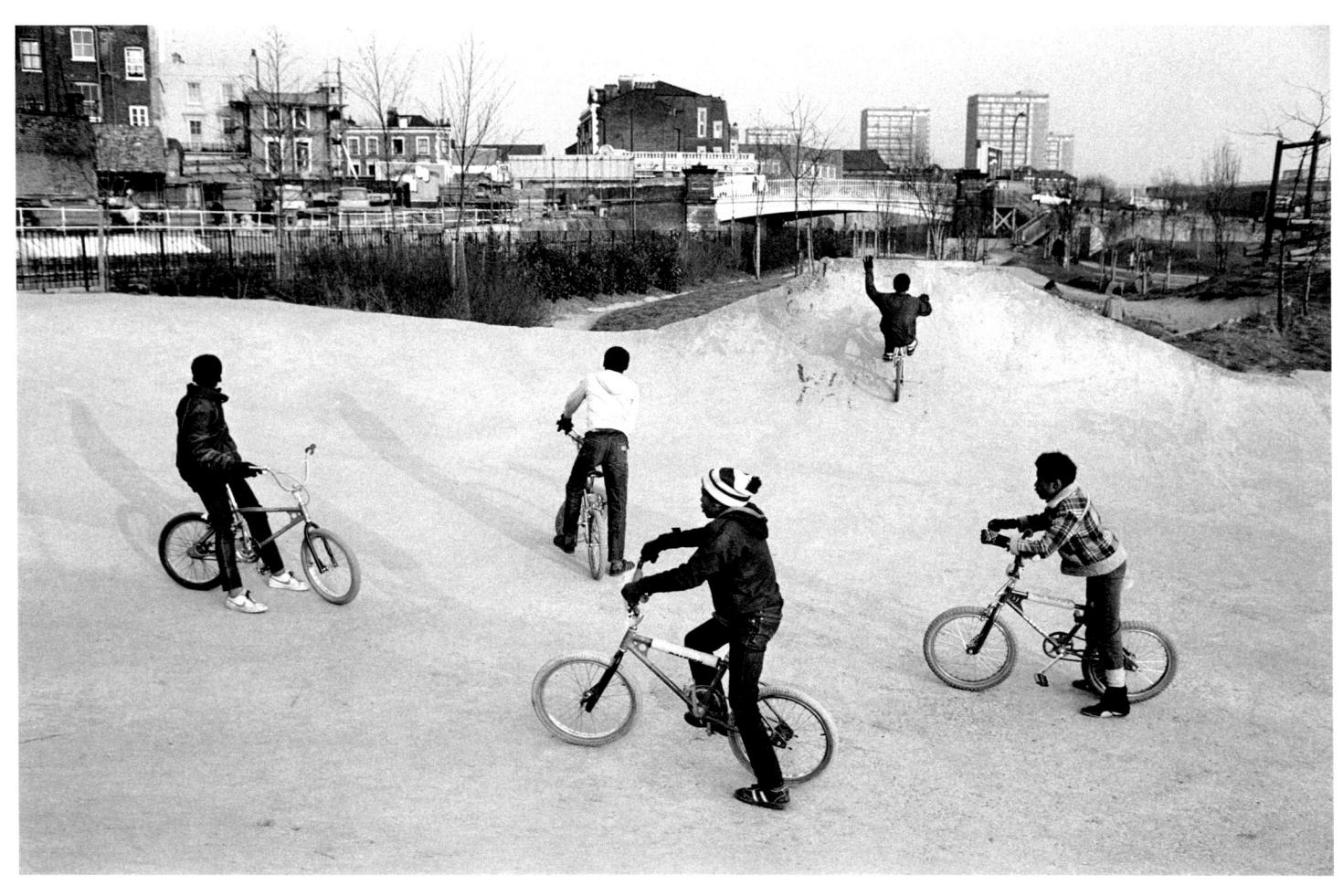

Above
Bikers on the first skateboard
bowl in Meanwhile Gardens, 1983.
Photo by Philip Wolmuth.

Opposite and next pages
MEANWHILE GARDENS POSTERS,
1976–1978, John Phillips

Founded by sculptor Jamie McCullough in 1976, *Meanwhile Gardens*, as its name implies, was an attempt turn a small strip of 'derelict' land into a temporary public gardens. Having gained momentum and community support the idea 'took root' and is now an important local facility and home to diverse communities from skateboarders to members of the mental health charity Mind, who tend part of the gardens.

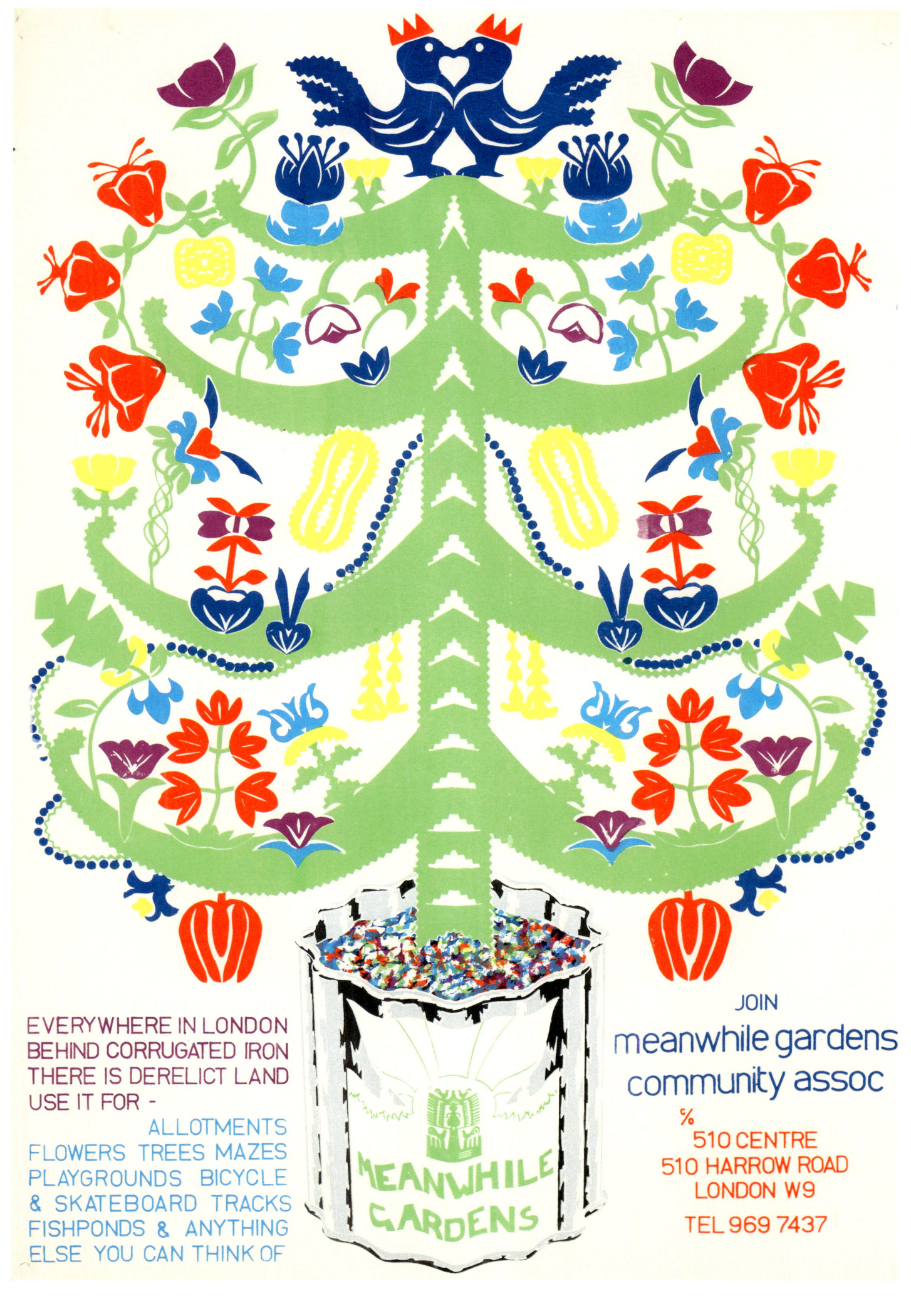

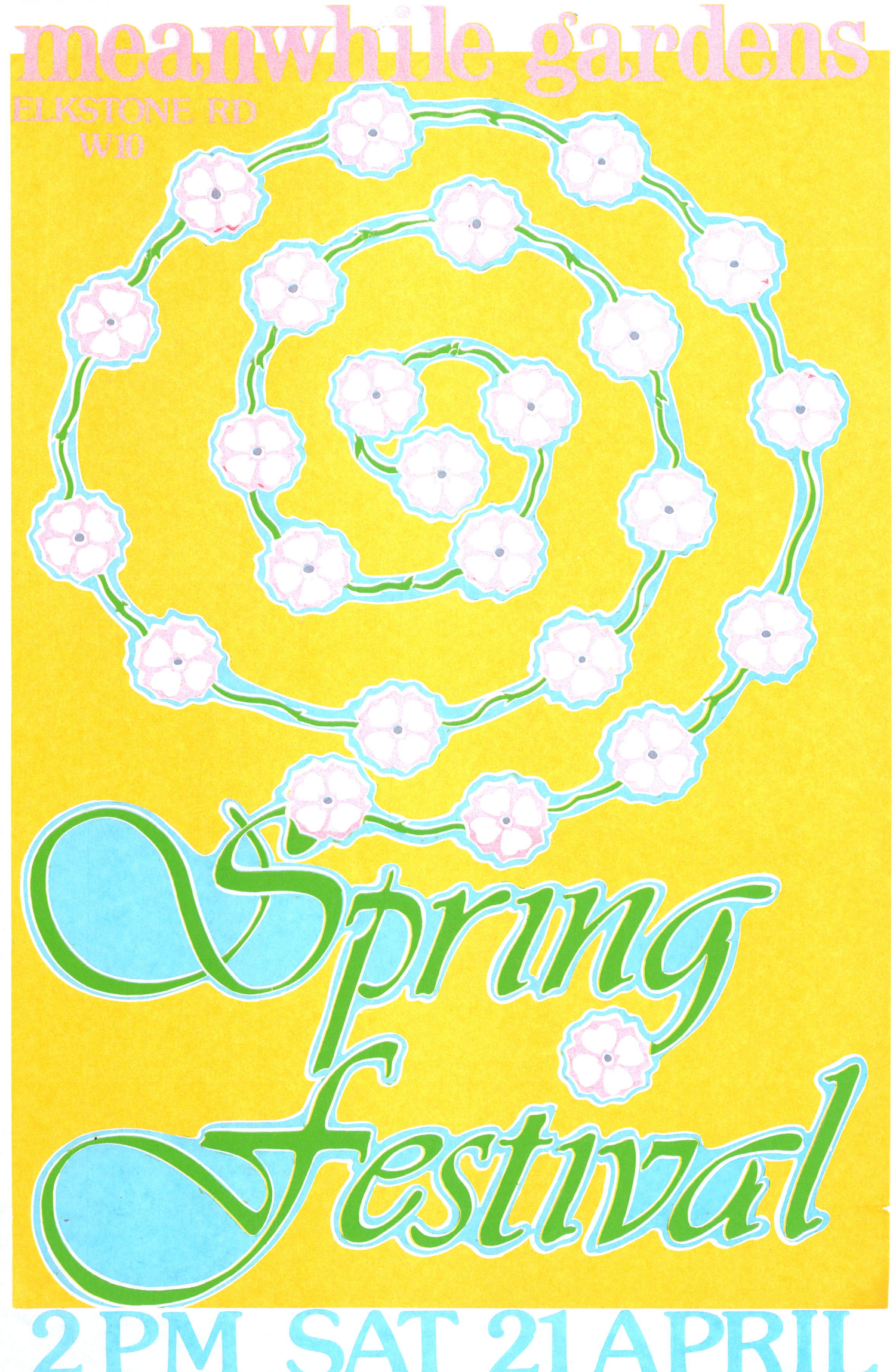

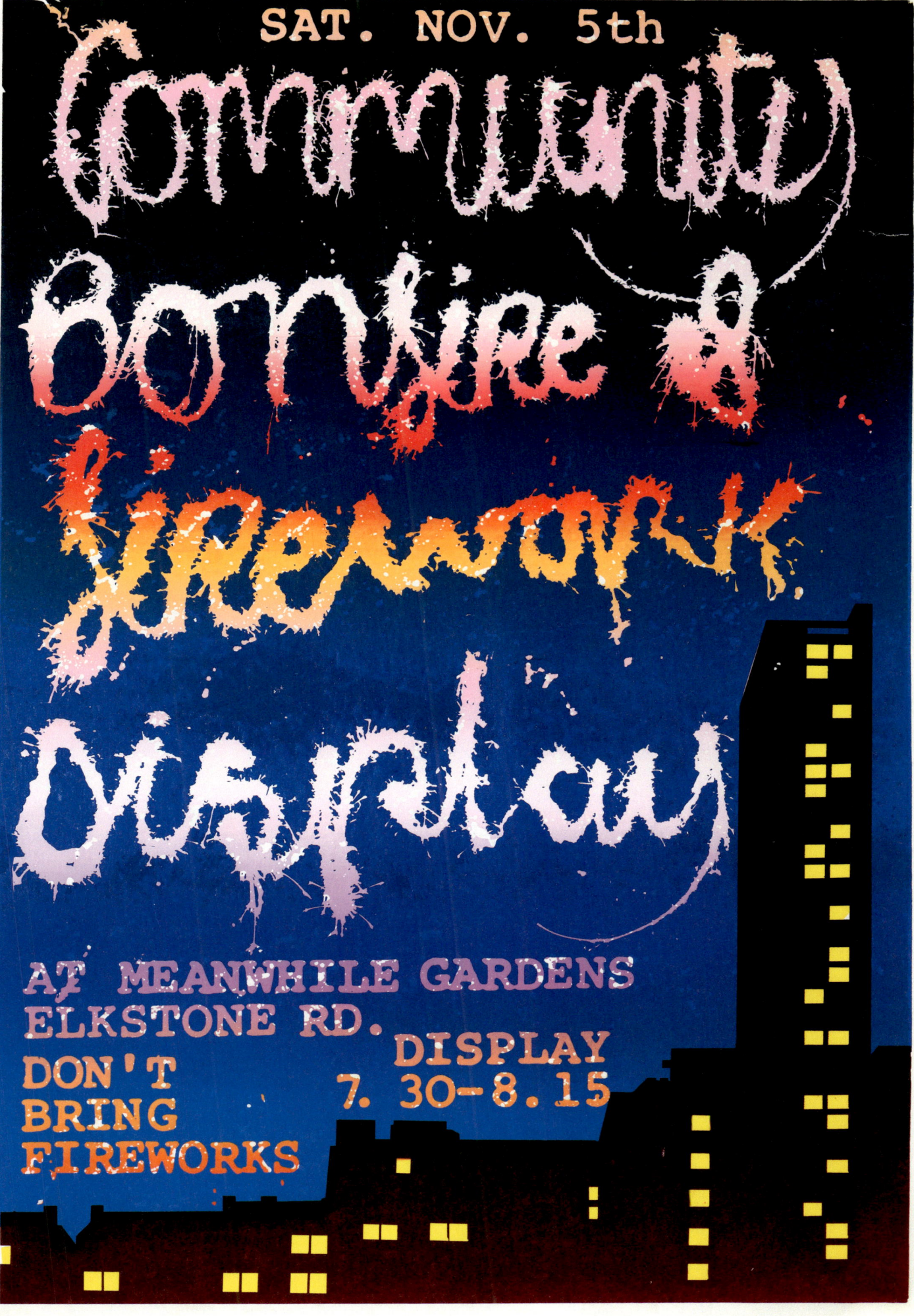

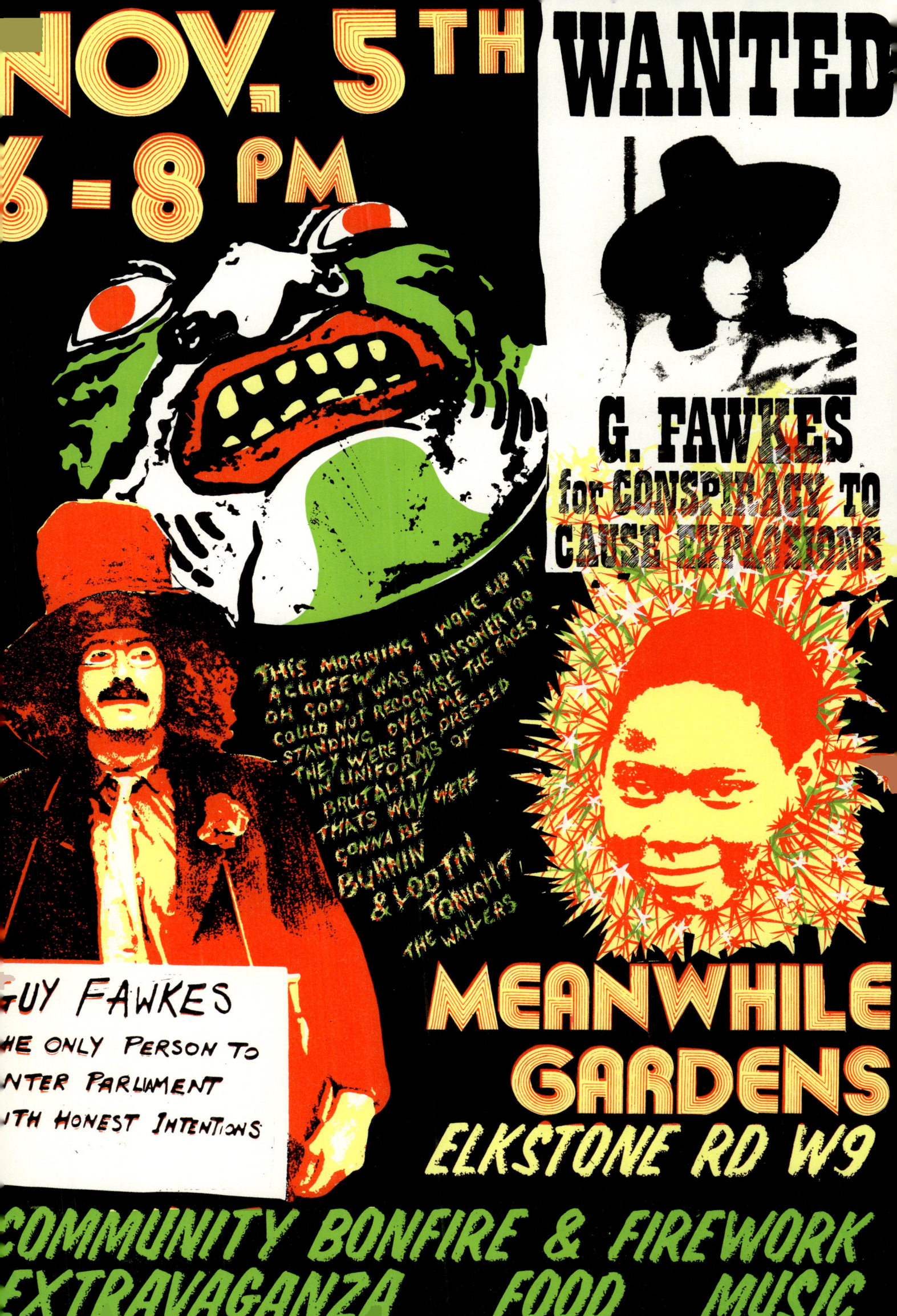

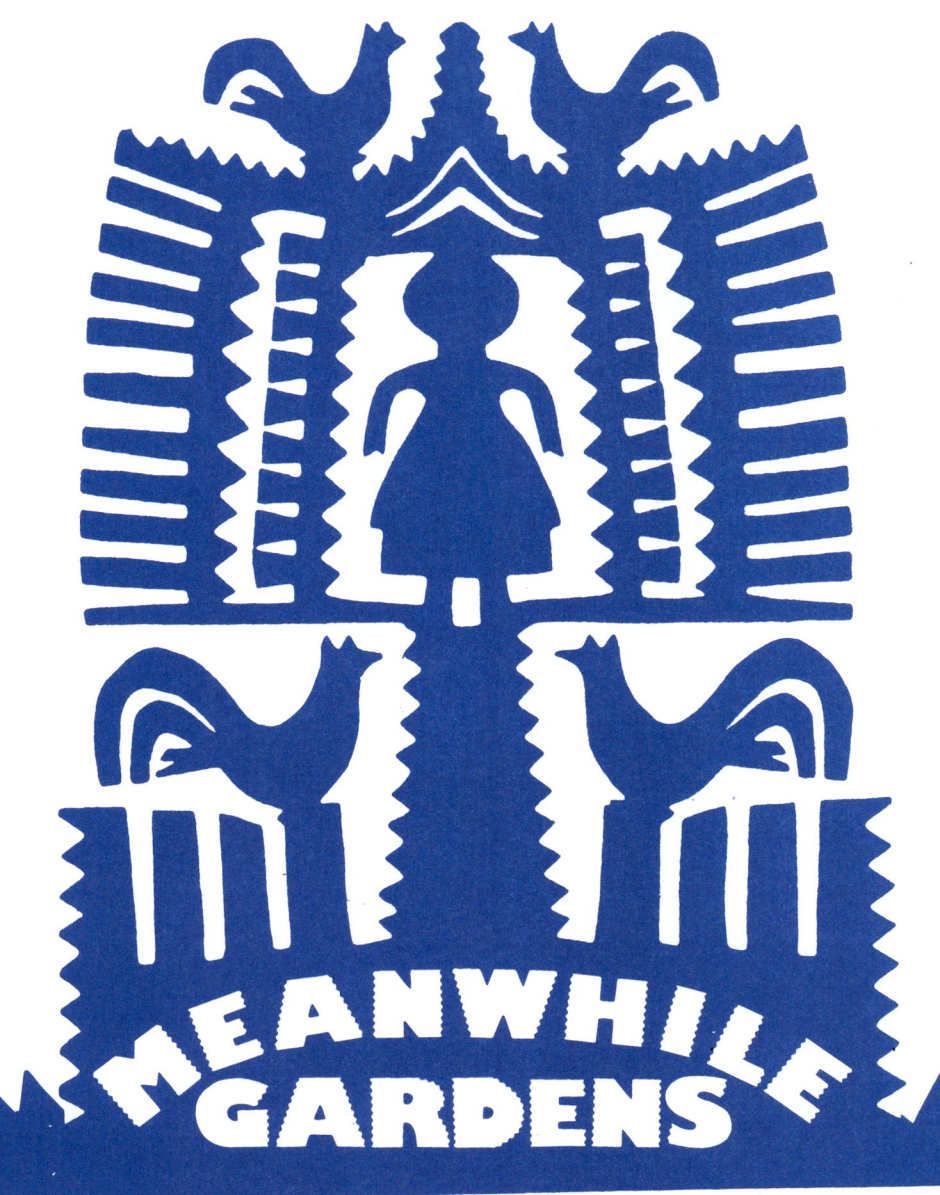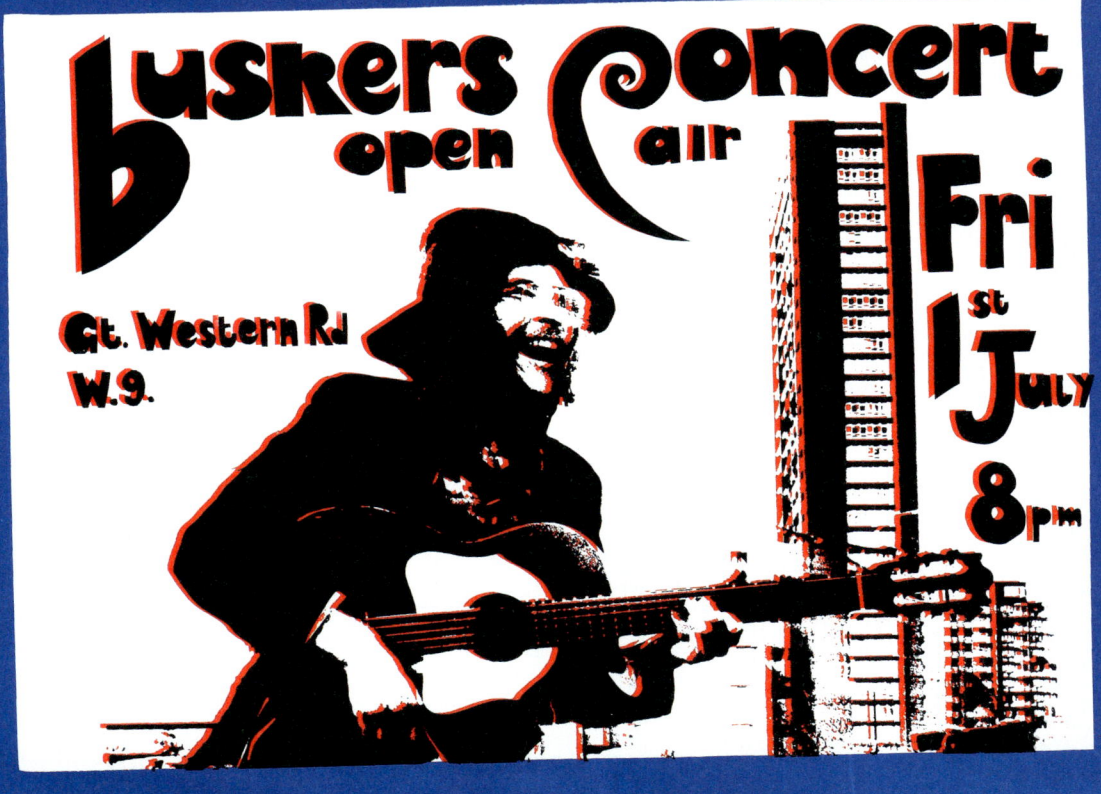

Next pages
BUSTOP, 1981, John Phillips

Designed by Jay Talbot and John Phillips, Bustop was the world's first audio-visual bus shelter. Located in a small garden area outside Paddington Printshop's premises at 1 Elgin Avenue, the shelter housed a back-projection screen and speakers alongside a community newspaper display and public information boards. At night, it showed tape slide-shows of local events such as carnival, and during the day it played music.

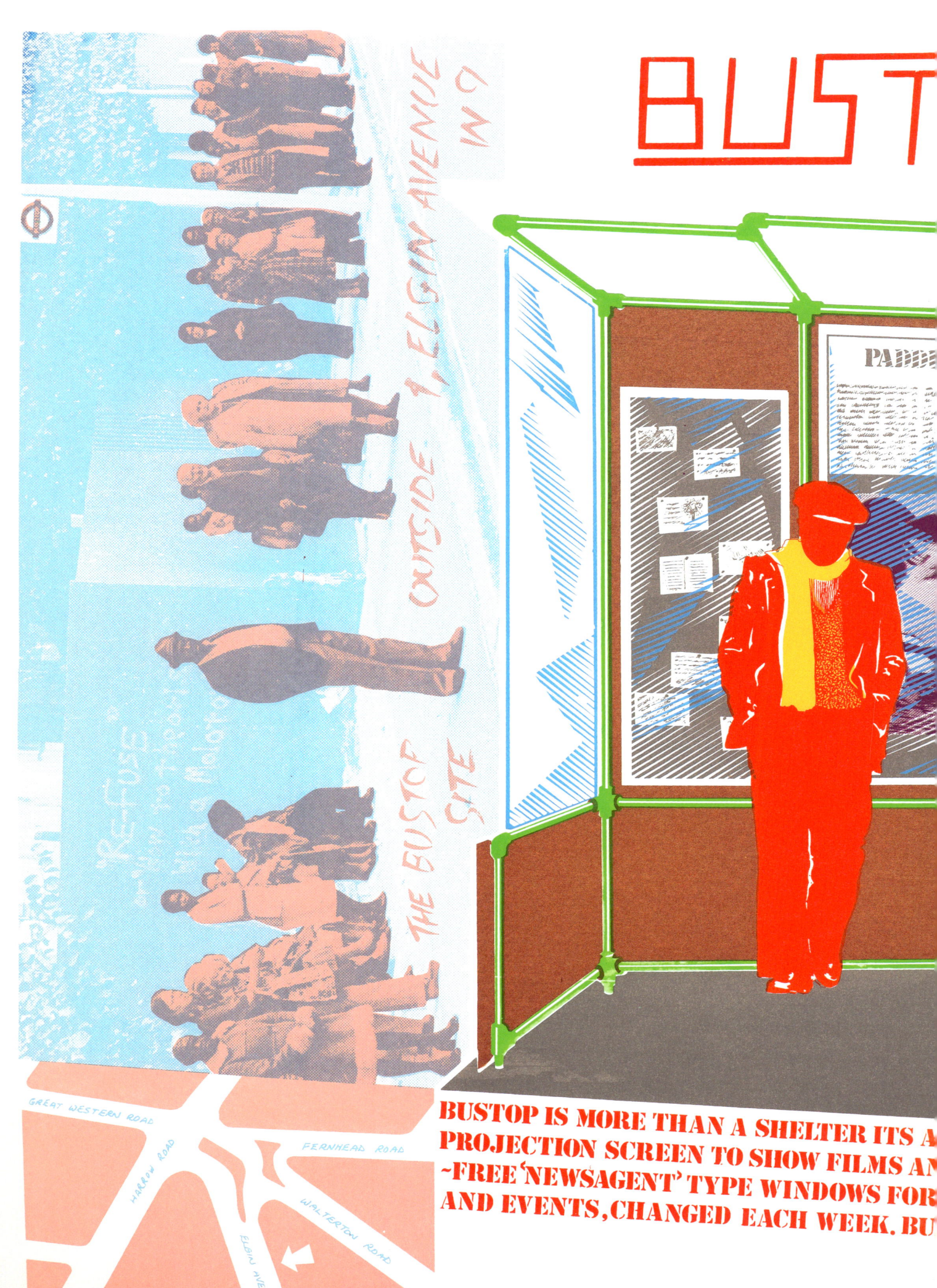

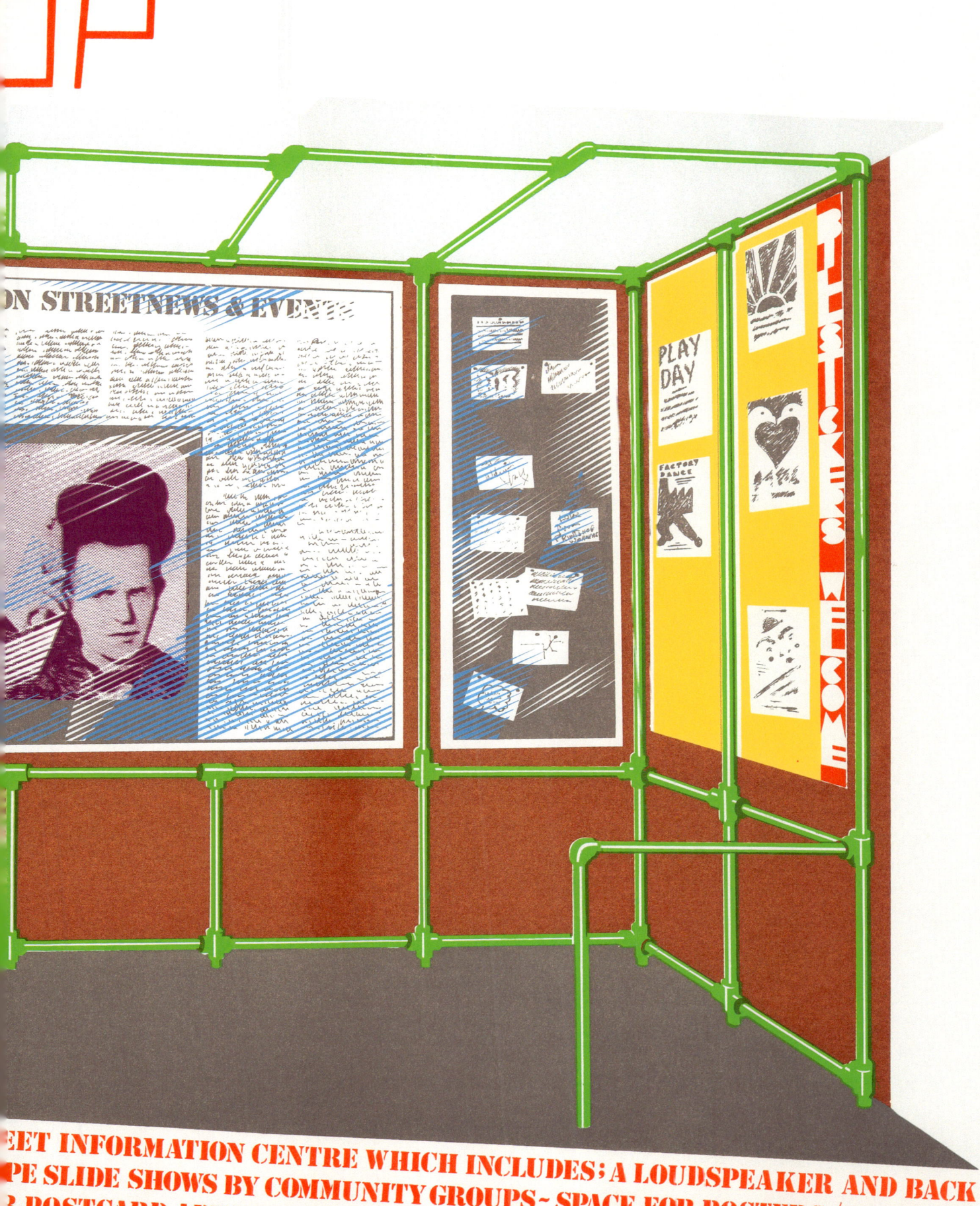

Opposite
WOMEN'S FESTIVAL, 1978, Anon

Next pages

ROUNDWOOD FESTIVAL,
1977, John Phillips and Kate McLean

ROUNDWOOD FESTIVAL,
1979, John Phillips and Kate McLean

PLAY DAY, 1977, Anonymous

From the outset, local festivals and celebrations were a common feature of community activism and engagement and posters promoting these events in different neighbourhoods were constantly in production in the print studio.

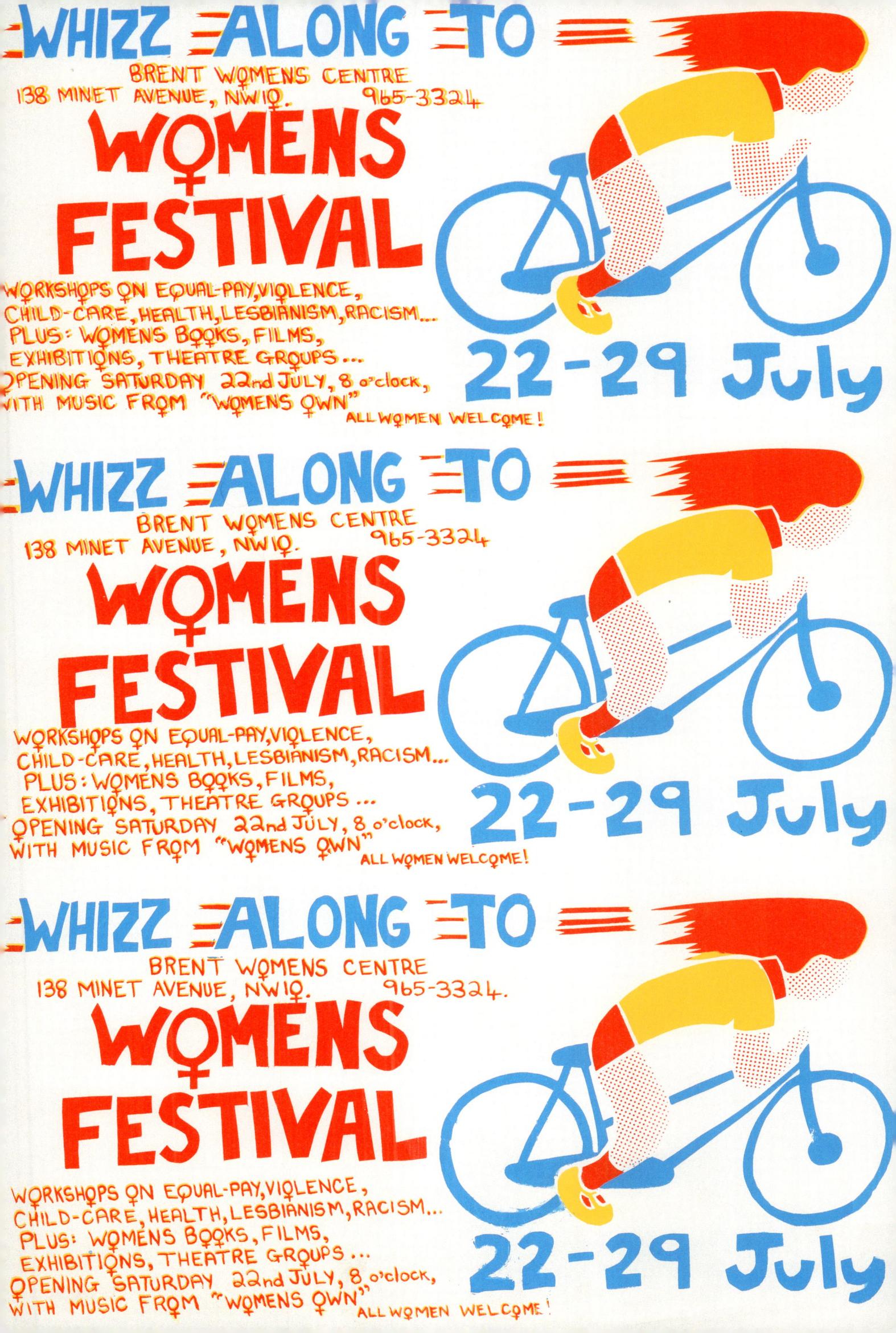

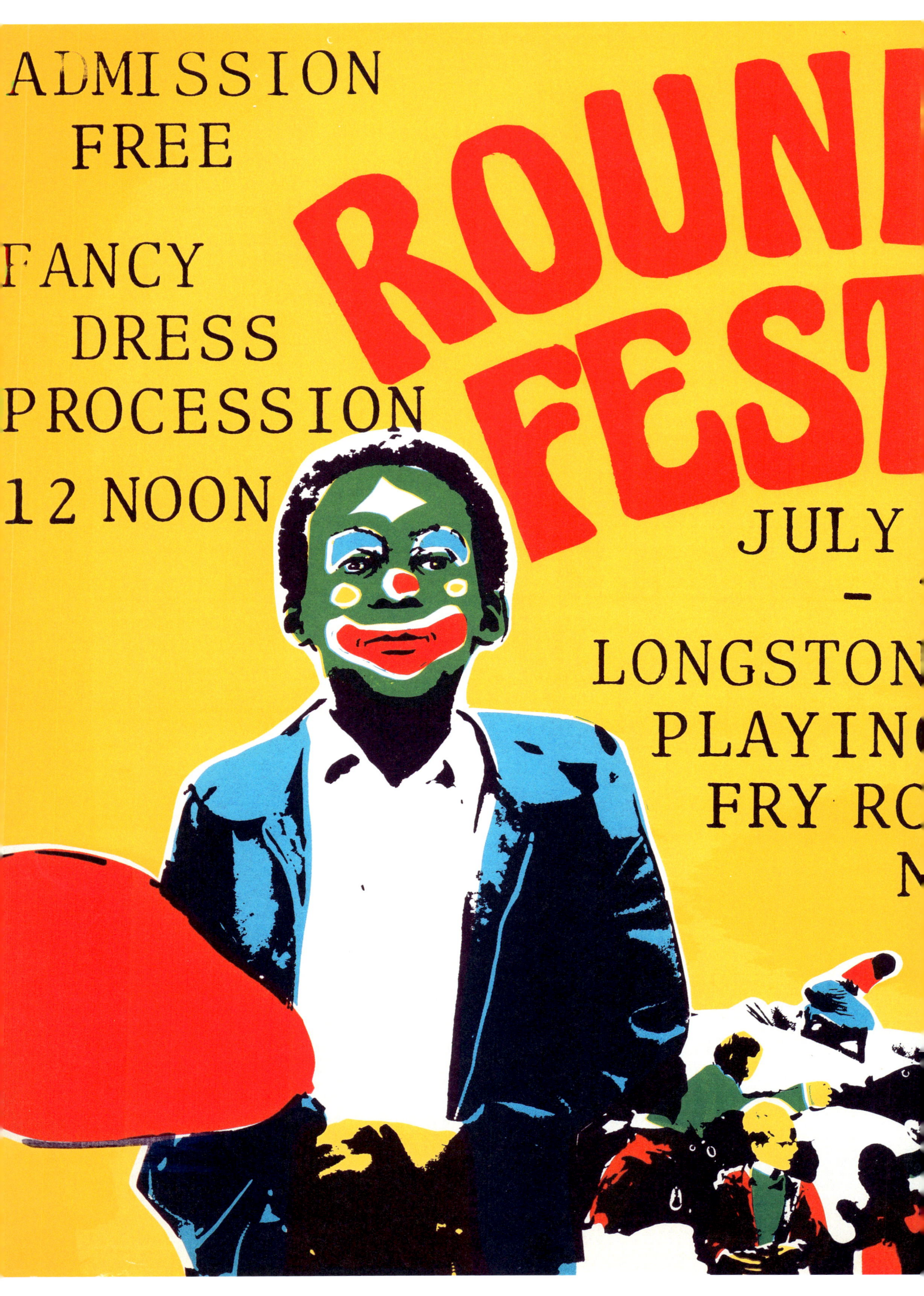

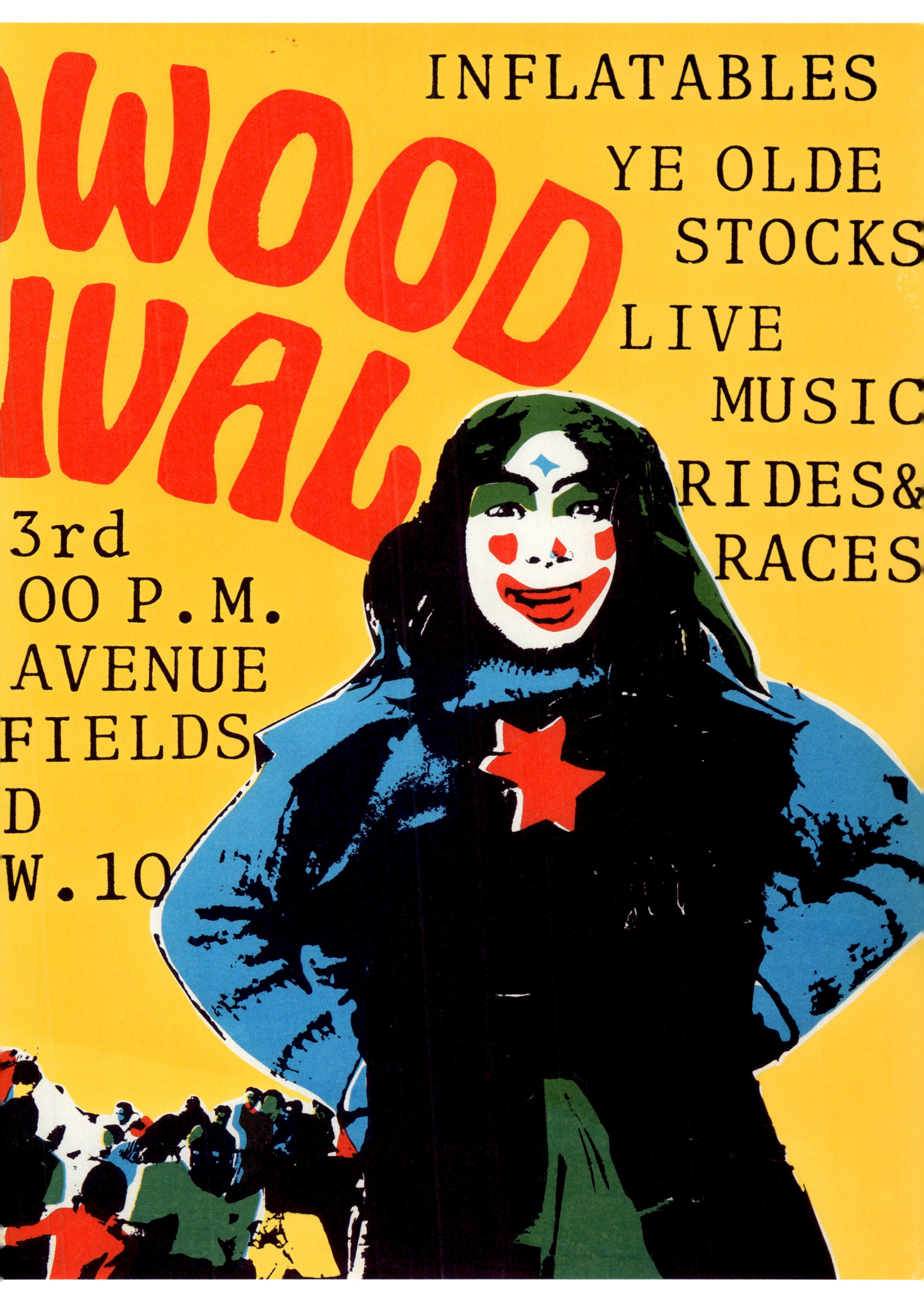

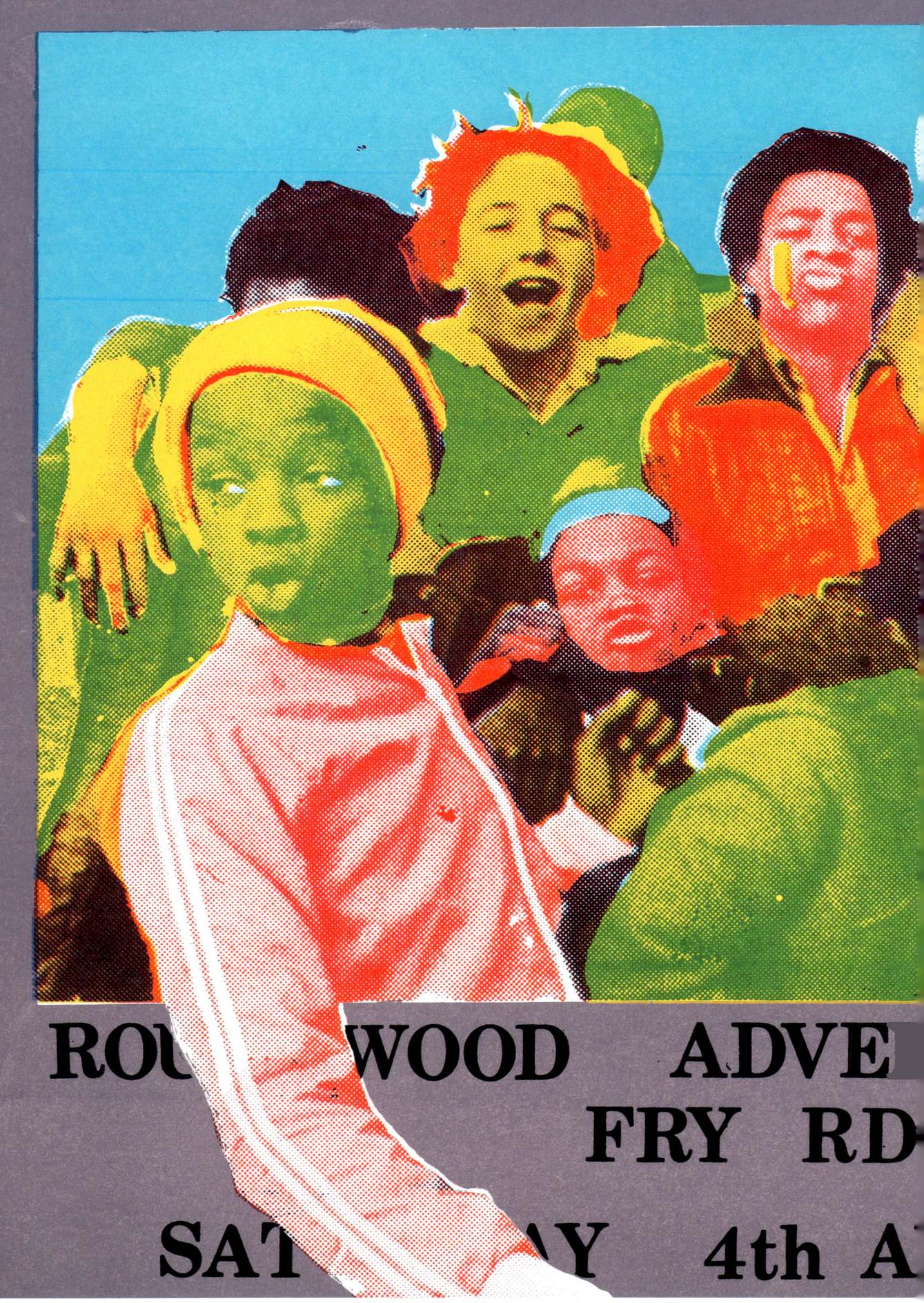

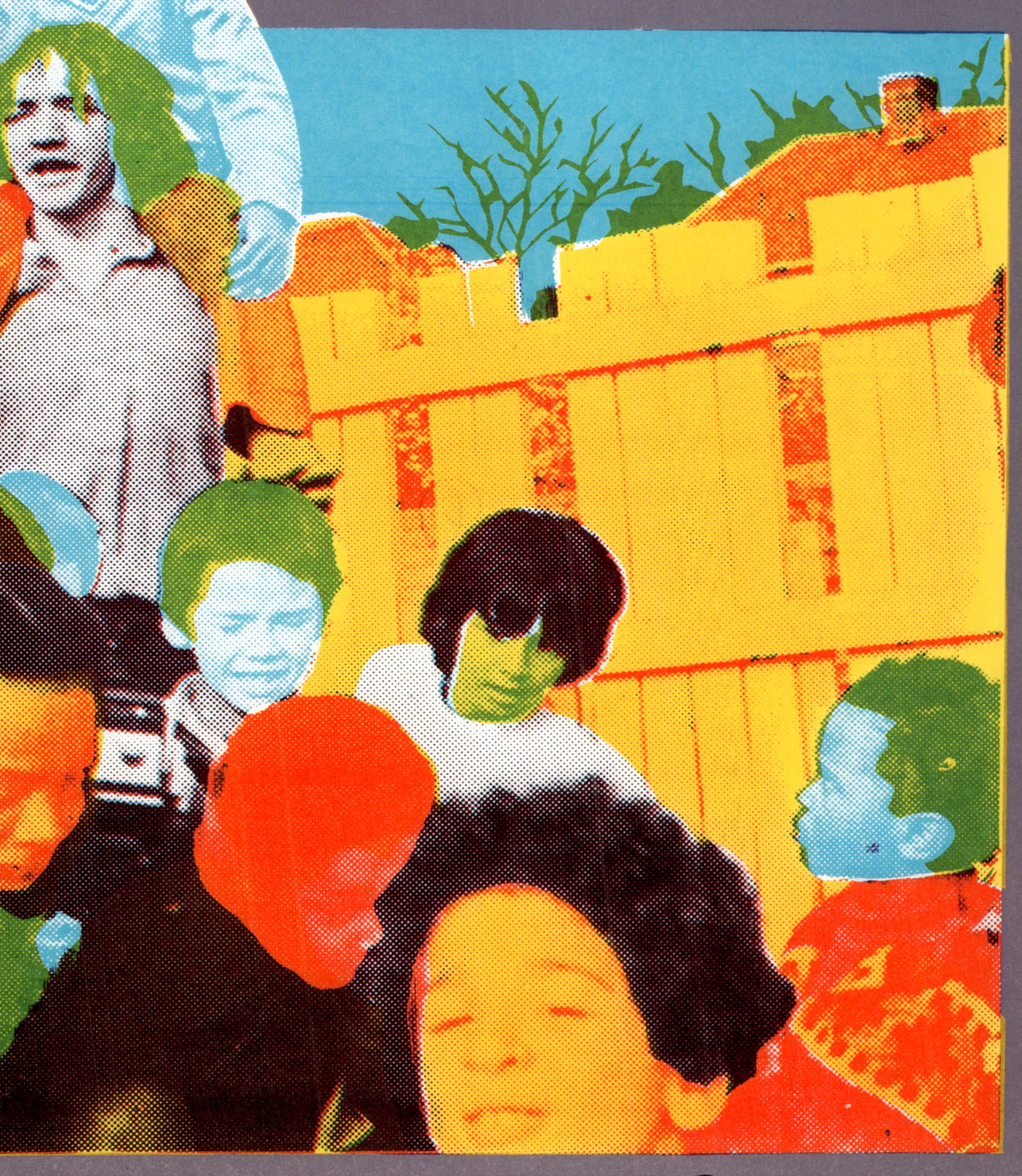

FESTIVAL

...TURE PLAYGROUND, NW10.

...GUST 79   12 am – 7pm

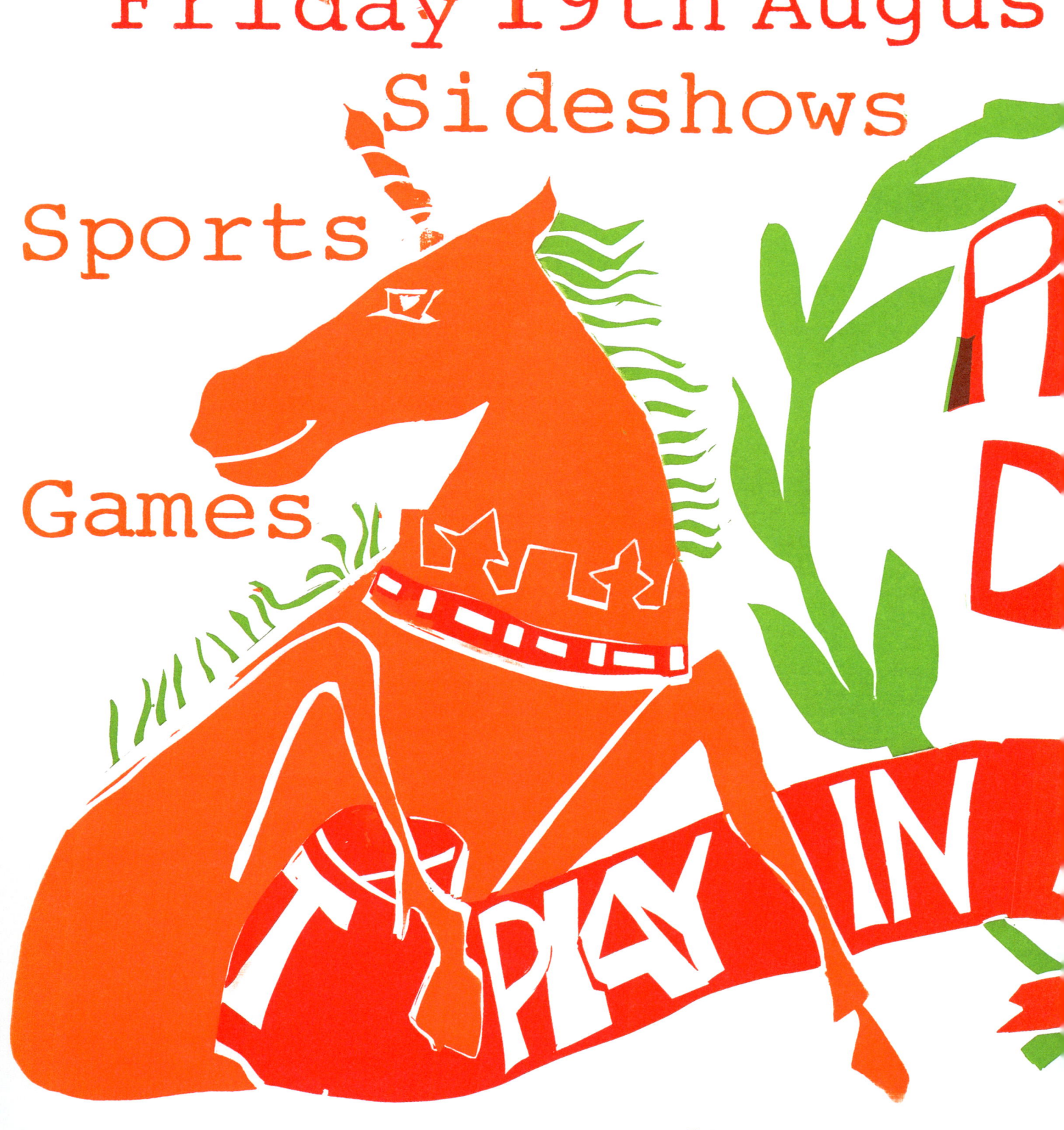

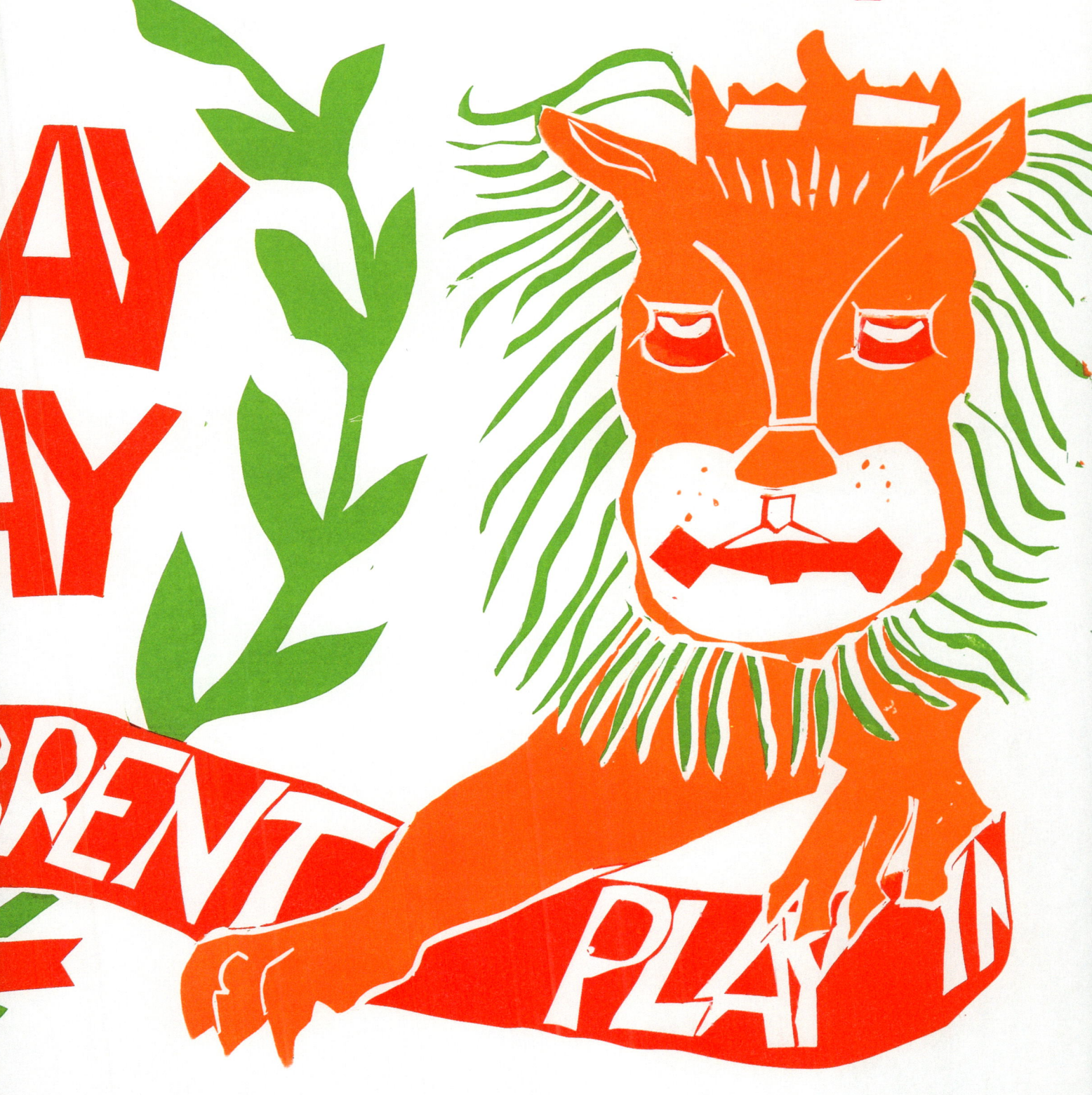

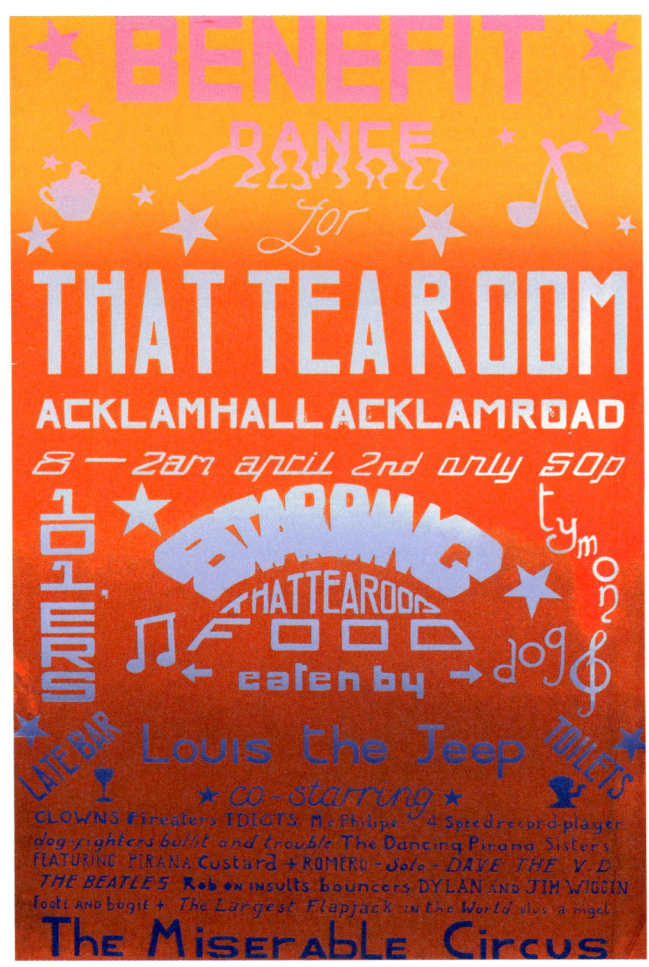
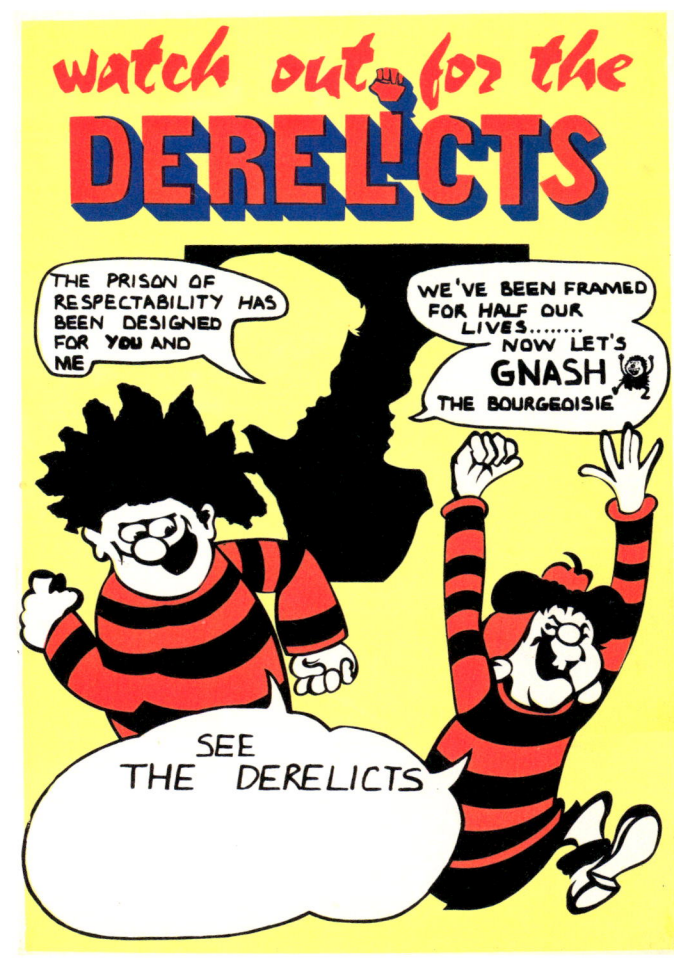

Above
BENEFIT DANCE – THAT TEA ROOM,
1975, Helen Cherry

That Tea Room was the neighbourhood squatter's café.

Above and opposite
WATCH OUT FOR THE DERELICTS,
1975, Barbara and Susan Gogan

Next pages

ALTERNATIVE CABARET,
c.1975, Tony Allen

HALLOWEEN MASKED BALL,
1980, John Phillips

CARIBBEAN EVENING, 1977,
Anonymous

STEEL 'N' SKIN, 1976, John Phillips

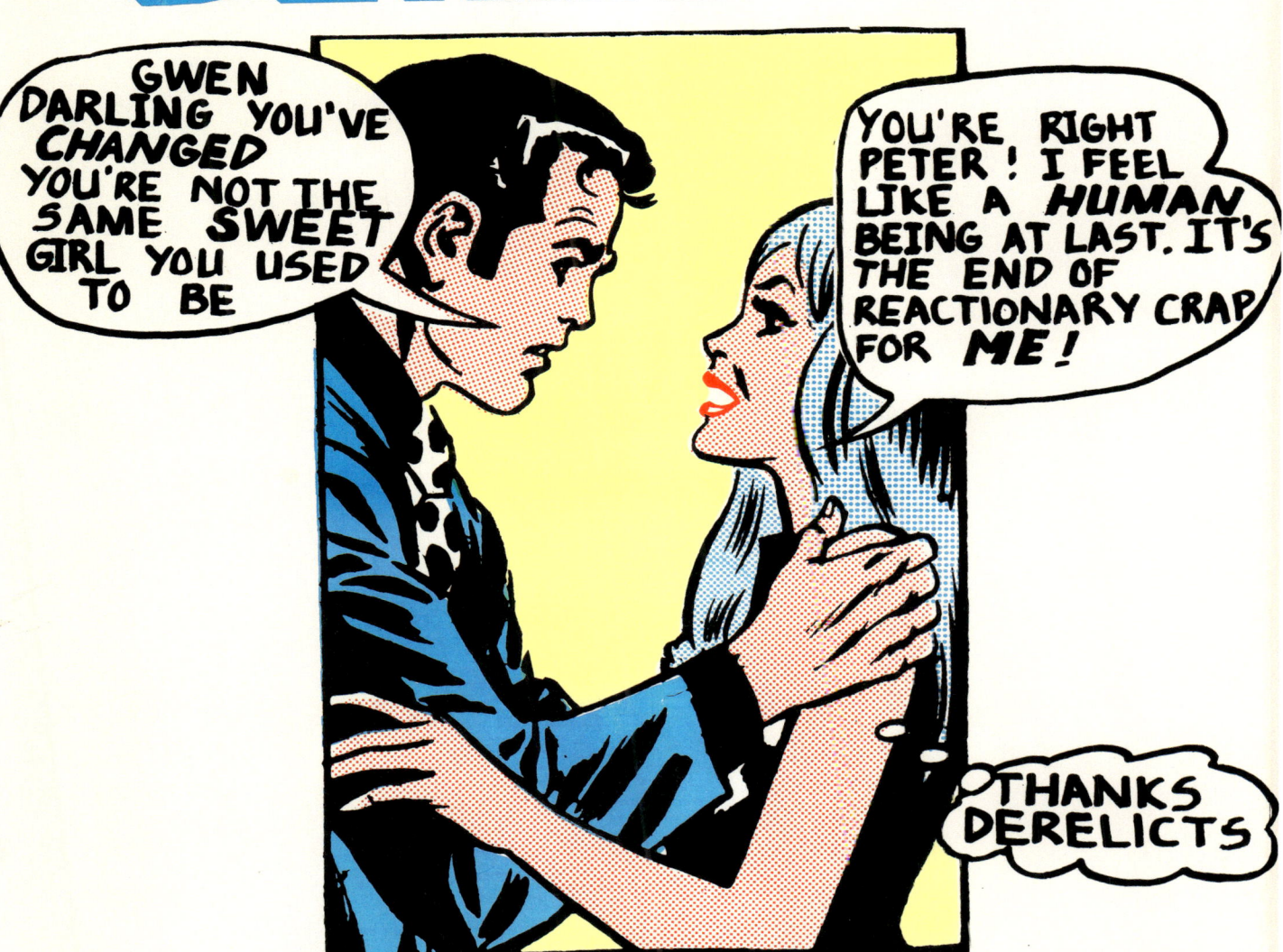

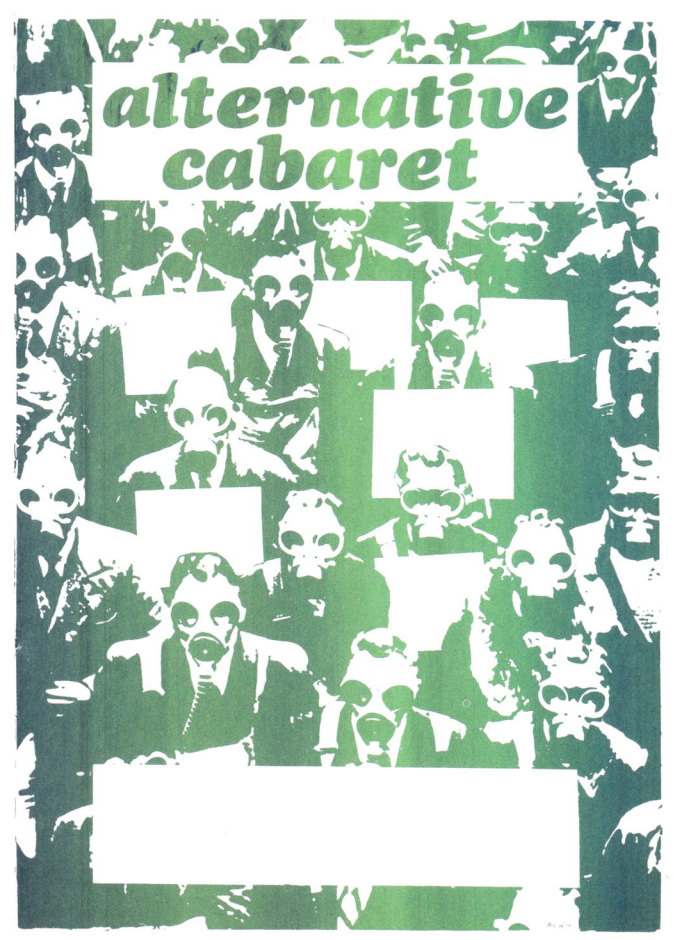
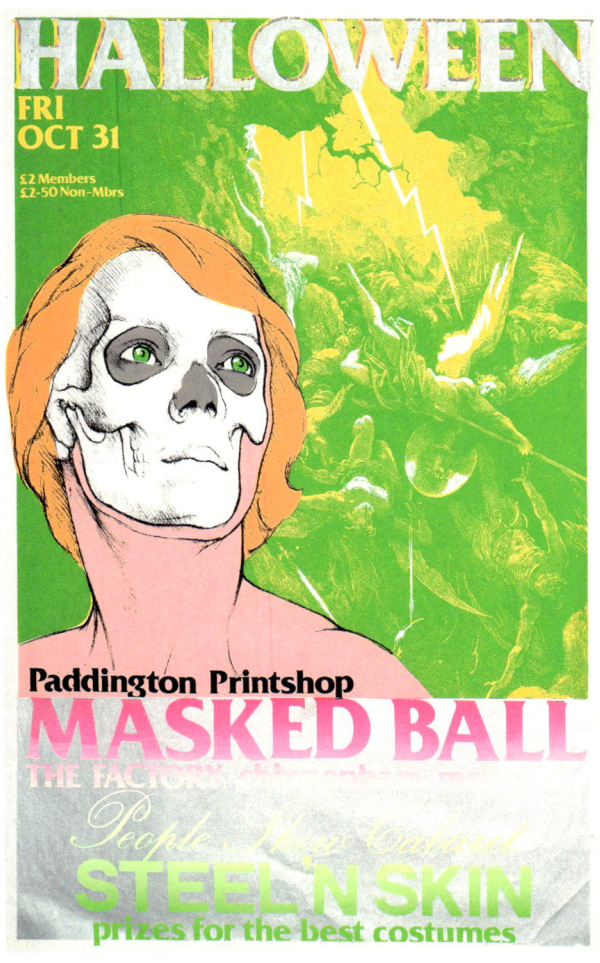
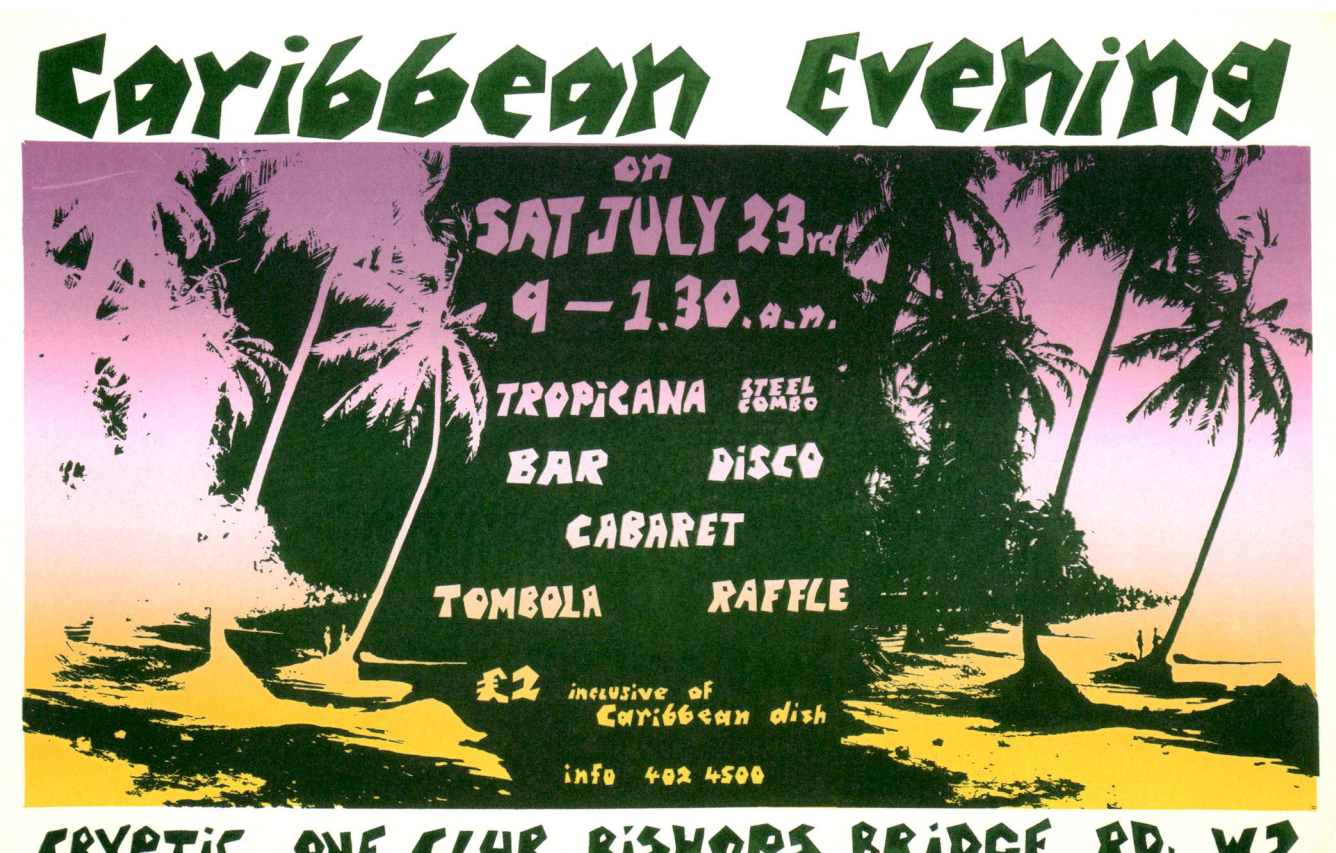

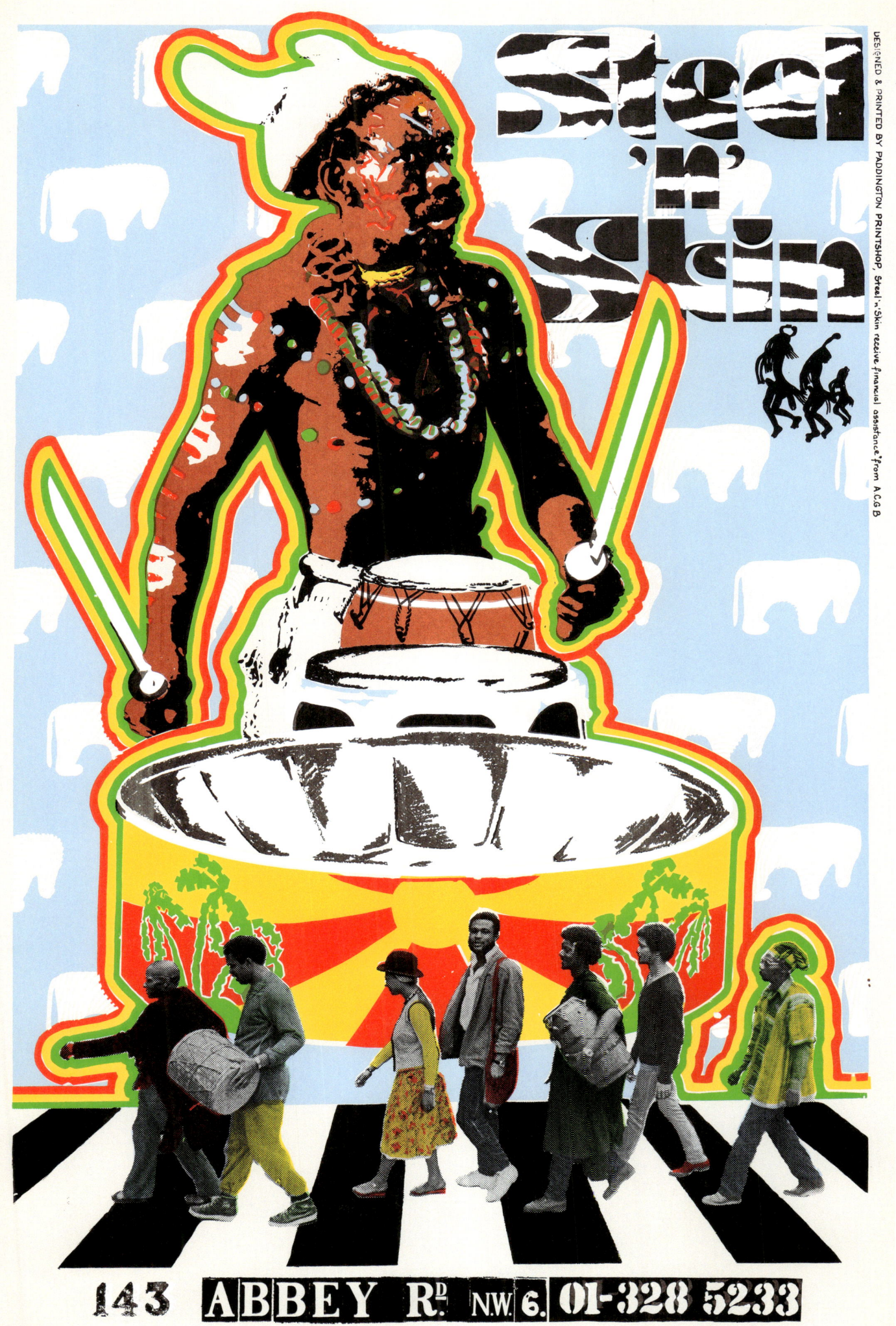

SUMMER FESTIVAL, 1982, Anonymous

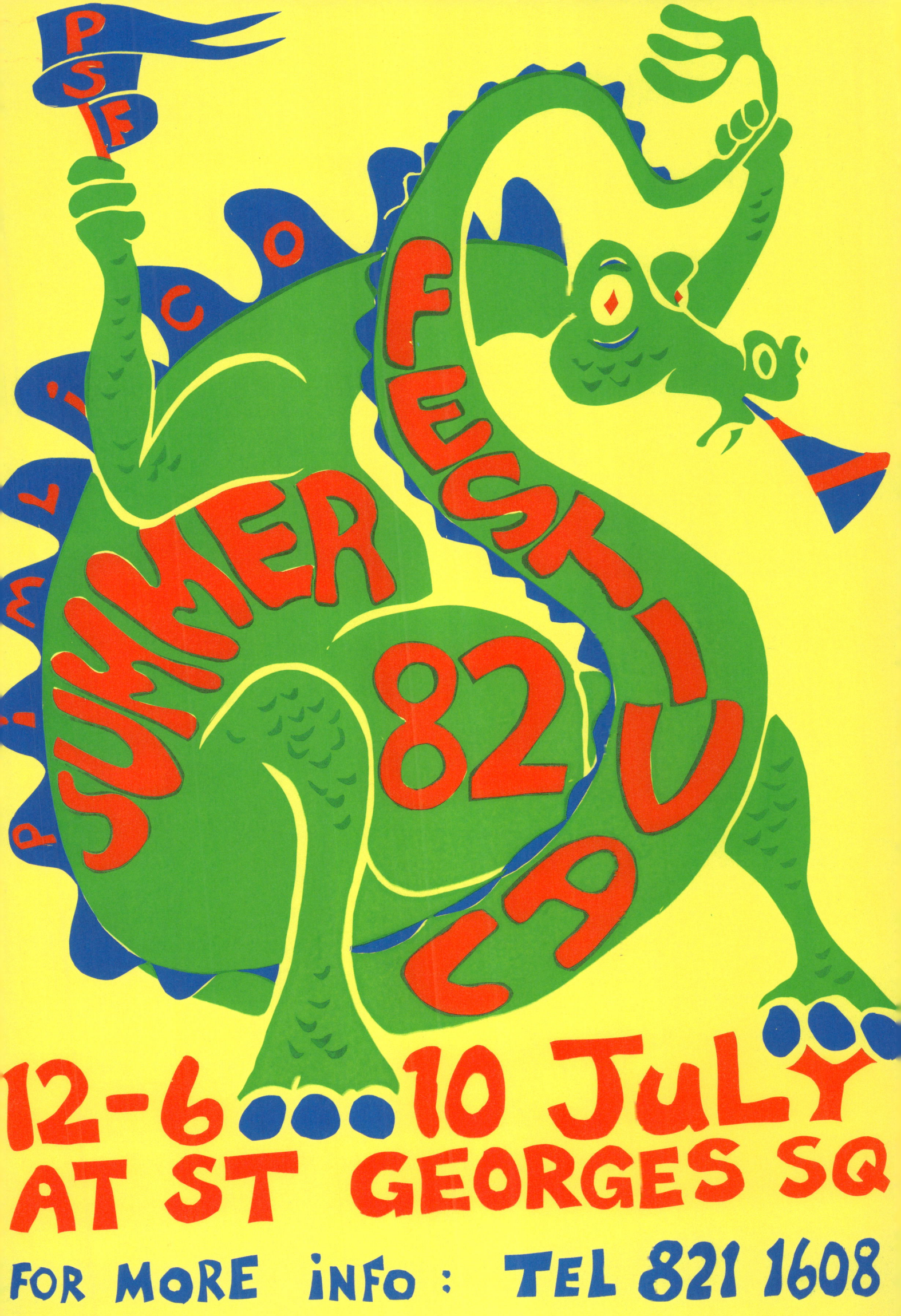

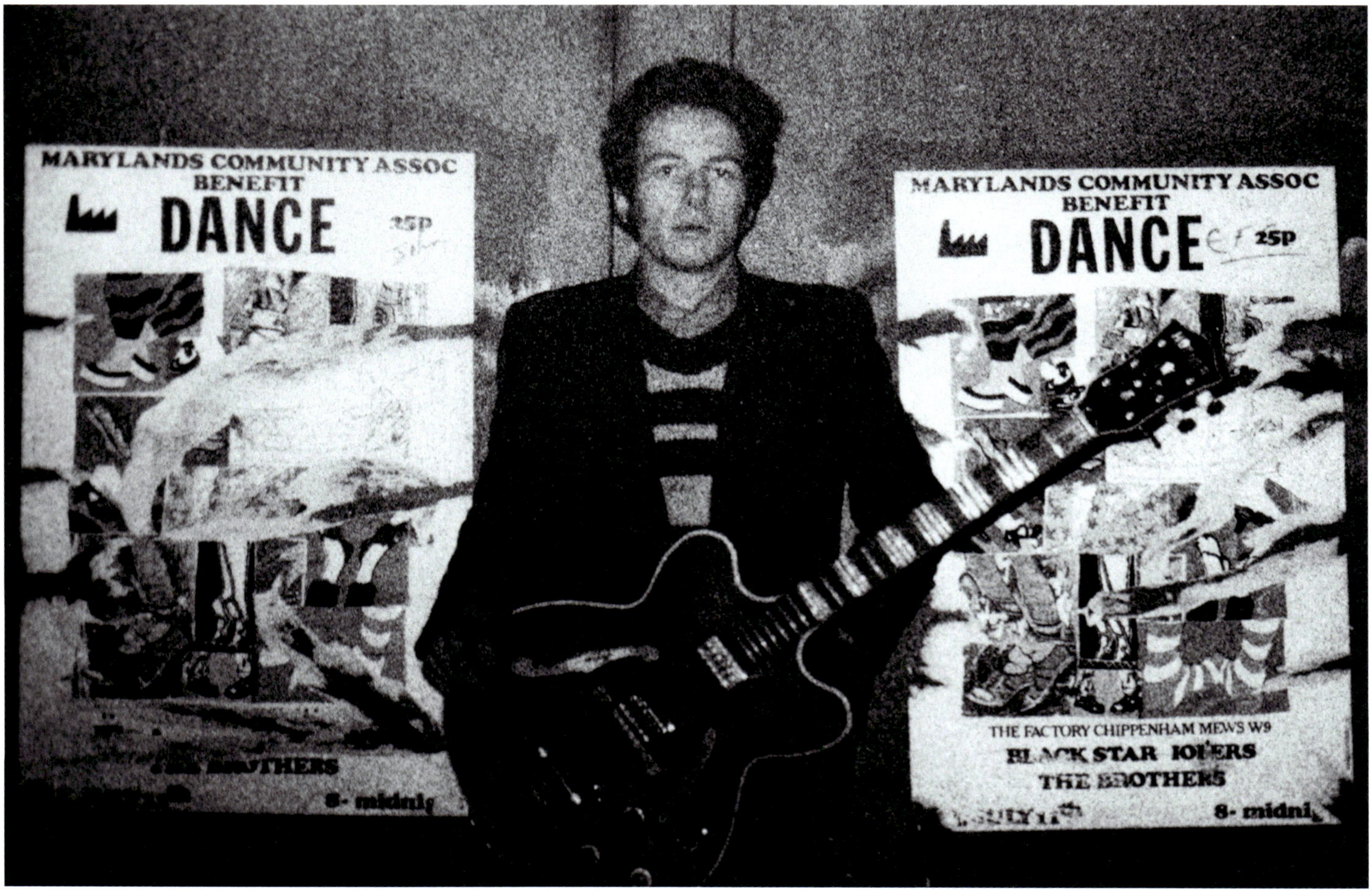

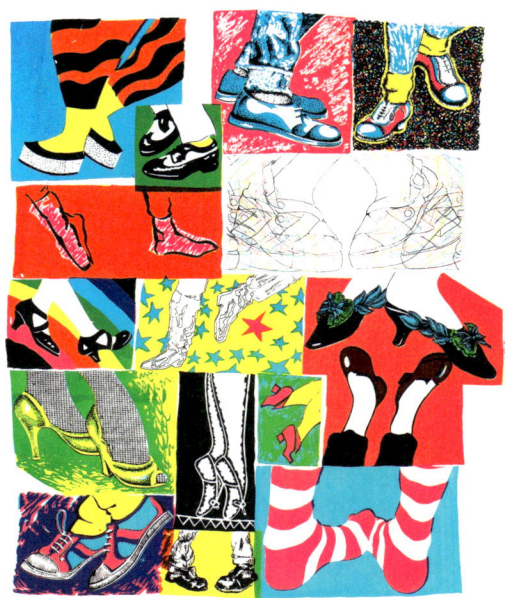

This page
MARYLANDS COMMUNITY
ASSOCIATION BENEFIT DANCE,
1975, John Phillips

Opposite
THE 101ERS, 1975, Joe Strummer

Named after the Maida Vale squat where they lived, The 101ers featured Joe Strummer, before he joined The Clash. In 1975, they had a residency at The Elgin pub, ending in January 1976 after noise complaints.

The 101'ers

R'n B

RAVE ON! ♪ ♪ ♪

EVERY MONDAY NIGHT at THE ELGIN

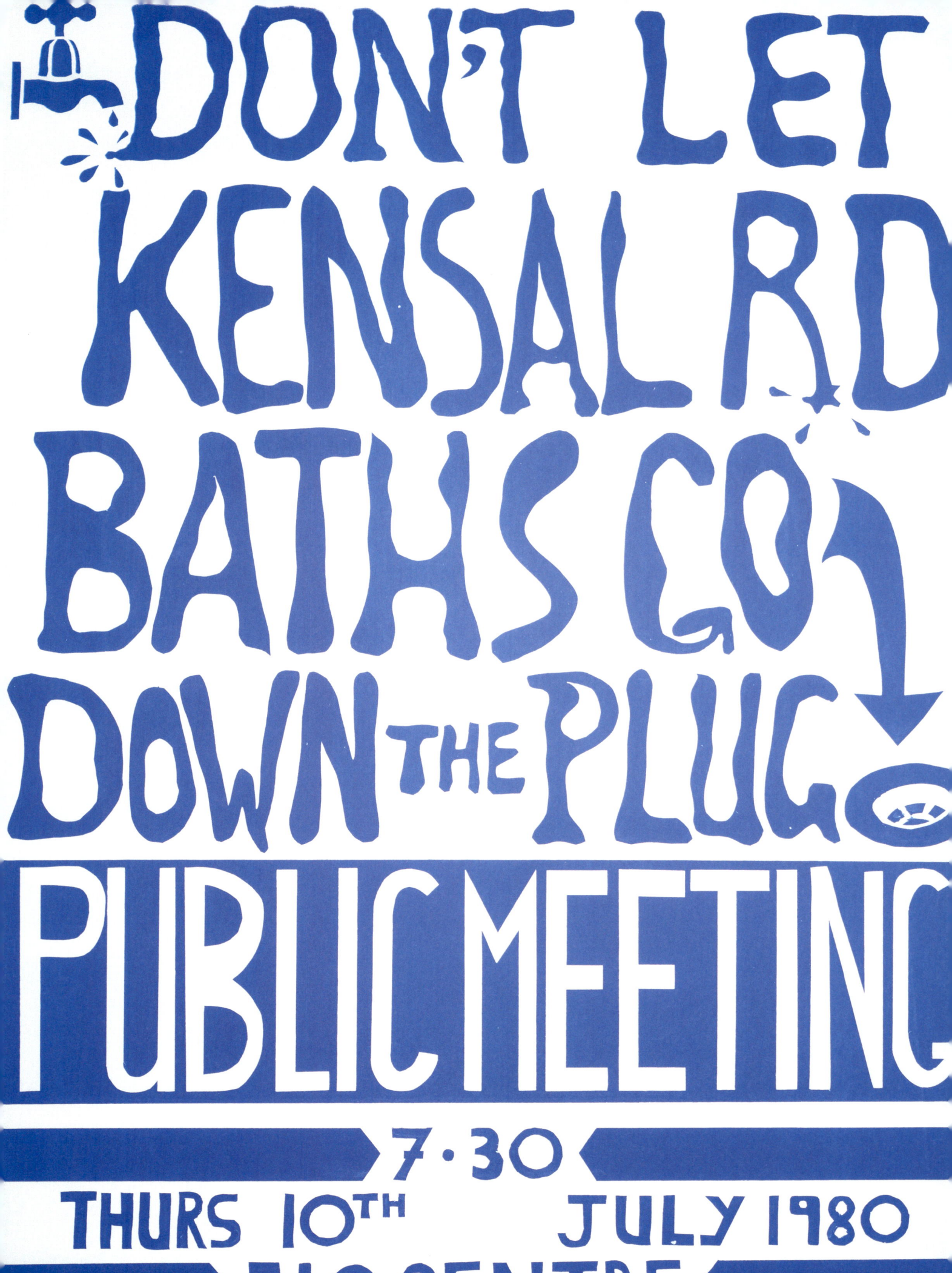

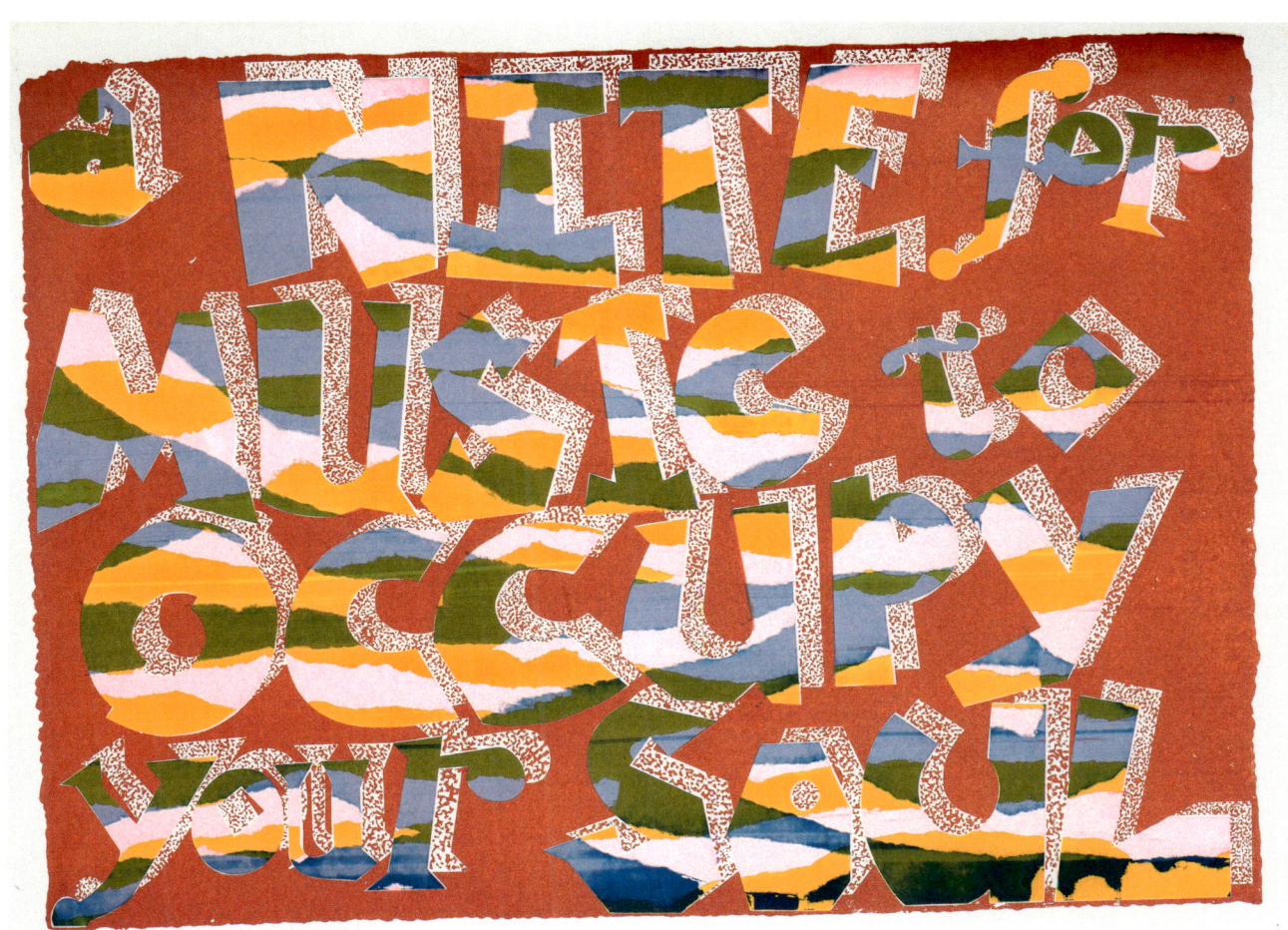

Opposite
KENSAL ROAD BATHS, 1980,
Simon Kenrick

Above
A NITE FOR MUSIC TO OCCUPY
YOUR SOUL, 1980, John Phillips

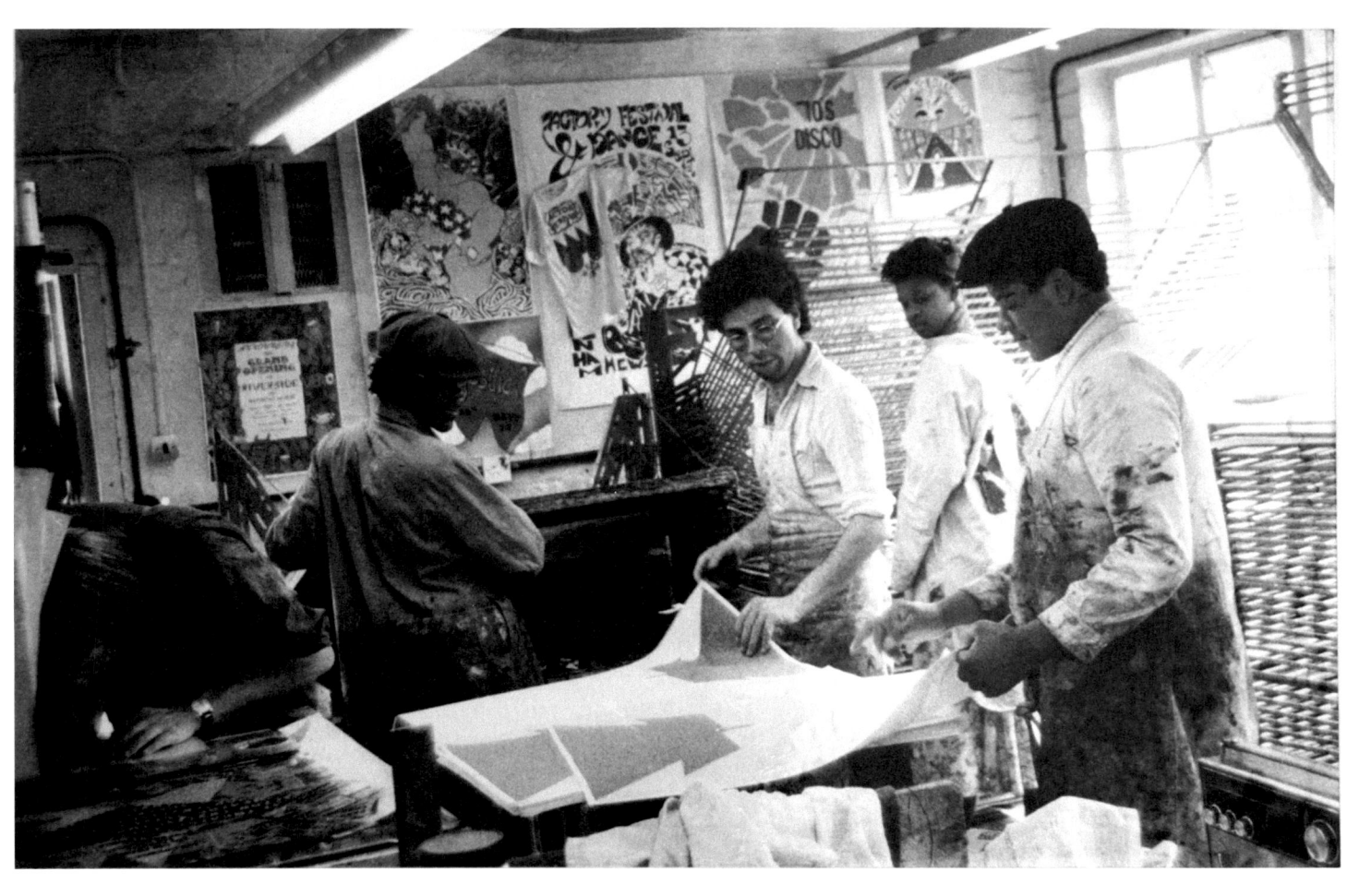

ROCKAS HOUSE, 1976,
Martin Stellman and Rockas Sound

As a youth worker in the 1970s, writer Martin Stellman worked with young sound systems in Lewisham, and Rockas Sound in particular. He drew on this experience to write and co-produce the film *Babylon* (1980).

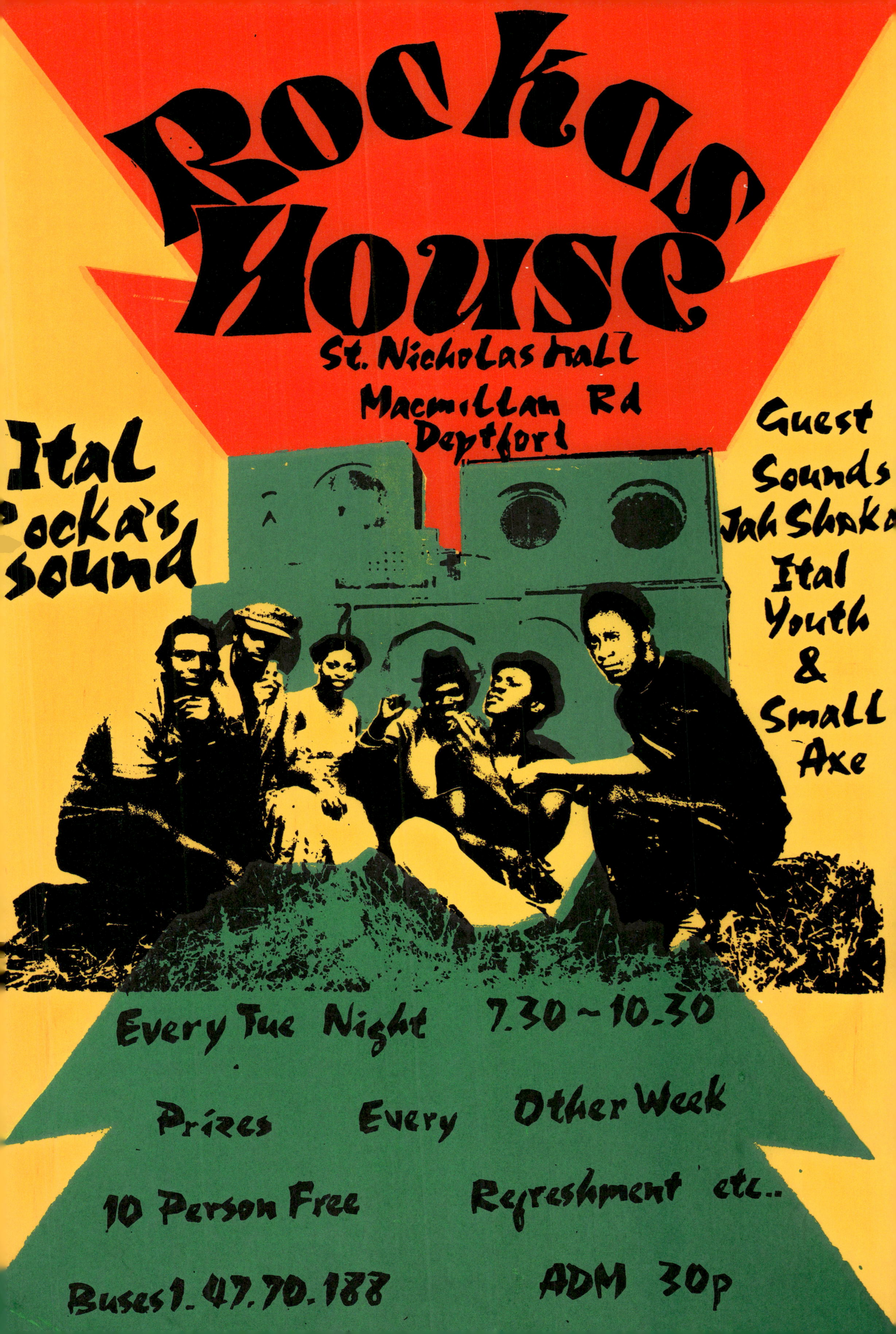

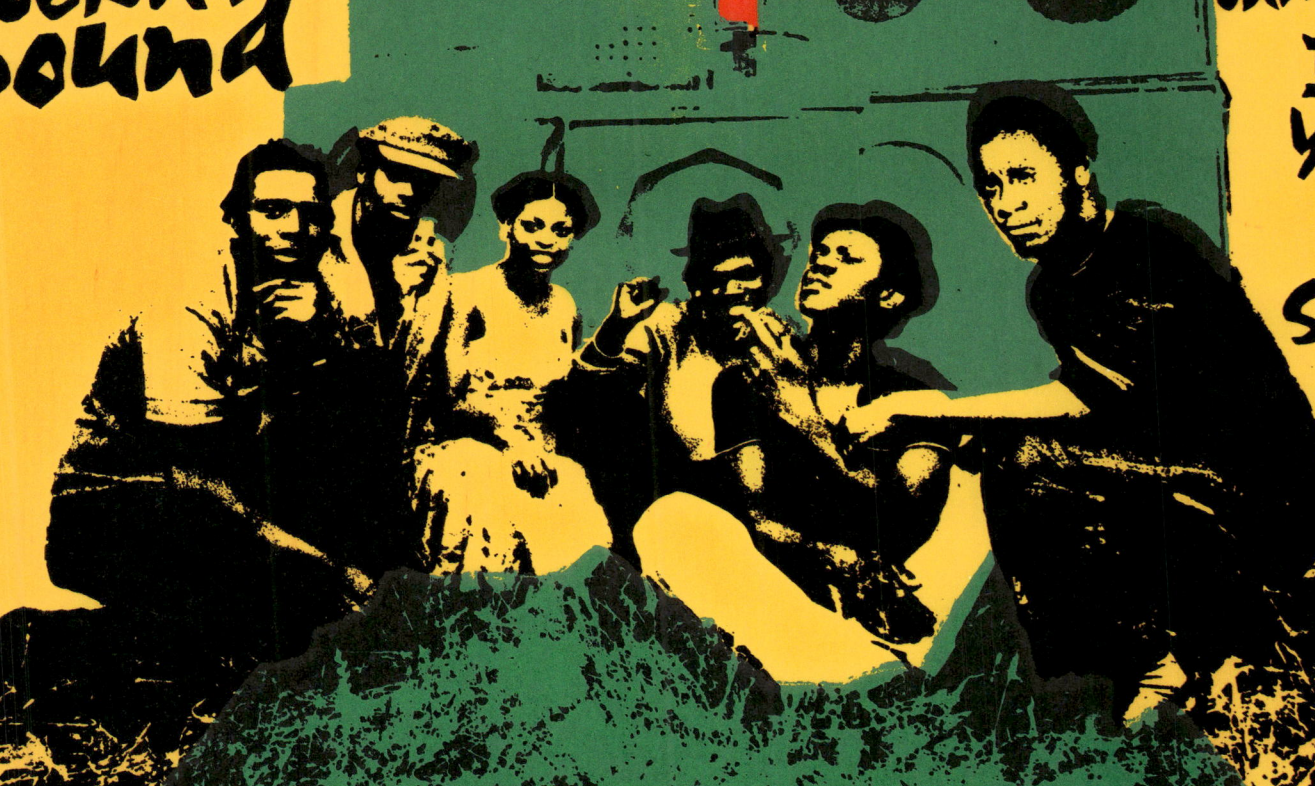

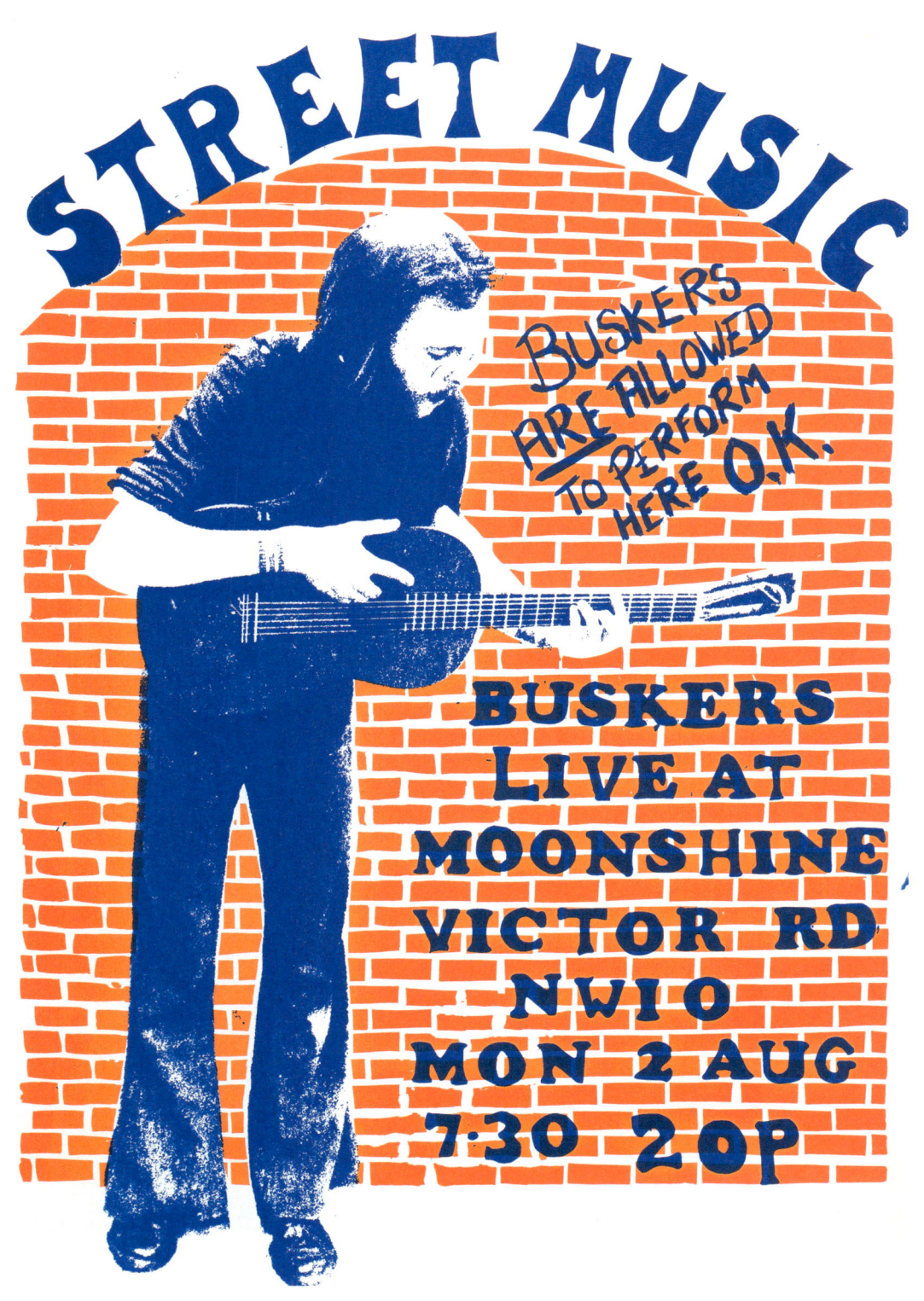

Above
STREET MUSIC, 1976, Richard Baker

Opposite
WORKSHOPS IN PHOTOGRAPHY, 1982, Simon Fell

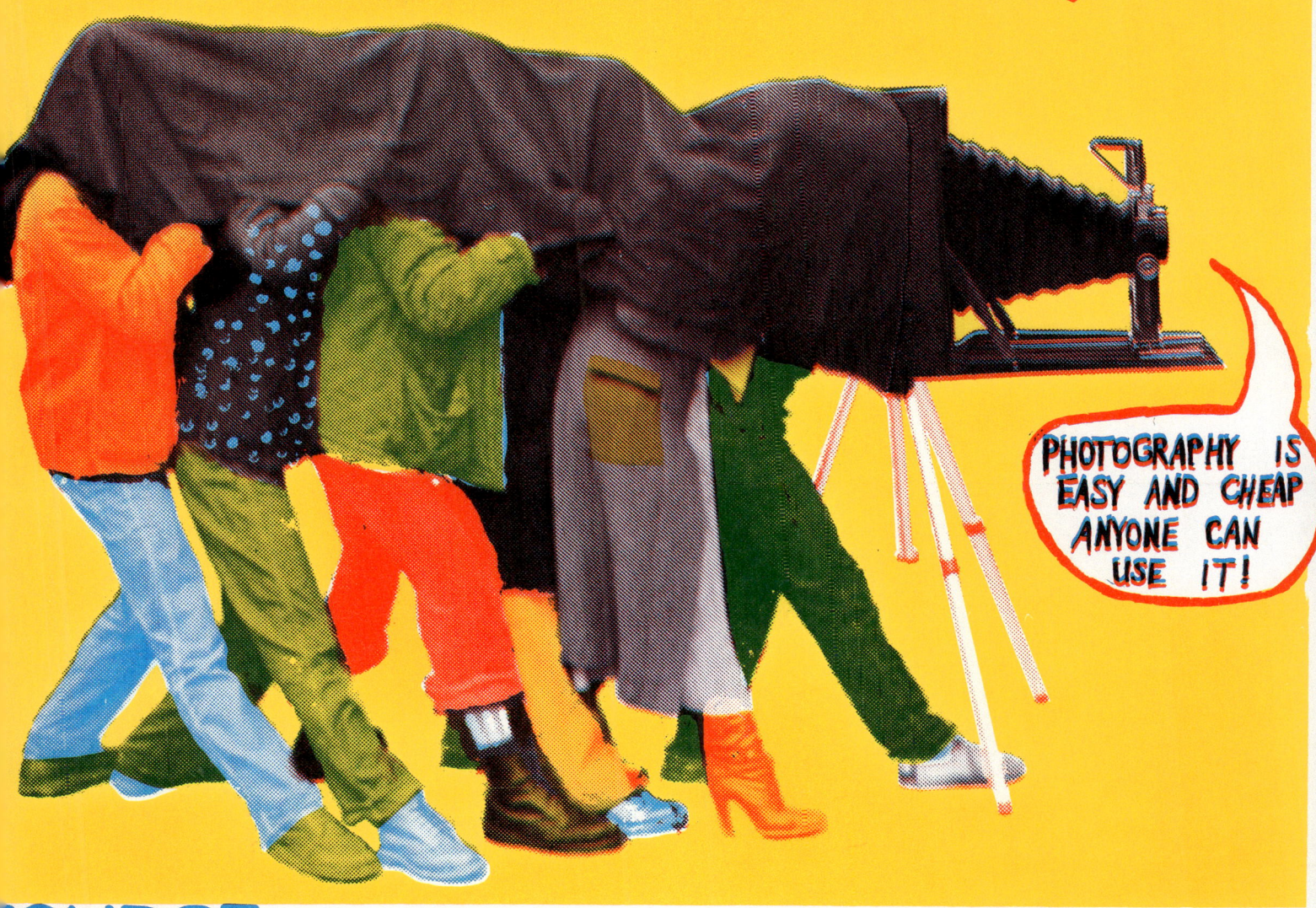

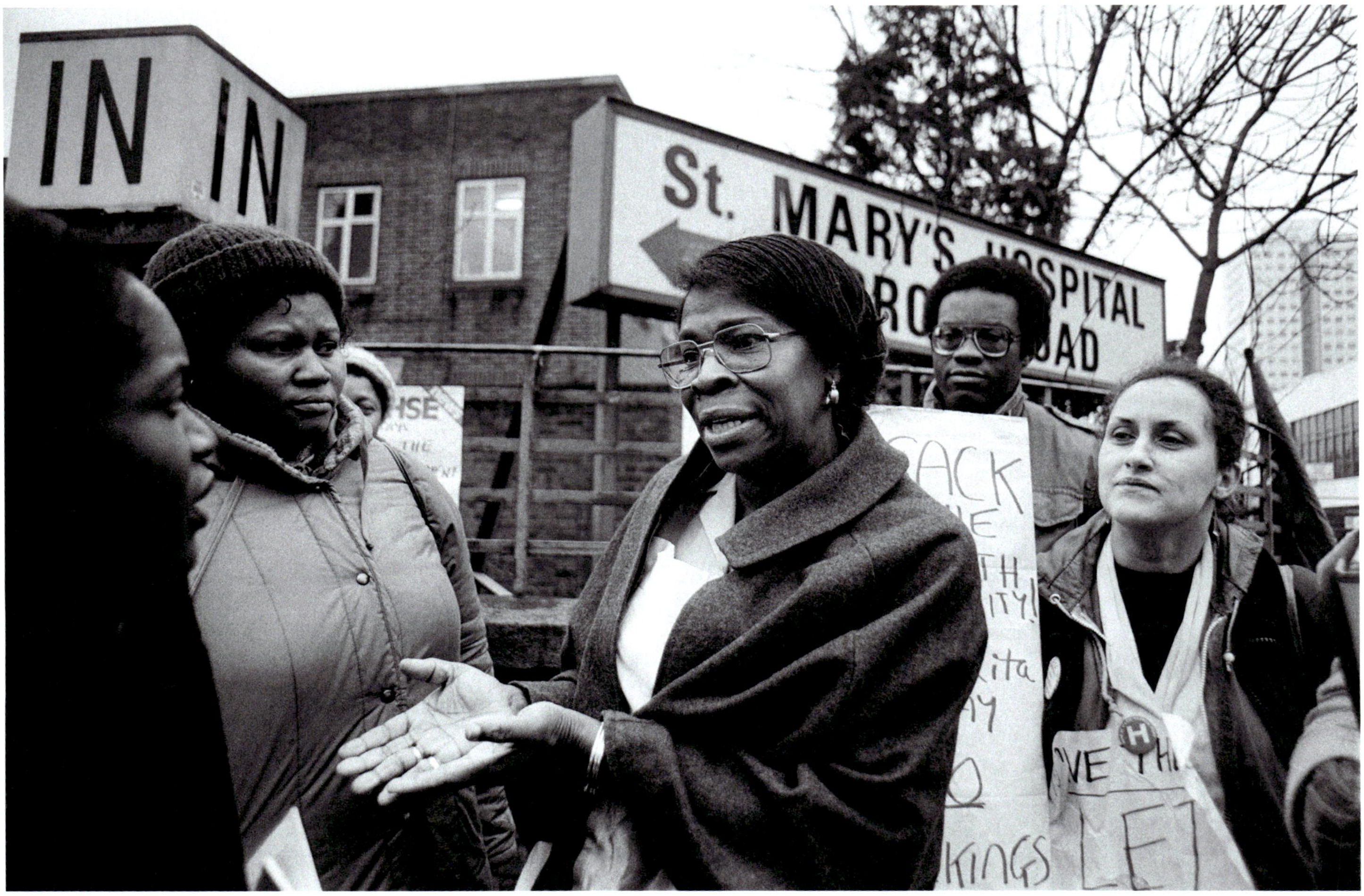

Above
Hospital worker Rita Maxim, speaking outside St Mary's Hospital, where she worked for 22 years, after being sacked for refusing to sign a new short term contract, 22 February, 1984. Photo by Philip Wolmuth.

This page
SAVE OUR HOSPITAL!,
1981, Jay Talbot

Opposite
SAVE ST MARY'S HOSPITAL,
1981, John Phillips

Since the late 1970s, St Mary's Hospital (Harrow Rd) had suffered bed cuts and lack of investment, which were vigorously opposed by staff and local residents, who objected to key local resources being lost and services being removed to another St Mary's, in Praed Street. Residents joined forces with hospital staff to protest the closure. On 26 June 1981 staff engaged in a work-in and carried out two occupations in different parts of the hospital. St Mary's (Harrow Rd) closed in 1986.

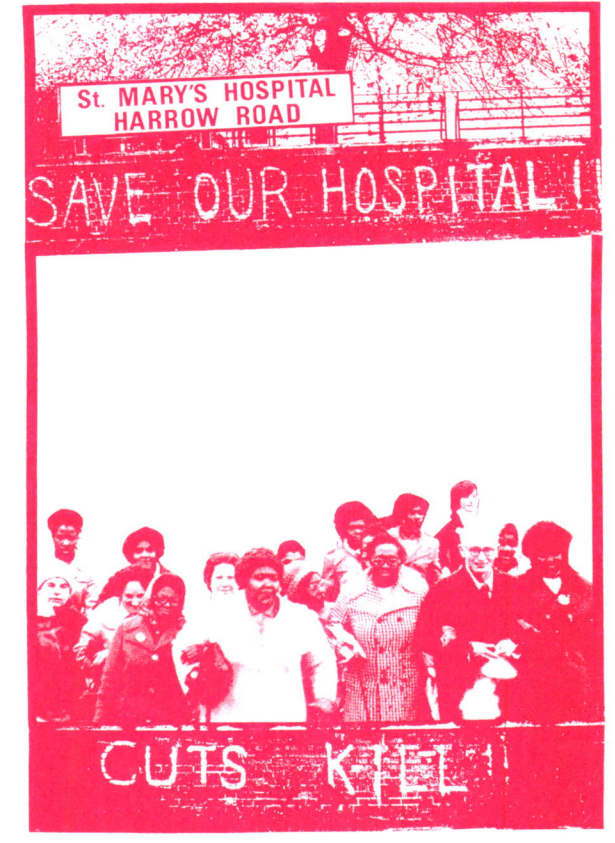

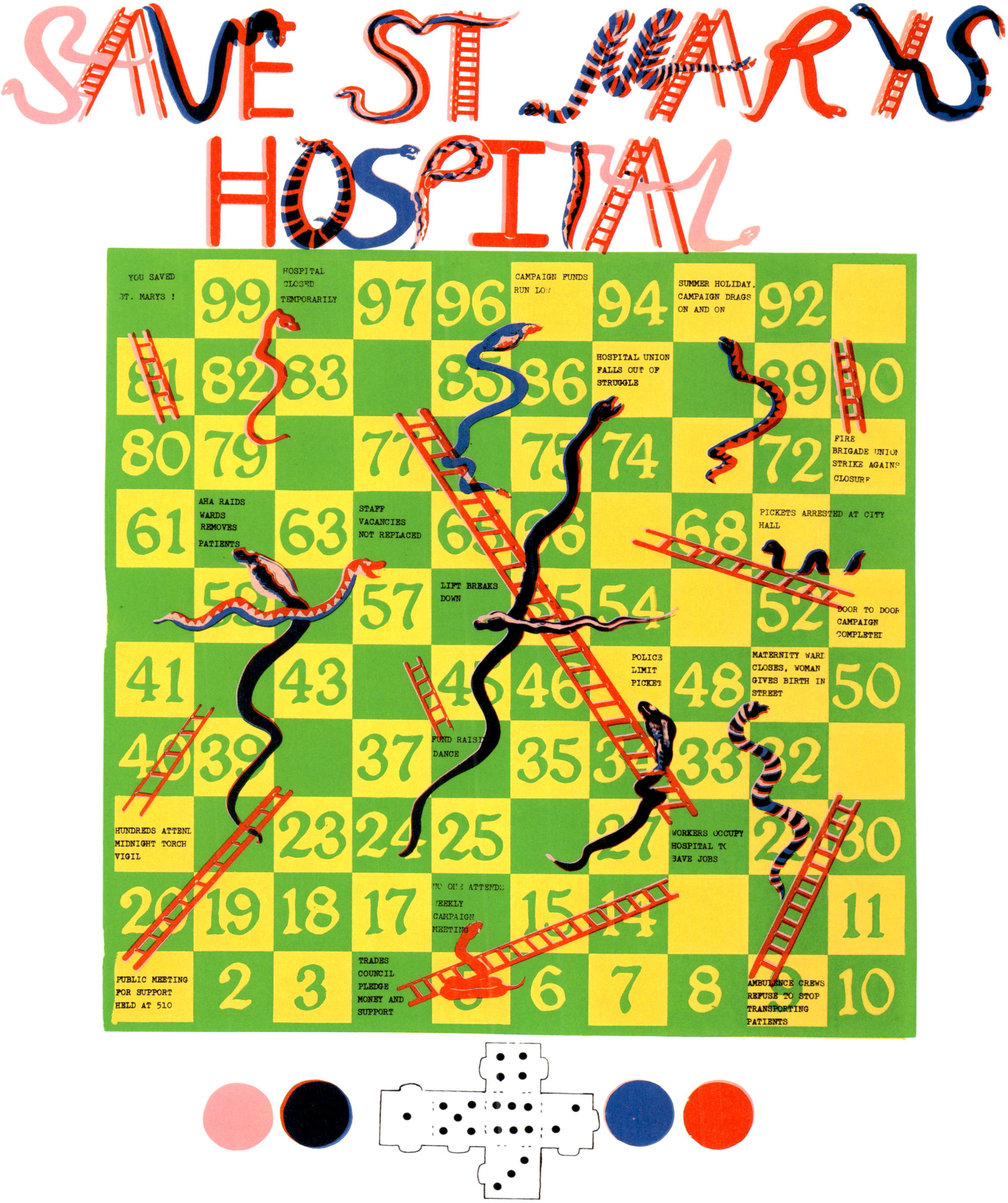

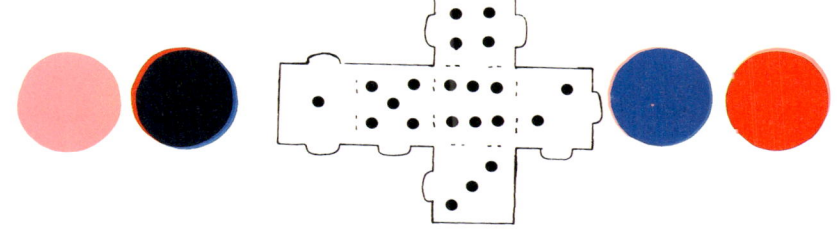

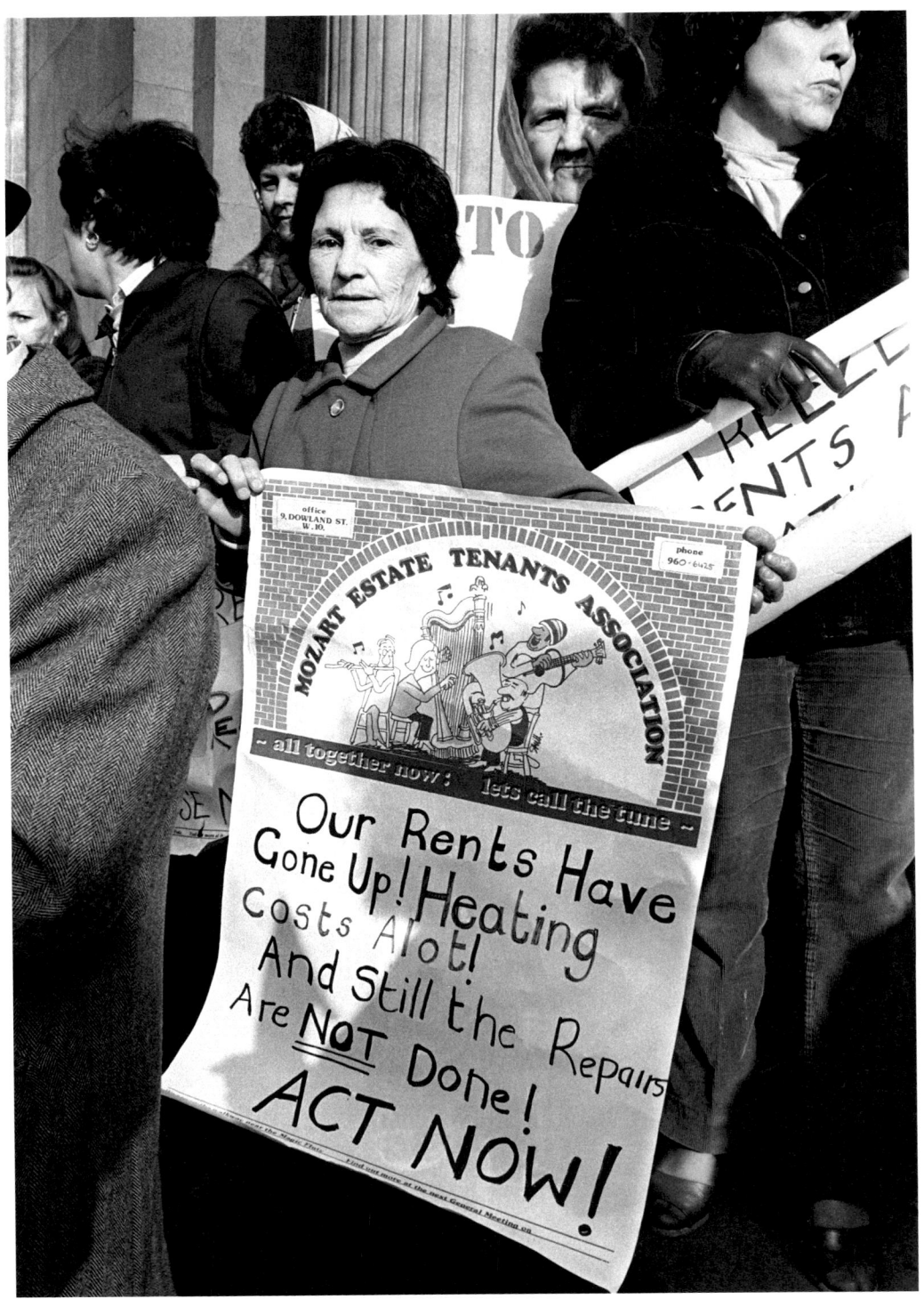

Above
Mozart Estate tenants picket Westminster Council House on Marylebone Road, 27 April 1981. Photo by Philip Wolmuth.

Opposite
DAMP AND HEATING BLUES, c.1980, Jay Talbot

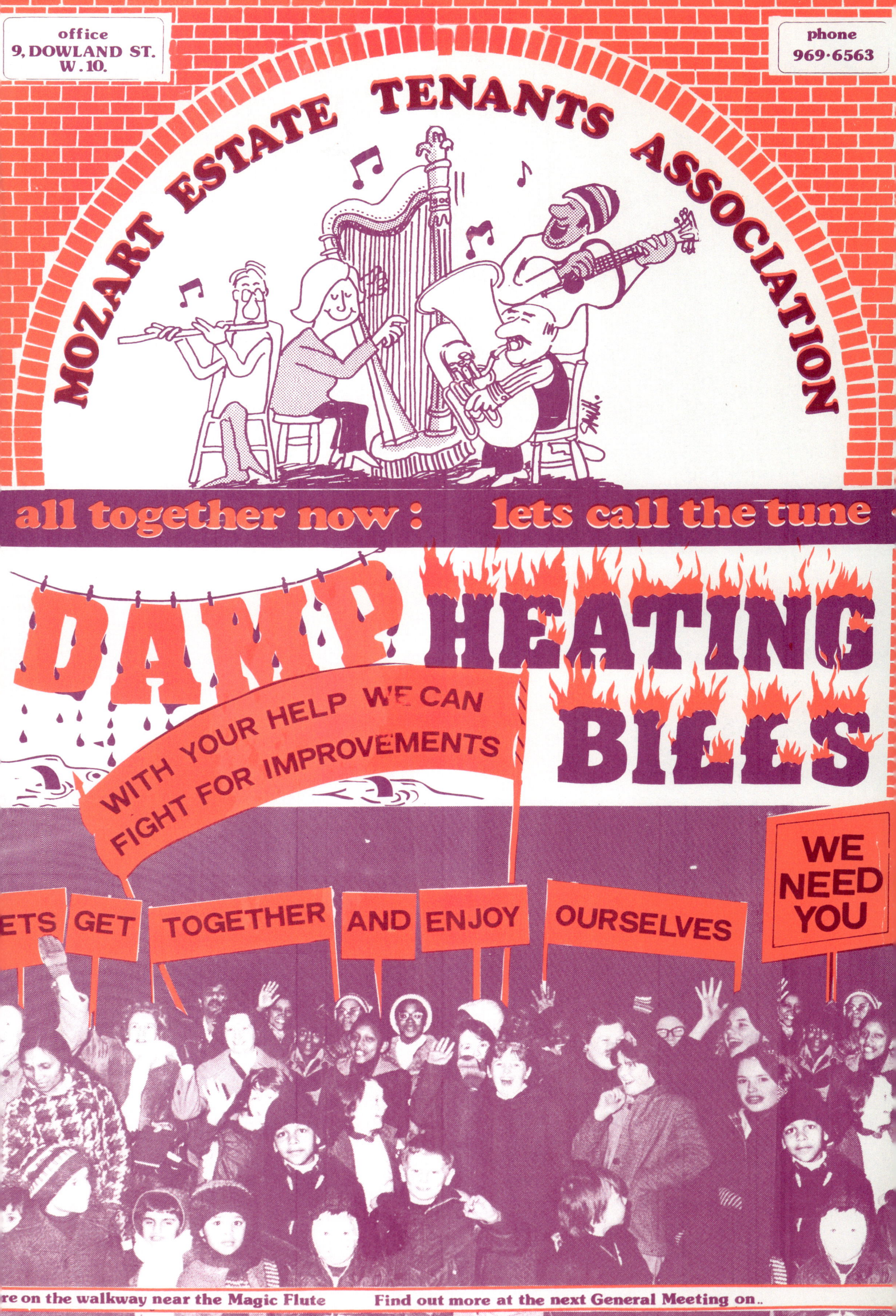

Opposite
NORTH PADDINGTON WOMEN'S
CENTRE, 1978, Anonymous

Next pages

YOUNG? UNEMPLOYED? A WOMAN?,
1982, Anonymous

WESTMINSTER YOUTH ADVISORY
SERVICE, c.1982, Simon Fell

Numerous projects and organisations
emerged within the neighbourhood:
some such as the Westminster Youth
Advisory Service were part of local
authority provision, while others, like
North Paddington Women's Centre,
were initiatives by local residents.

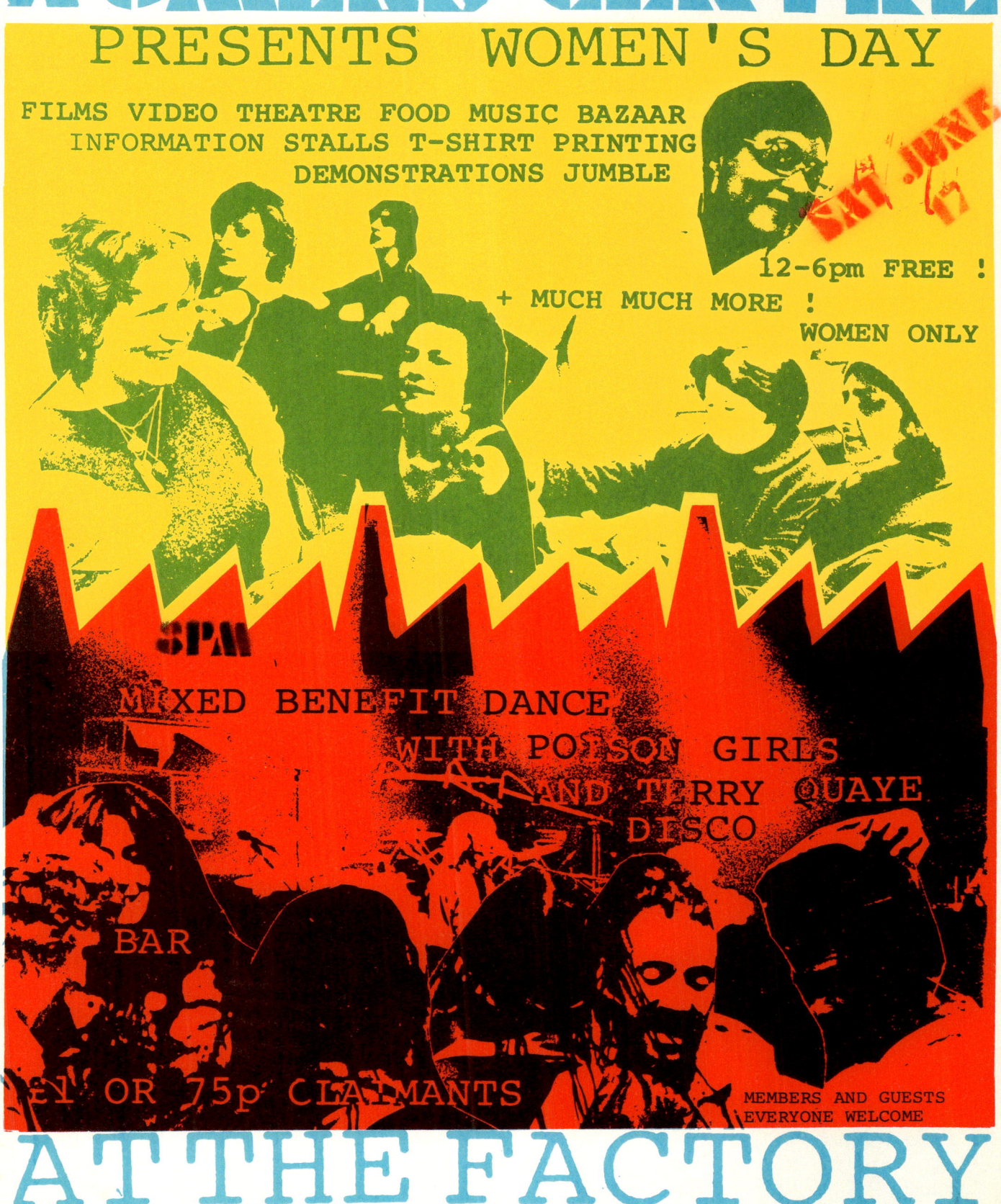

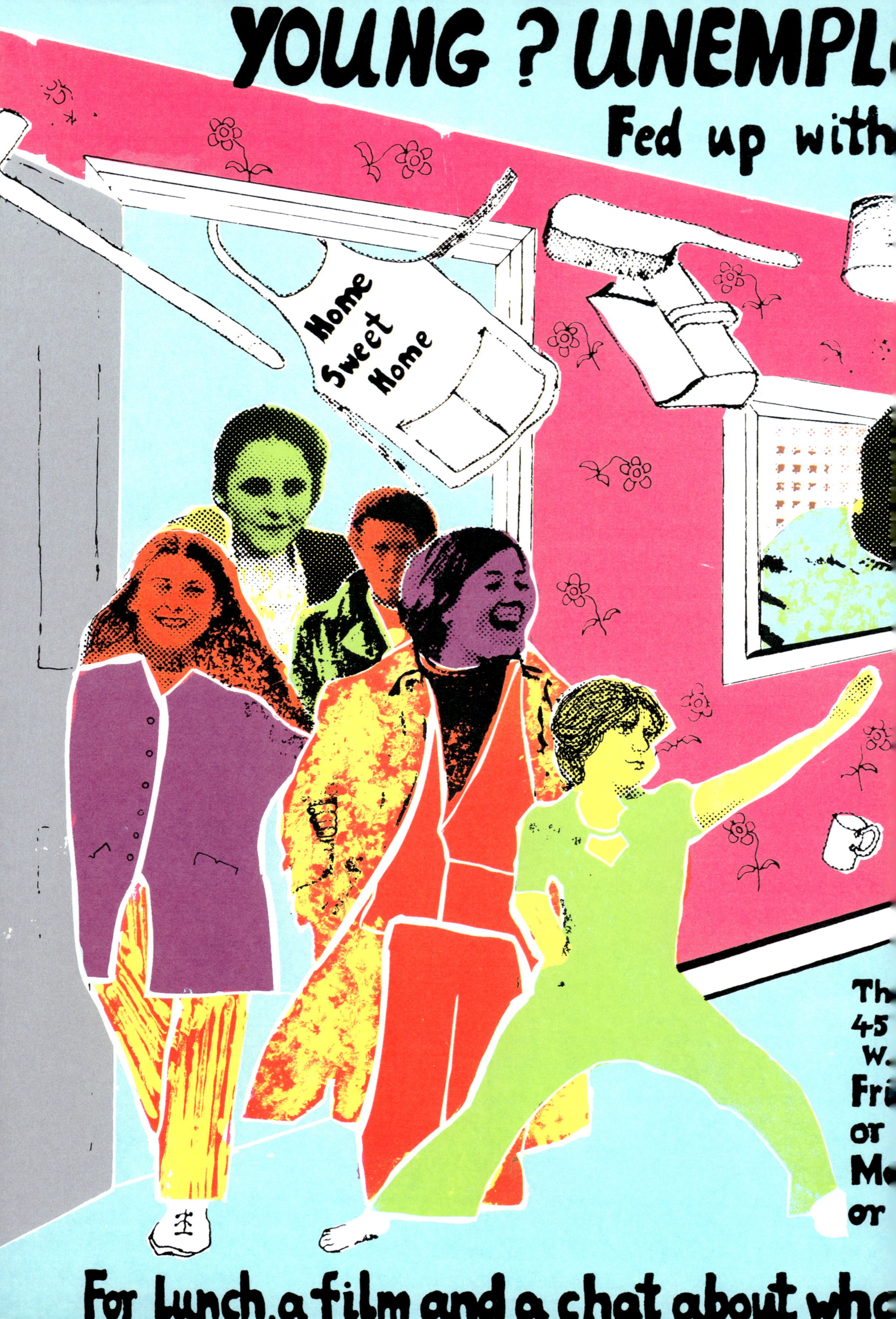

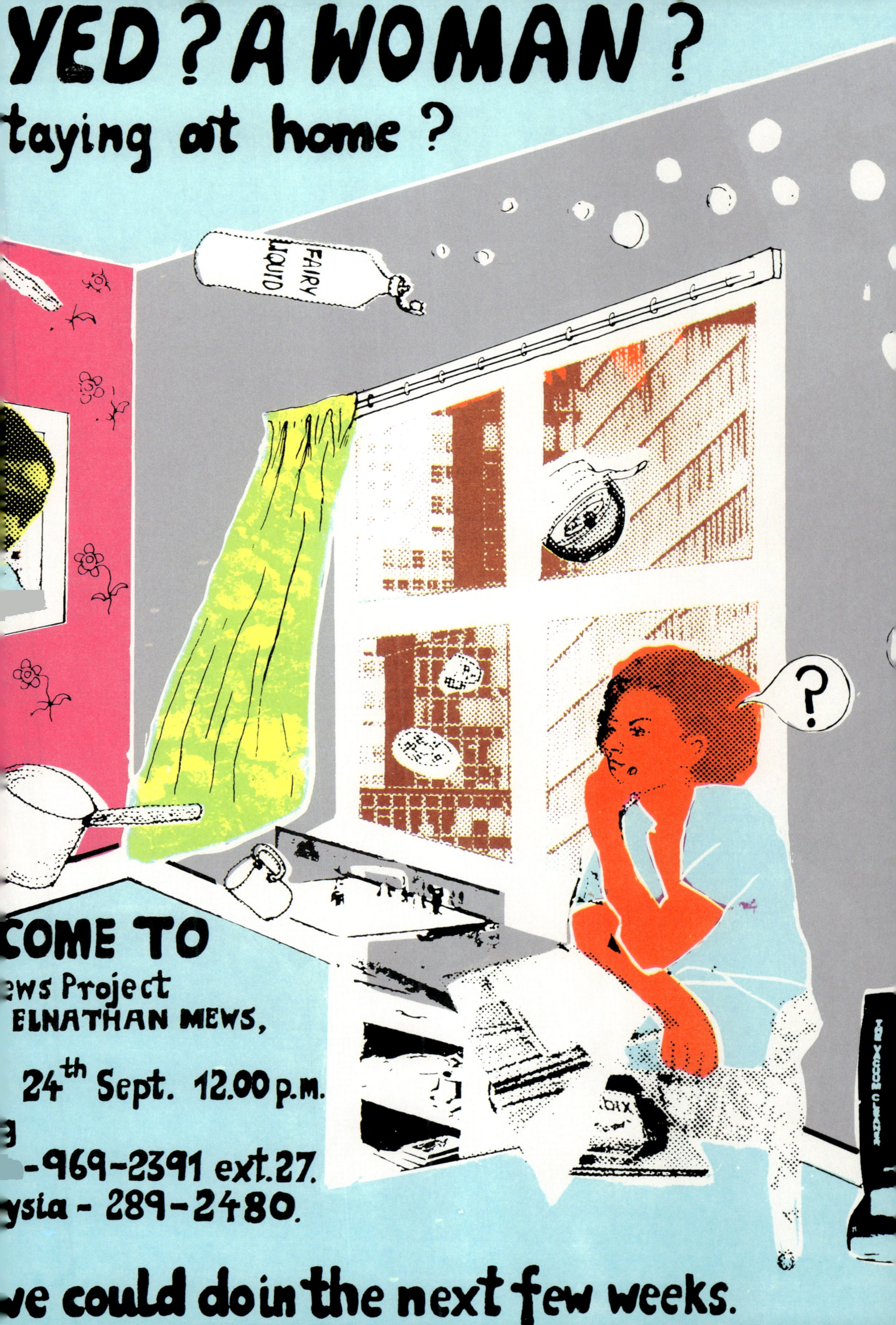

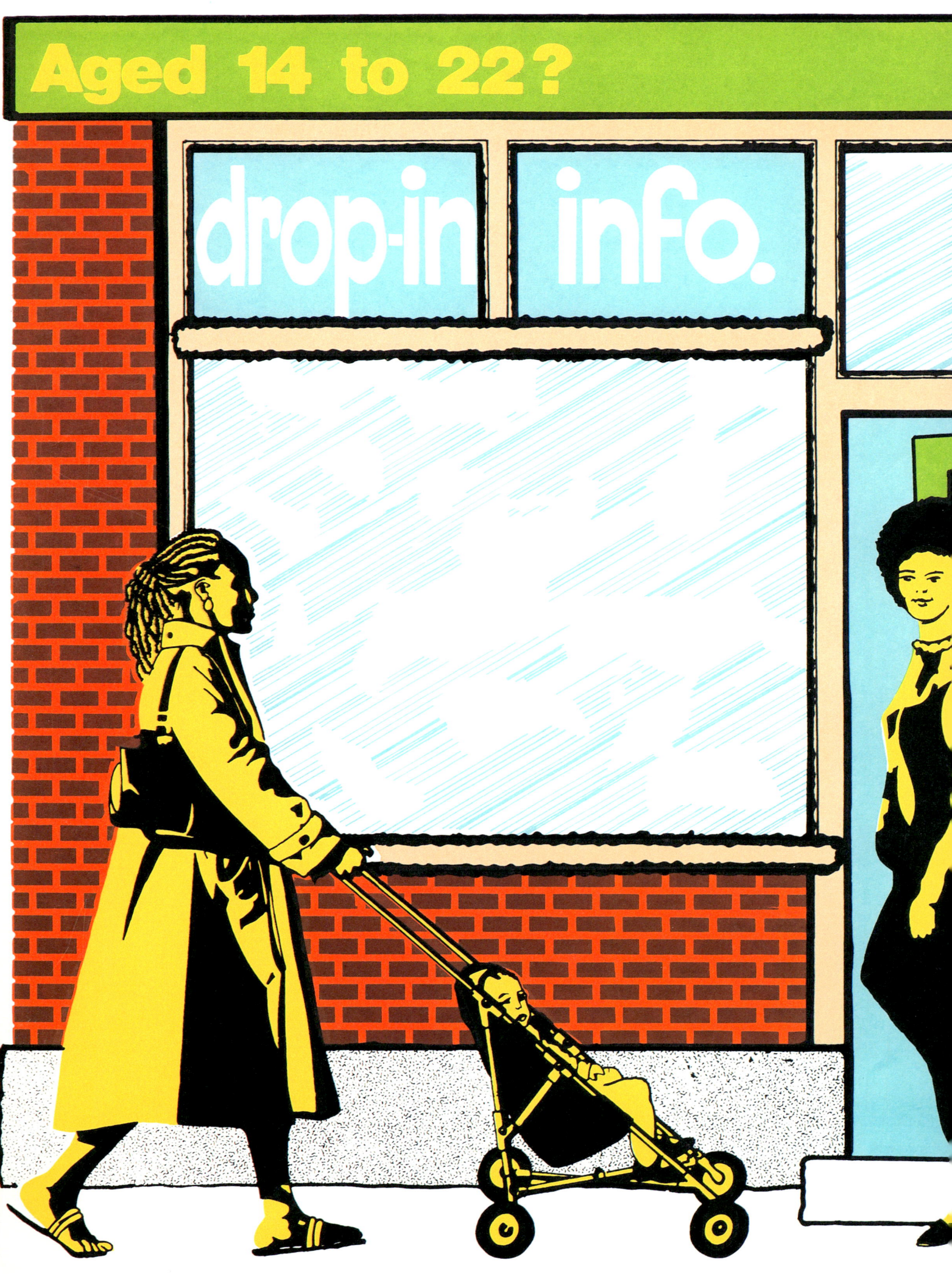

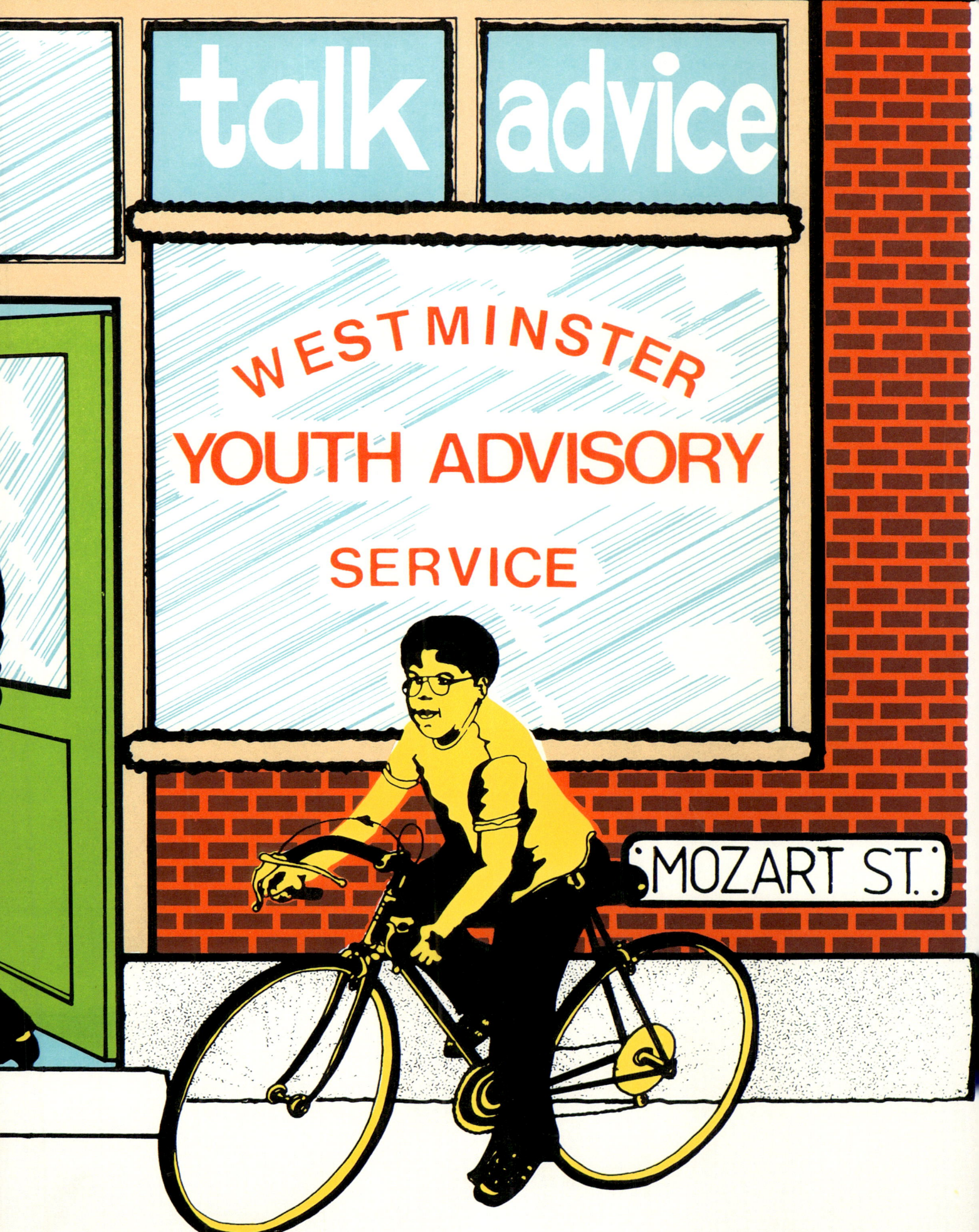

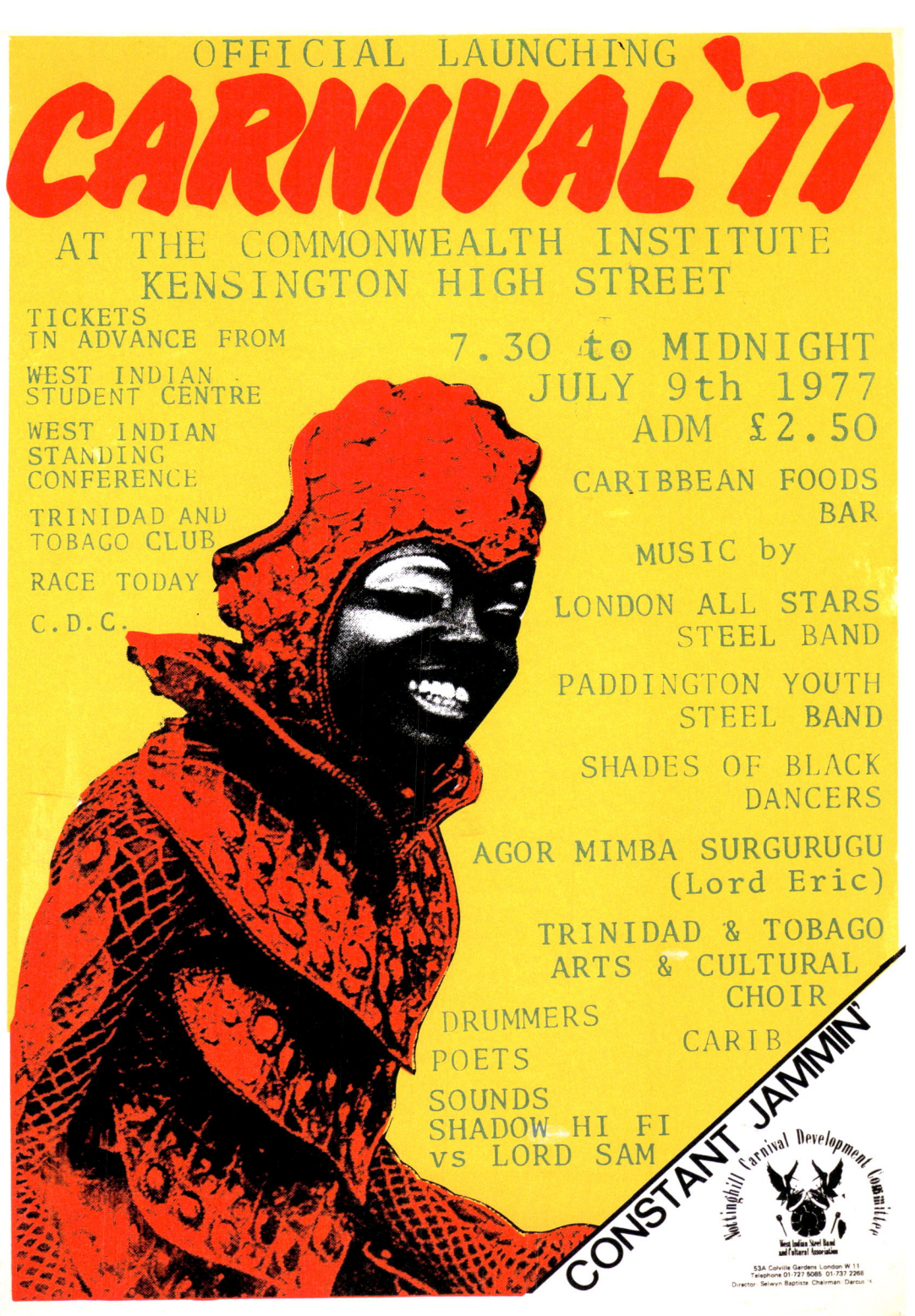

Above
CARNIVAL 77, 1977, John Phillips

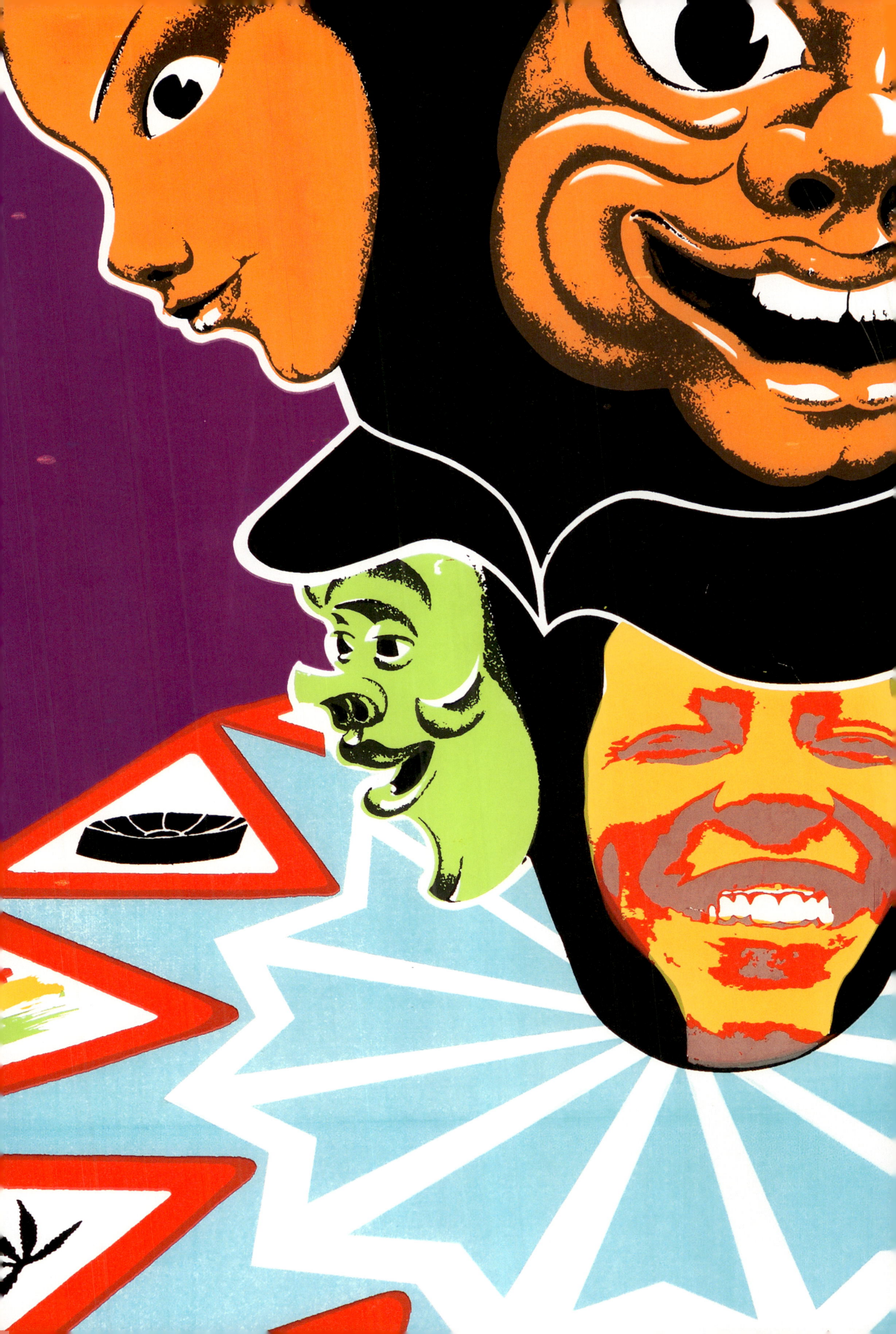

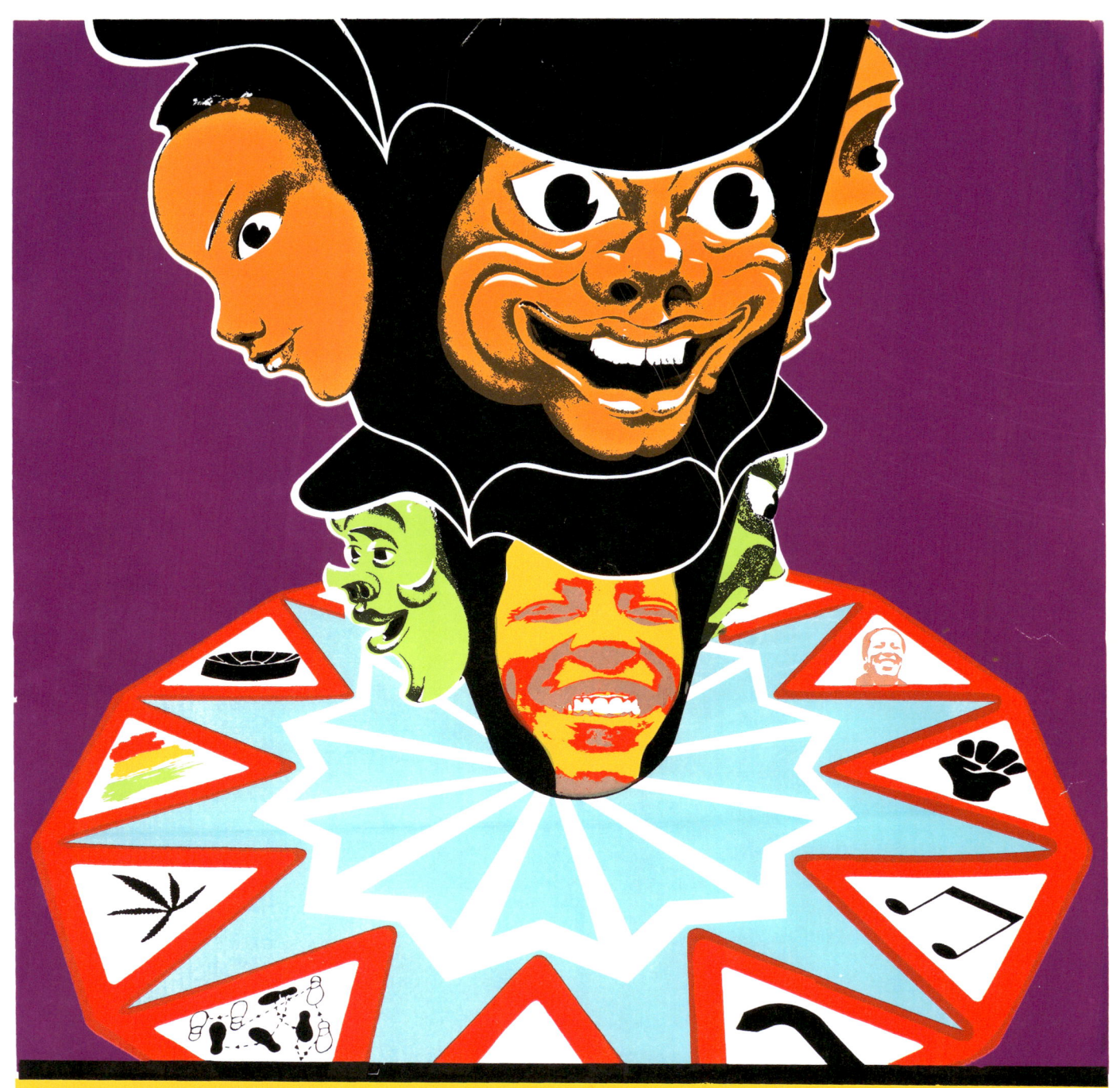

Opposite
THE STREETS BELONG TO
THE PEOPLE, KEEP CARNIVAL
IN THE STREETS, 1976, John Phillips

In the early 1970s, Notting Hill Carnival grew from a neighbourhood party into an international festival of Caribbean cultures, mingling Jamaican sound systems and Trinidadian masquerade together with the traditions and celebrations of the many other islands to create a unique London hybrid. As the festival grew, so did the tensions surrounding it, including proposals to move it away from 'the Ghetto' as Notting Hill was then known, and into the open space of Hyde Park. The Printshop worked with numerous carnival bands to produce t-shirts, costume decorations and posters for events. It made this poster in response to proposals to move the festival away from the neighbourhood.

Next pages
STOP POLICE REPRESSION
OF CLOWNS, 1976, John Phillips

Posters were usually requested by established organisations and campaigns, but some were made spontaneously in response to events. On 21 February 1976, for example, the performer Daniel Rovai was beaten and arrested while performing peacefully to a small crowd in Portobello Market. The performer launched a publicity campaign in his own defence to which the Printshop contributed this poster.

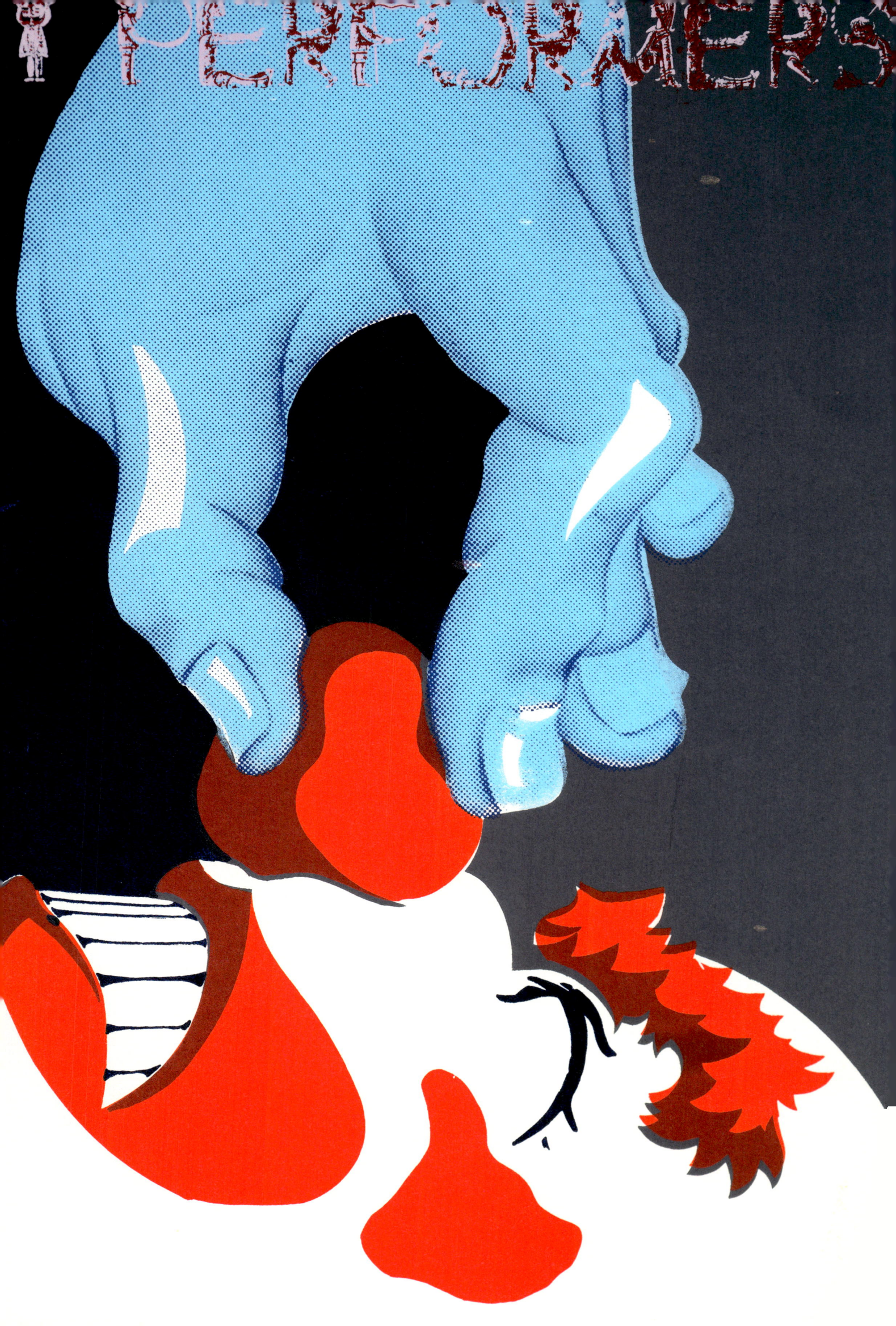

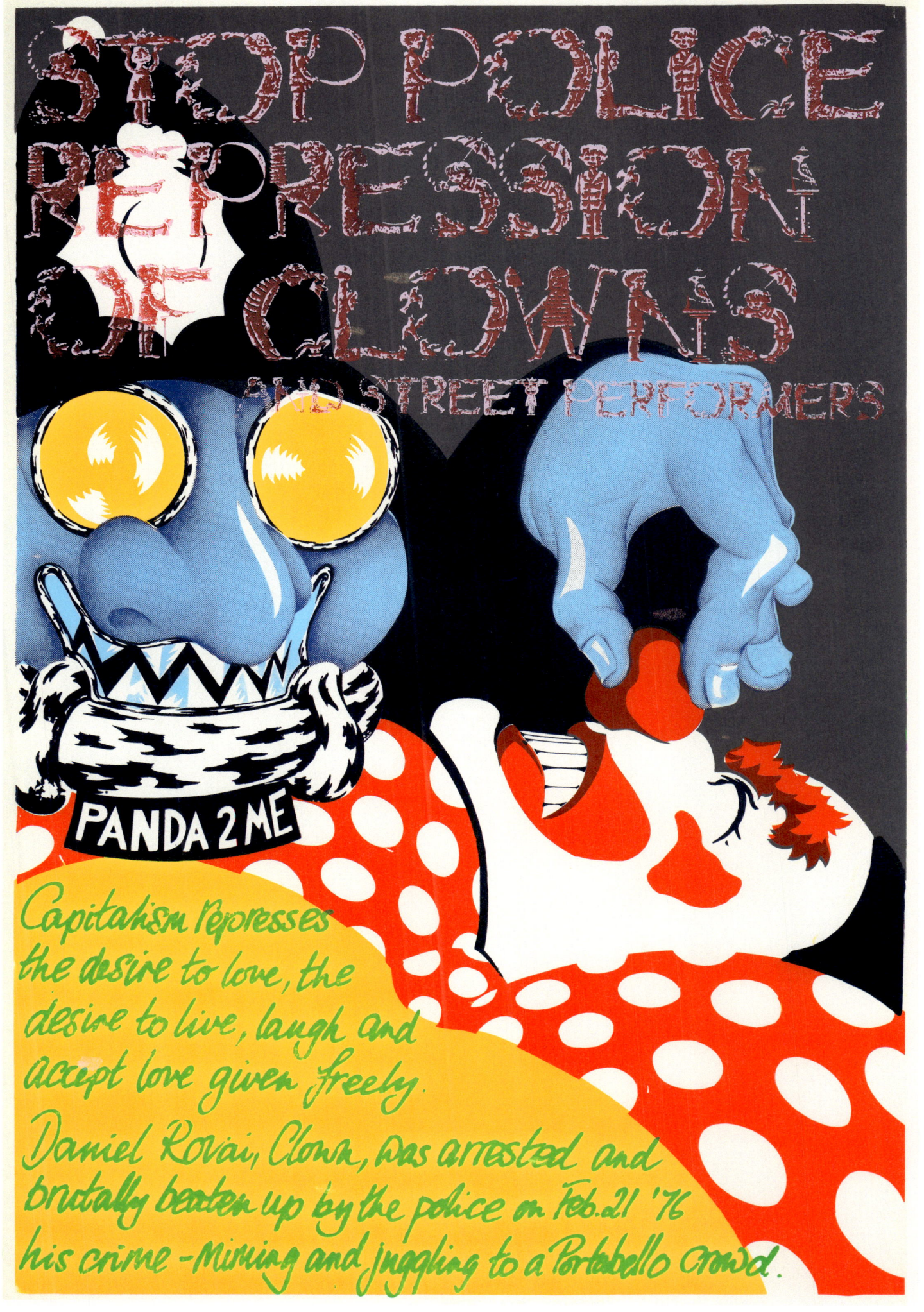

FREE GEORGE INCE

LOBBY! National Lobby of Members of Parliament followed by Candle-light Vigil

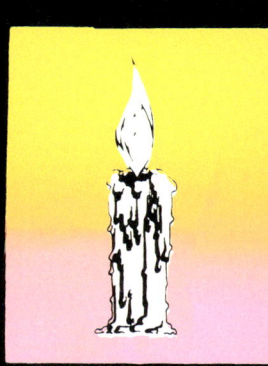

AT The House of Commons, Westminster at 6pm on Wednesday 27th April 1977

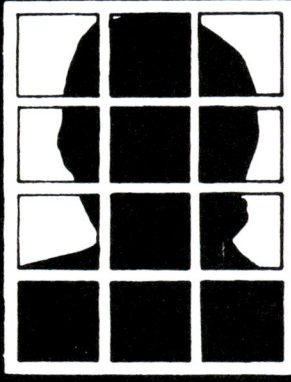
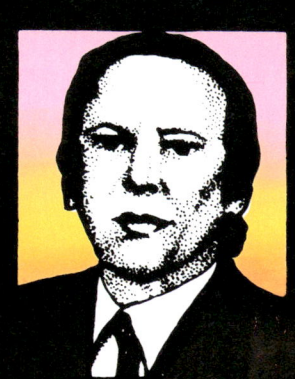
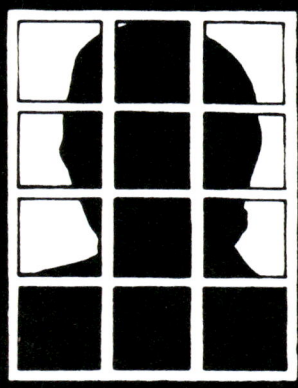

5 years ago George Ince was sentenced to fifteen years imprisonment for his alleged part in a robbery. He was convicted on the evidence of 2 police officers who had seen photographs of him before the identification parade.

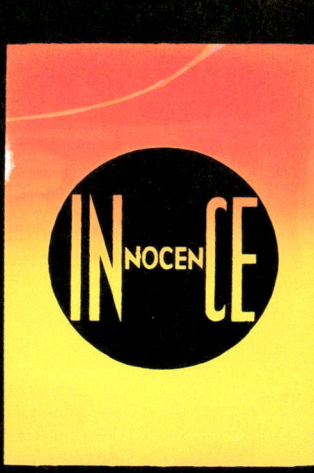

The Devlin Report has recommended that identification evidence alone is not sufficient to convict.

George Ince has constantly maintained his innocence.

We demand his immediate release.

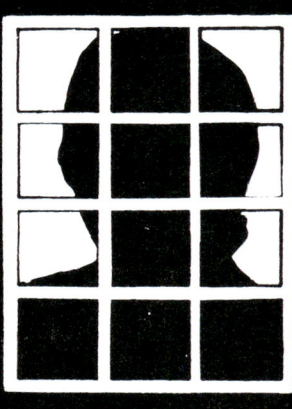
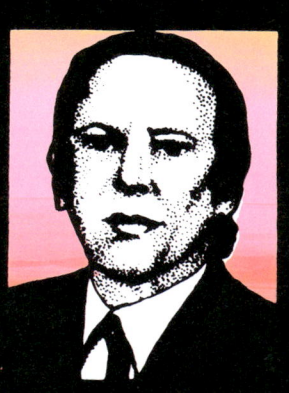
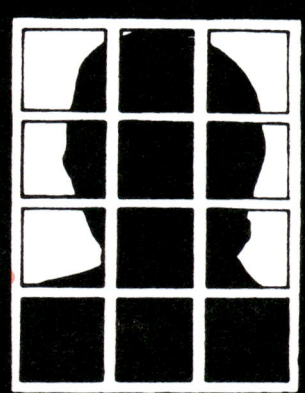

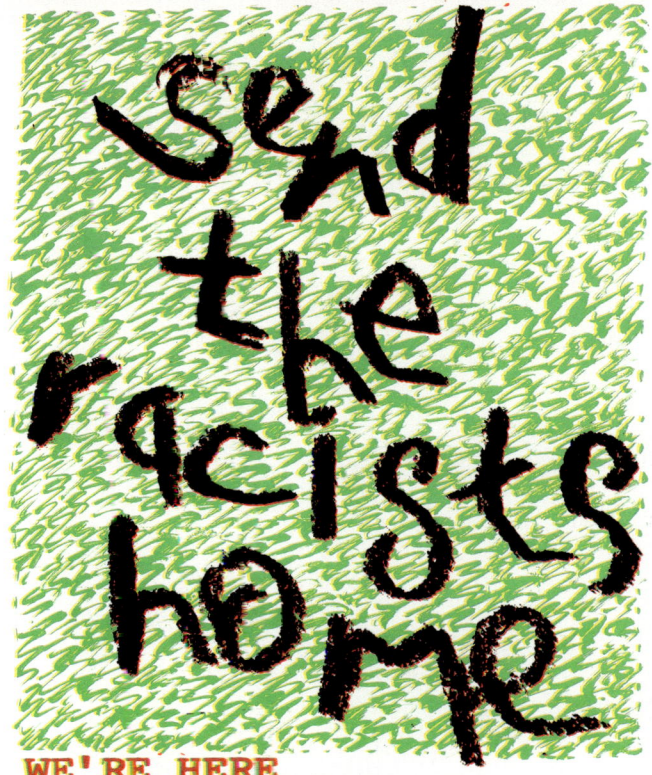

Opposite
FREE GEORGE INCE, 1977, Anon

George Ince was arrested and tried for a murder which he had not committed. The main evidence used against him was fabricated identification by police officers, and his trial eventually collapsed. Following his release, Ince was again arrested, charged and found guilty of a different crime on the basis of identification by a police officer seven months after the crime. He remained in jail until being paroled in 1980.

Above
SEND THE RACISTS HOME, 1978, John Phillips

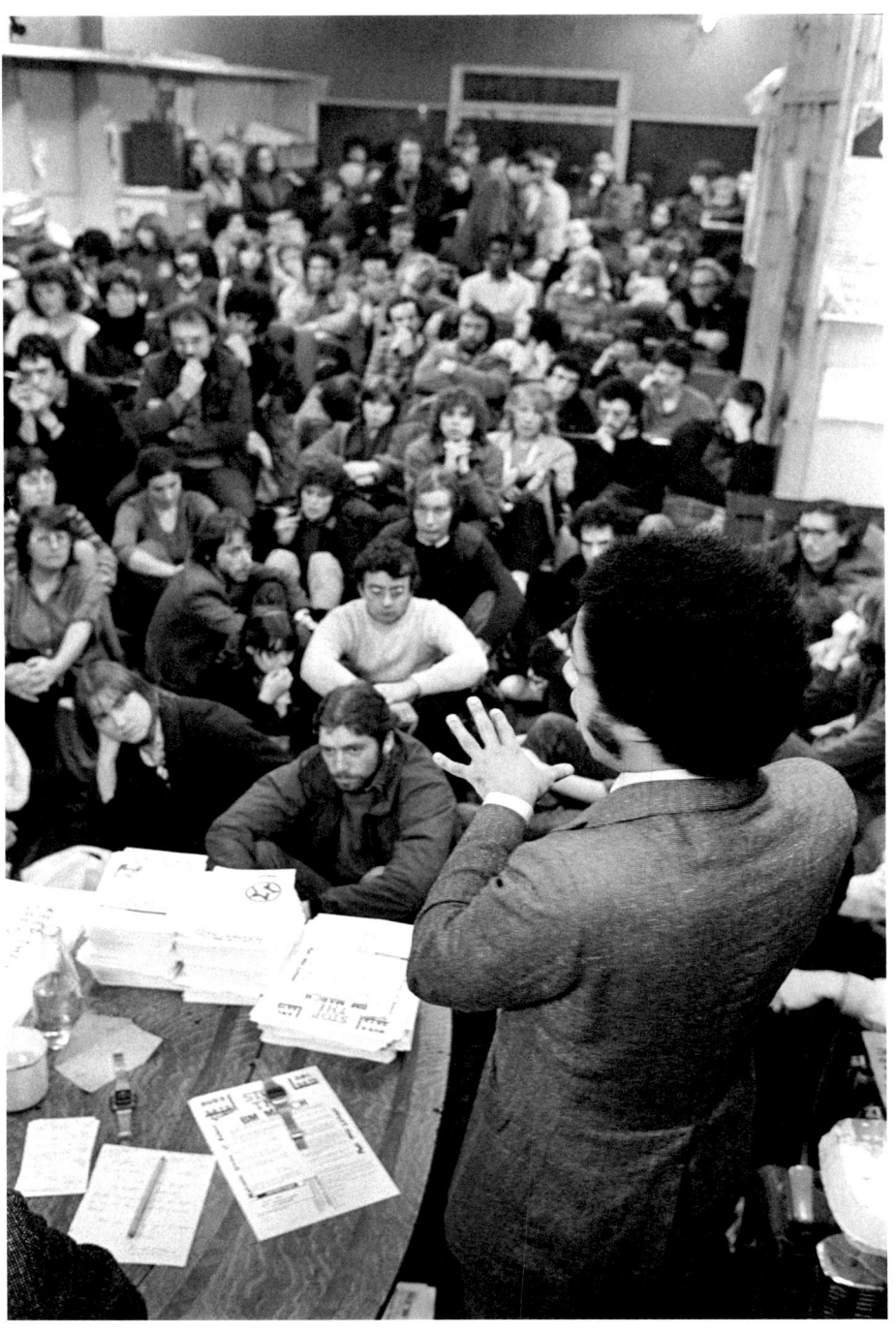

Above
Paul Boetang, then working at Paddington Law Centre, addresses a meeting of Paddington Campaign against Racism at the 510 Centre, Harrow Road, called to organise a counter-demonstration to a local march planned by the neo-Nazi British Movement, November 1980. Photo by Philip Wolmuth.

Opposite
PADDINGTON CAMPAIGN AGAINST RACISM, 1977, John Phillips

The Paddington Campaign Against Racism formed from a broad coalition of local organisations following a 'visitation' by members of the National Front (a prominent right wing and racist party) canvassing for recruits in the area. The Printshop was asked to create an authoritative image that could be distributed widely throughout the neighbourhood. The result was the black and white *Paddington Campaign Against Racism* mask-like logo.

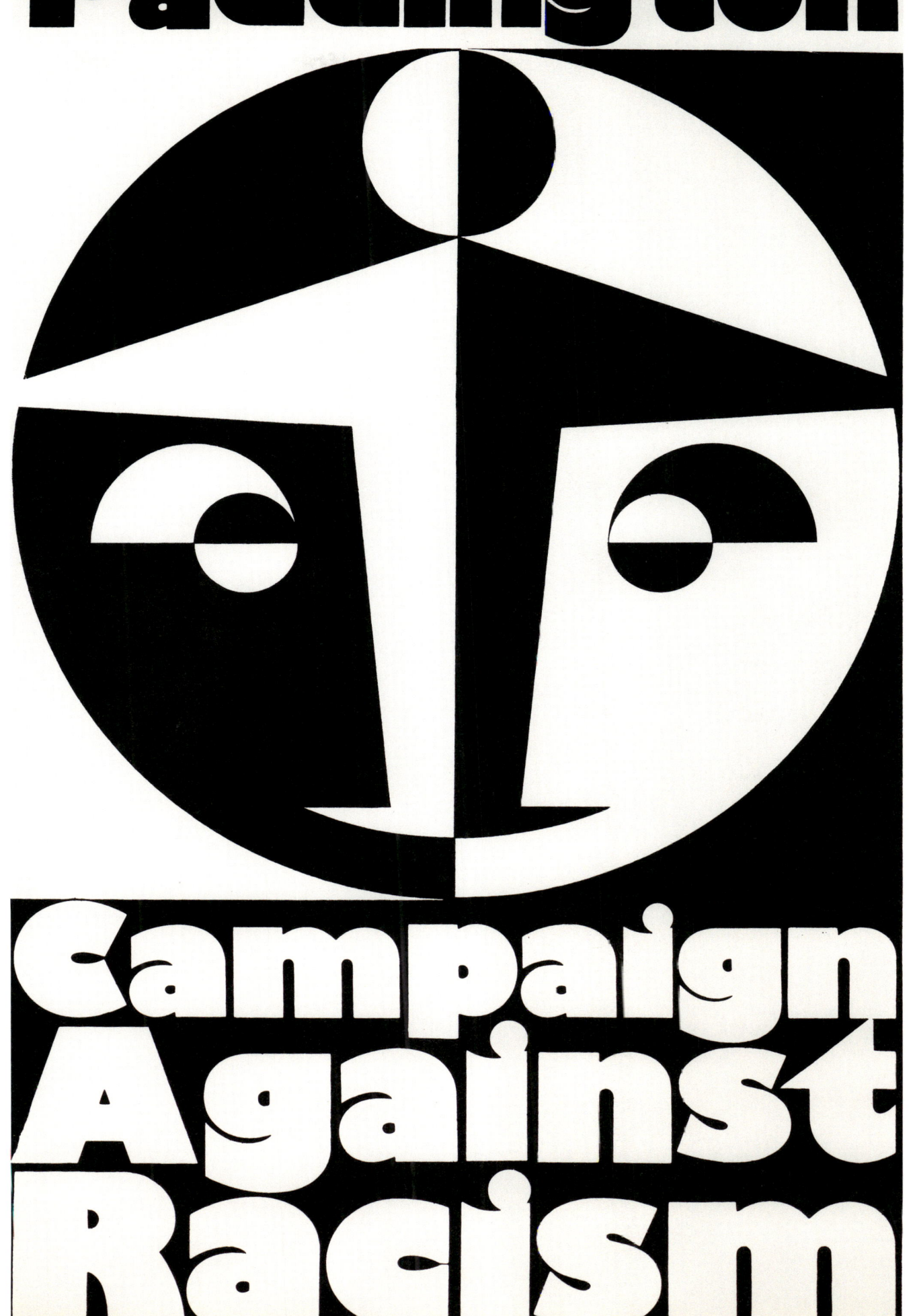

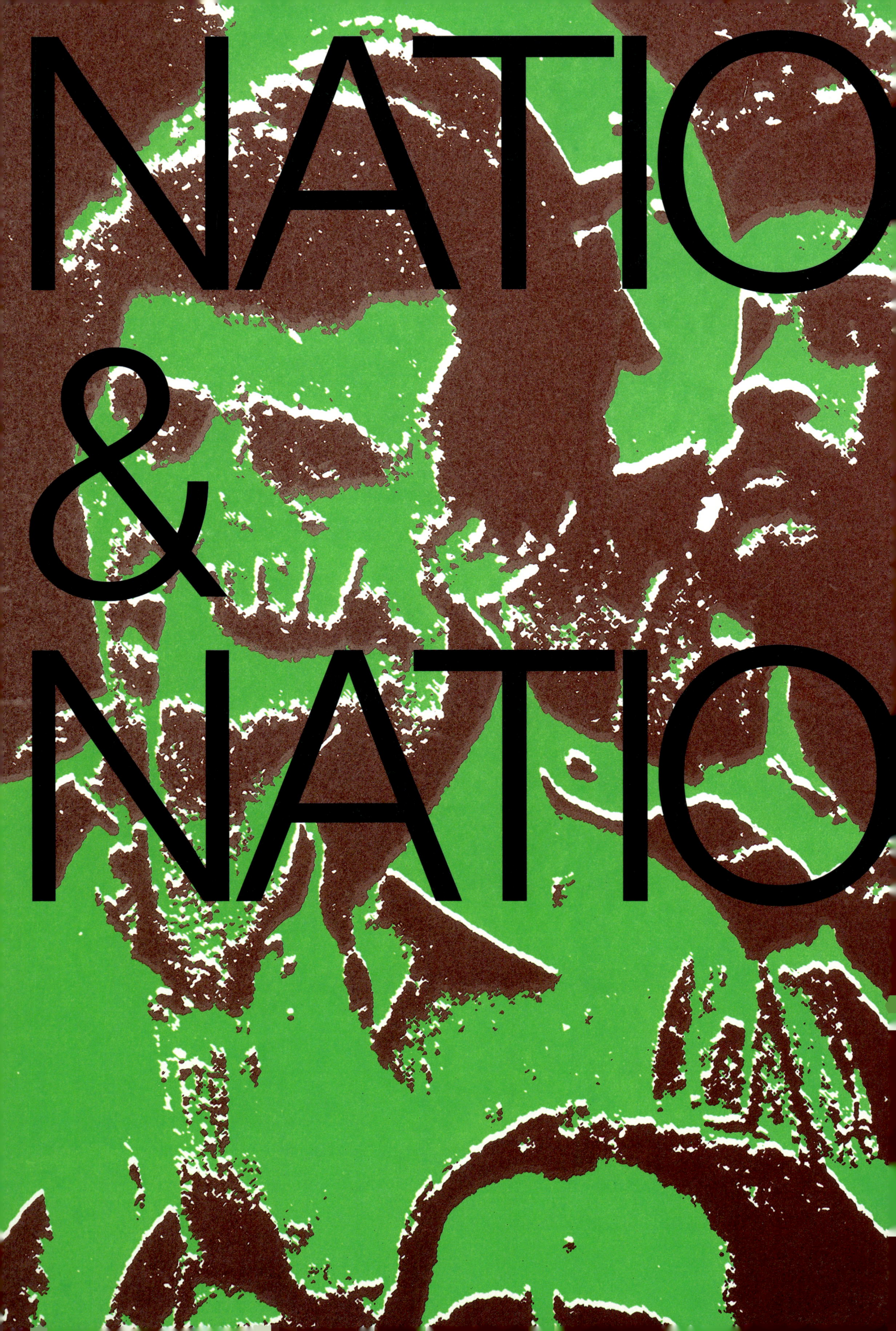

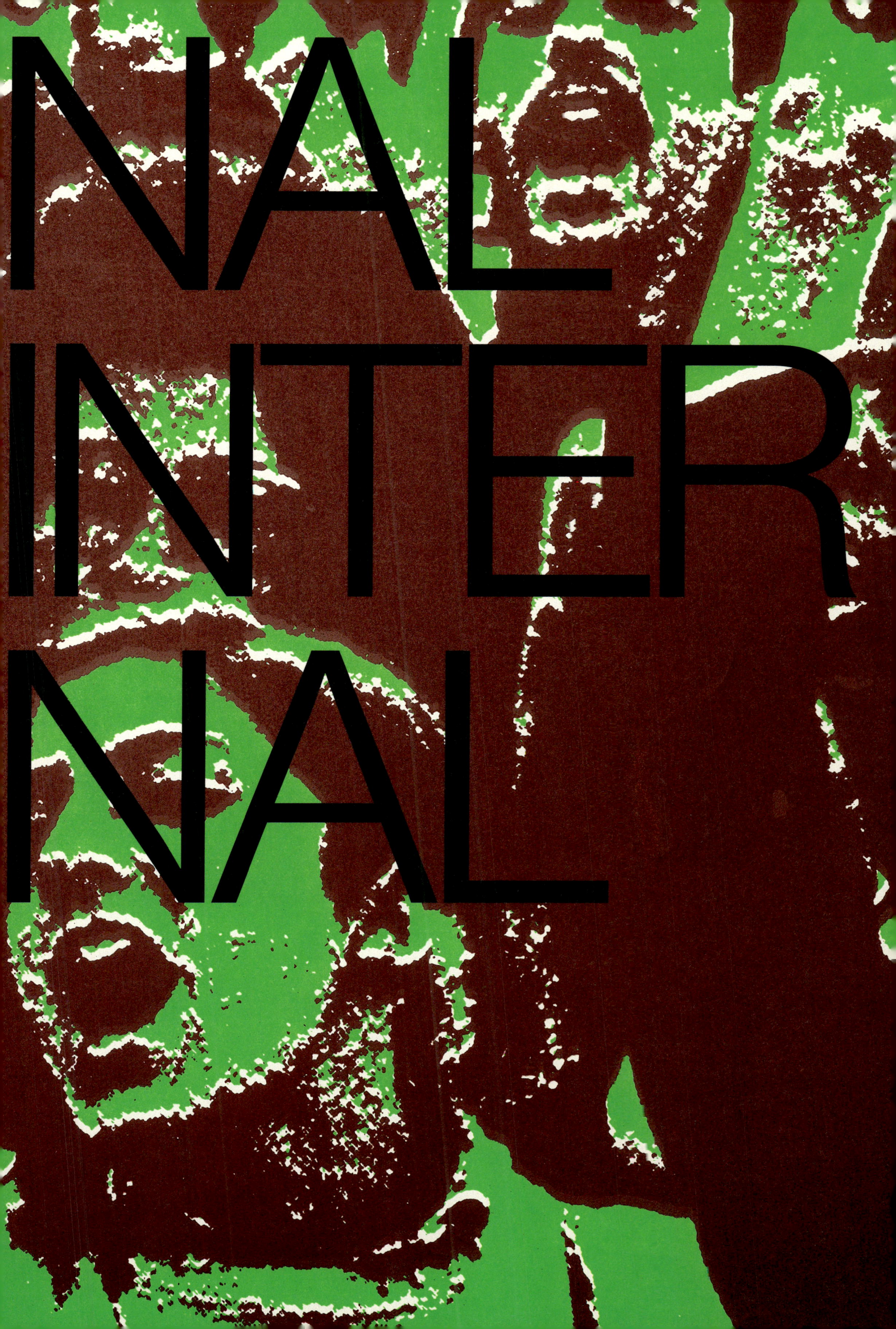

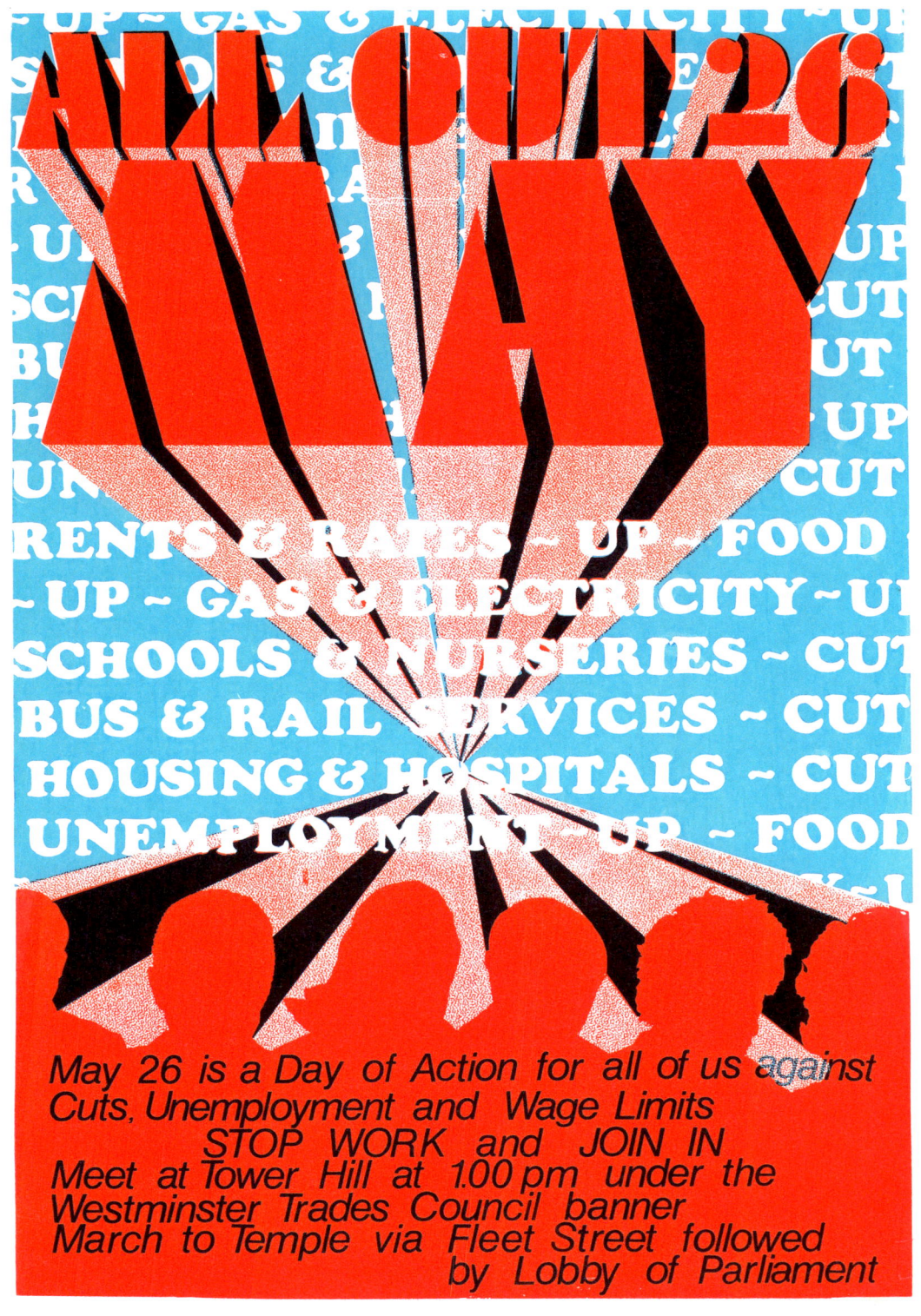

Above
ALL OUT 26 MAY, 1976, John Phillips

Opposite
KEEP FARES DOWN, 1982, Anne Dundon

Next pages

BUCKINGHAM PALACE VIEW
FROM THE NORTH, 1976, John Phillips

LOOK WHAT THEY GAVE TO THE
MAYOR TODAY, c.1976, John Phillips

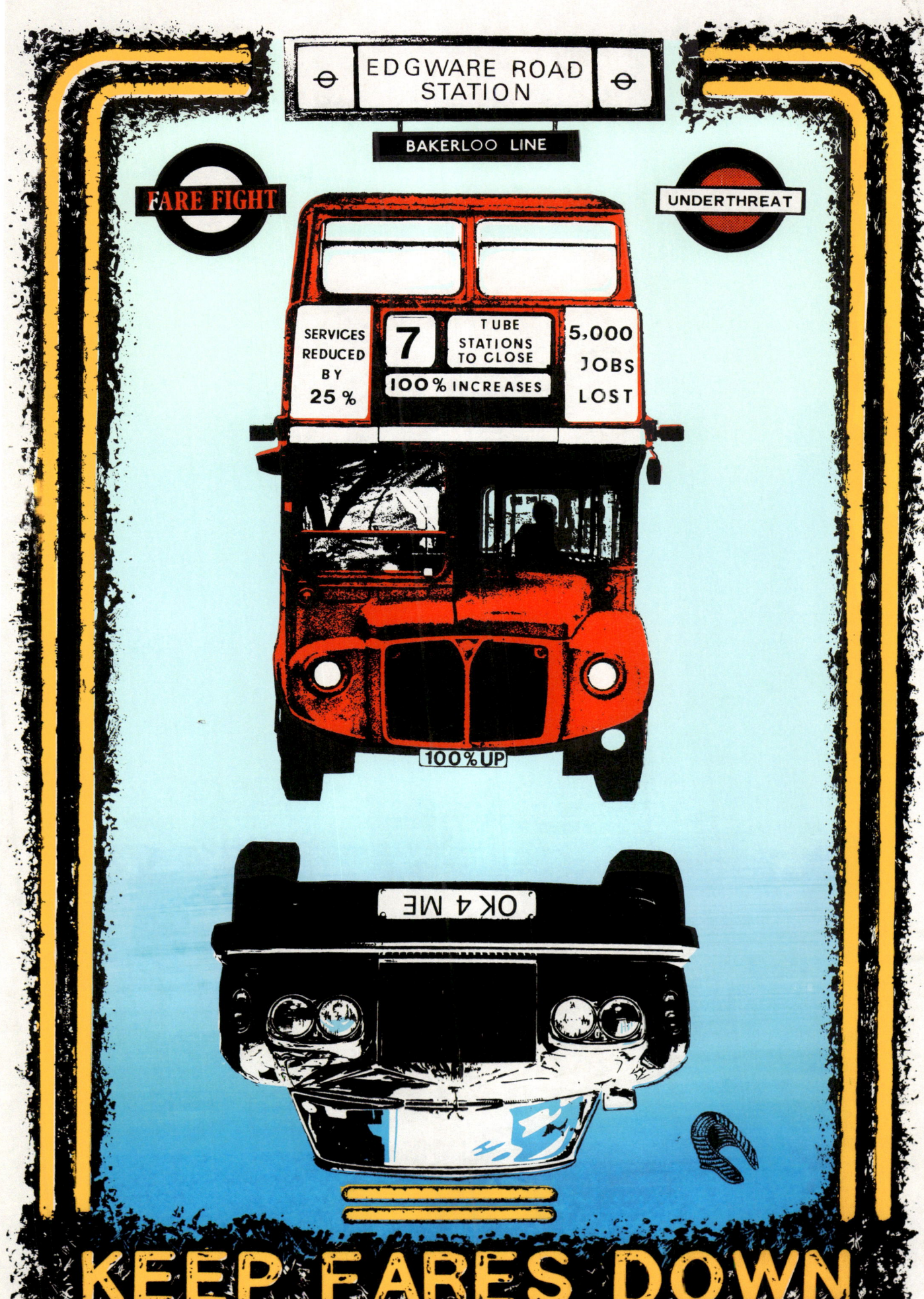

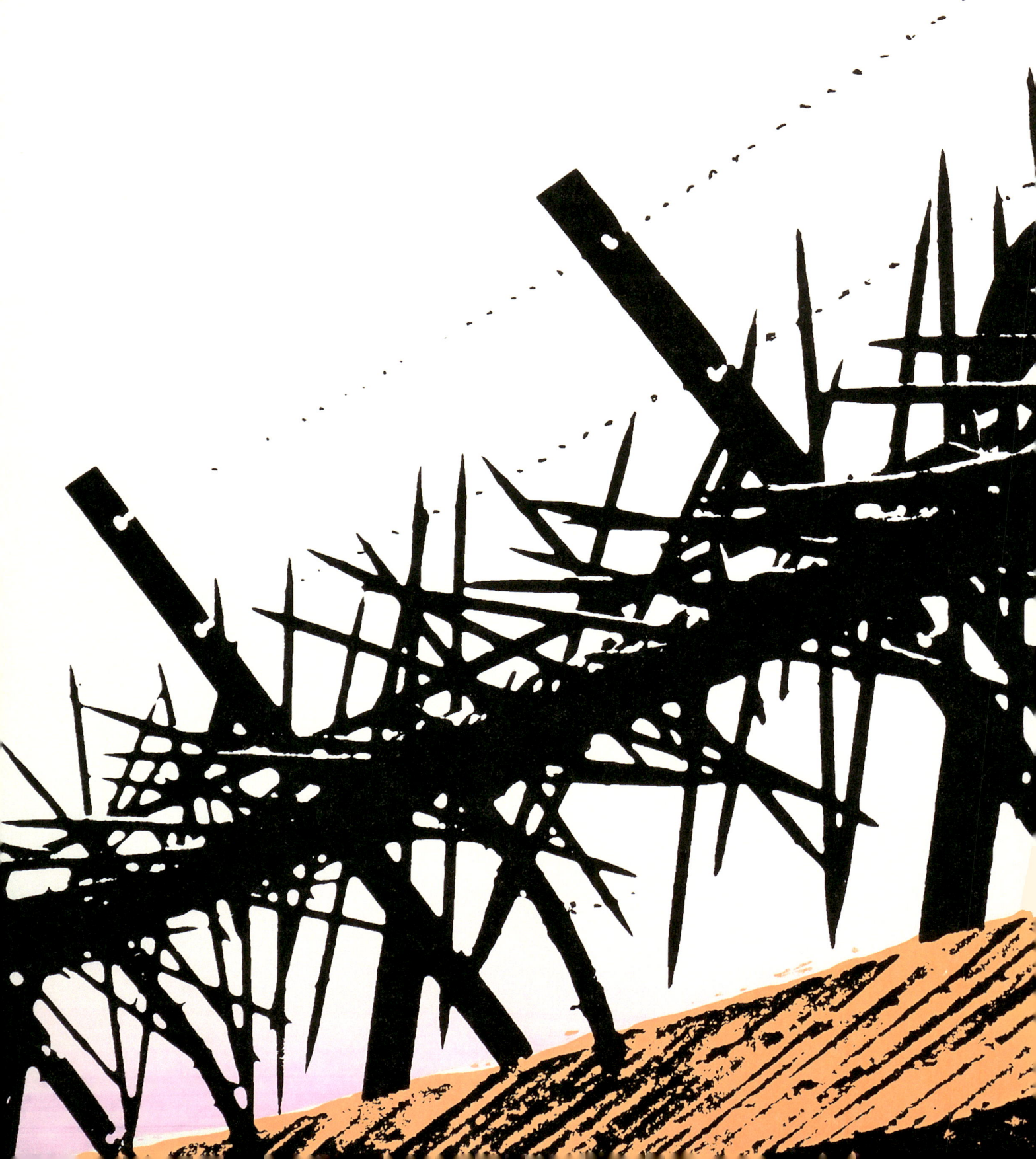

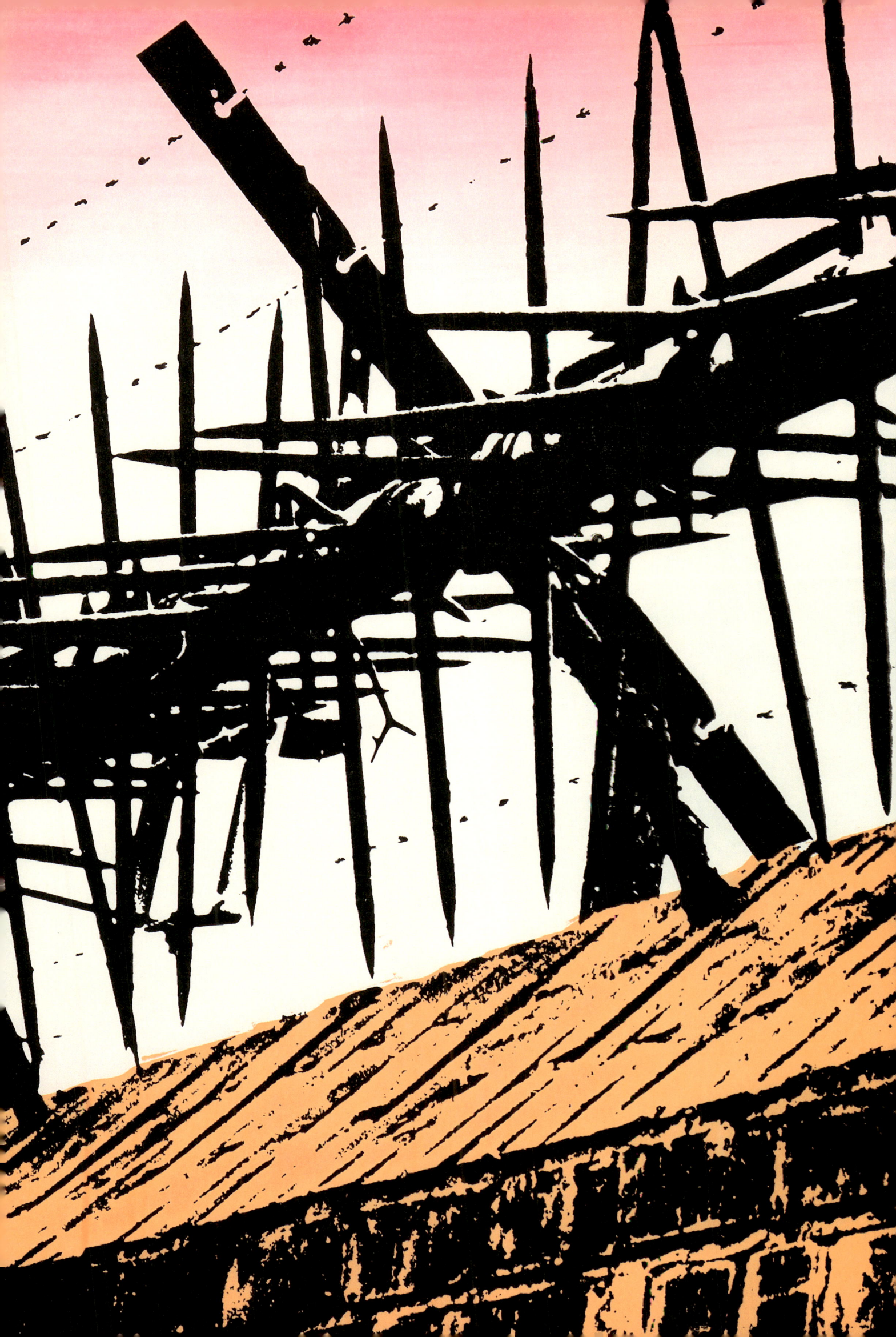

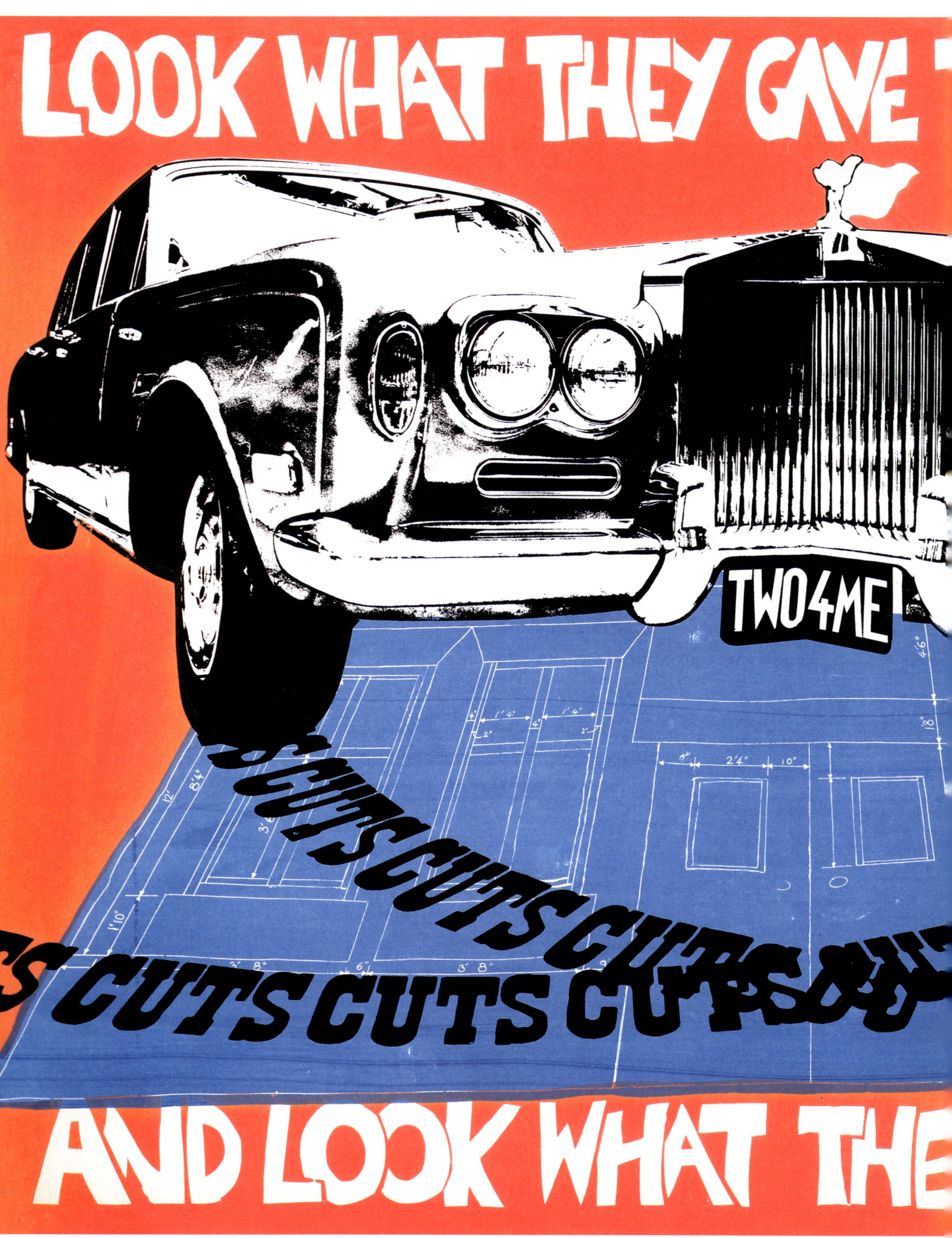

THE MAYOR TODAY...

In order to put money into industry and make profits for British shareholders the Government has ordered severe cuts in Public Expenditure. When Westminster City Council dole out the money they make very sure that we are the only people to suffer – not their own kind.

At a recent Westminster City Council meeting: CUT – £100,000 for Grosvenor Estate and Lisson Green Estate Halls, places for thousands of people to meet and have fun. PASSED – £120,000 for the upkeep of 1 Lord Mayor, including 2 Rolls Royces and 2 chauffeurs, so he doesn't have to meet Westminster people on the buses.

FIGHT BACK NOW!
ALL OUT FOR DAY OF ACTION

MAY 26th

MEET 1PM TOWER HILL
(ASSEMBLE UNDER WESTMINSTER TRADES COUNCIL BANNER)

TOOK FROM US!

Opposite
NUCLEAR POWER: IT'S CHILD'S
PLAY, 1979, John Phillips

Created in the aftermath of the Three Mile Island incident in Pennsylvania in 1979. The partial meltdown of one of the site's reactors resulted in increased public concern around safety in the growing nuclear power industry.

Next pages
STAND TOGETHER, 1977,
Chris Thomas

On 20th August 1976 a small group of workers, mainly Asian women, walked out of a film processing factory in protest over working conditions. They had joined the trade union APEX (Association of Professional, Executive, Clerical and Computer Staff) and requested recognition from the factory owners. The company's owners were vehemently opposed to unionism and were members of a consortium of small companies that had created a 'fighting fund' to support any member company that became embroiled in a union dispute. The Grunwick strikers sustained a picket outside the factory gates for weeks and gradually gained support from the predominantly white and male-dominated trade union movement. By the following summer, with TUC backing, as many as many as 20,000 supporters joined the daily mass picket confronting non-unionised workers bussed into the factory under police escort. The strike ultimately collapsed following a House of Lords ruling and fading support from other unions.

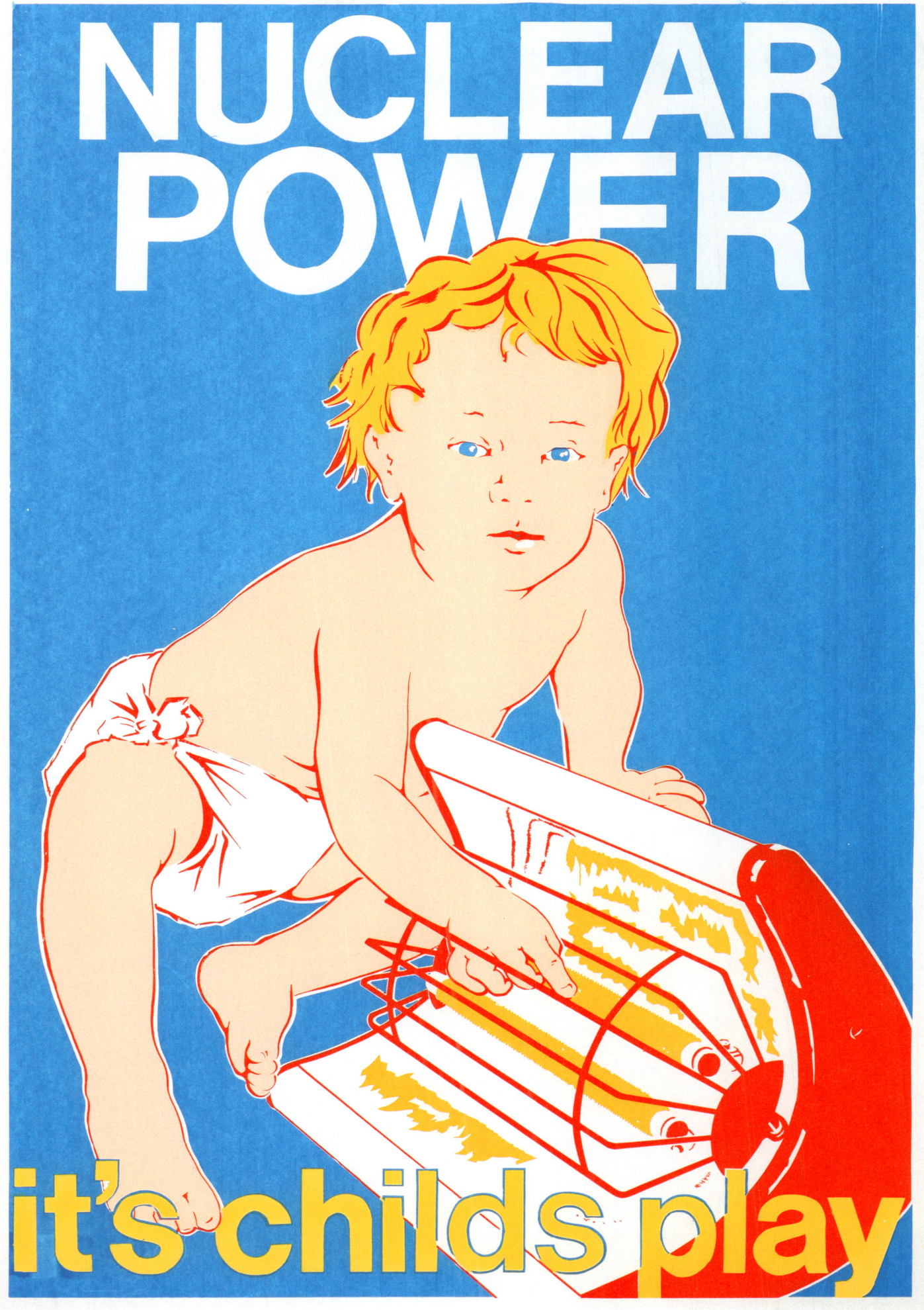

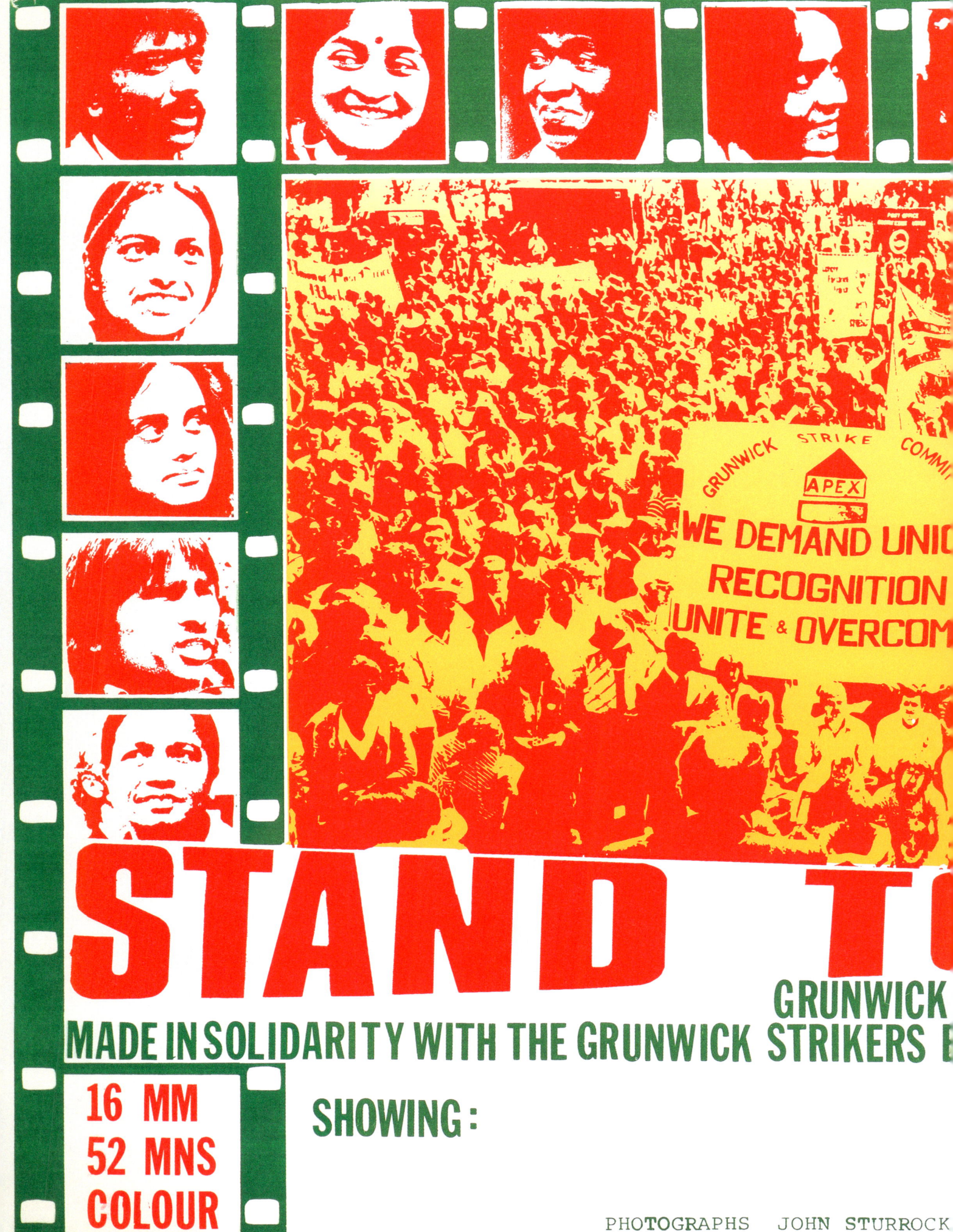

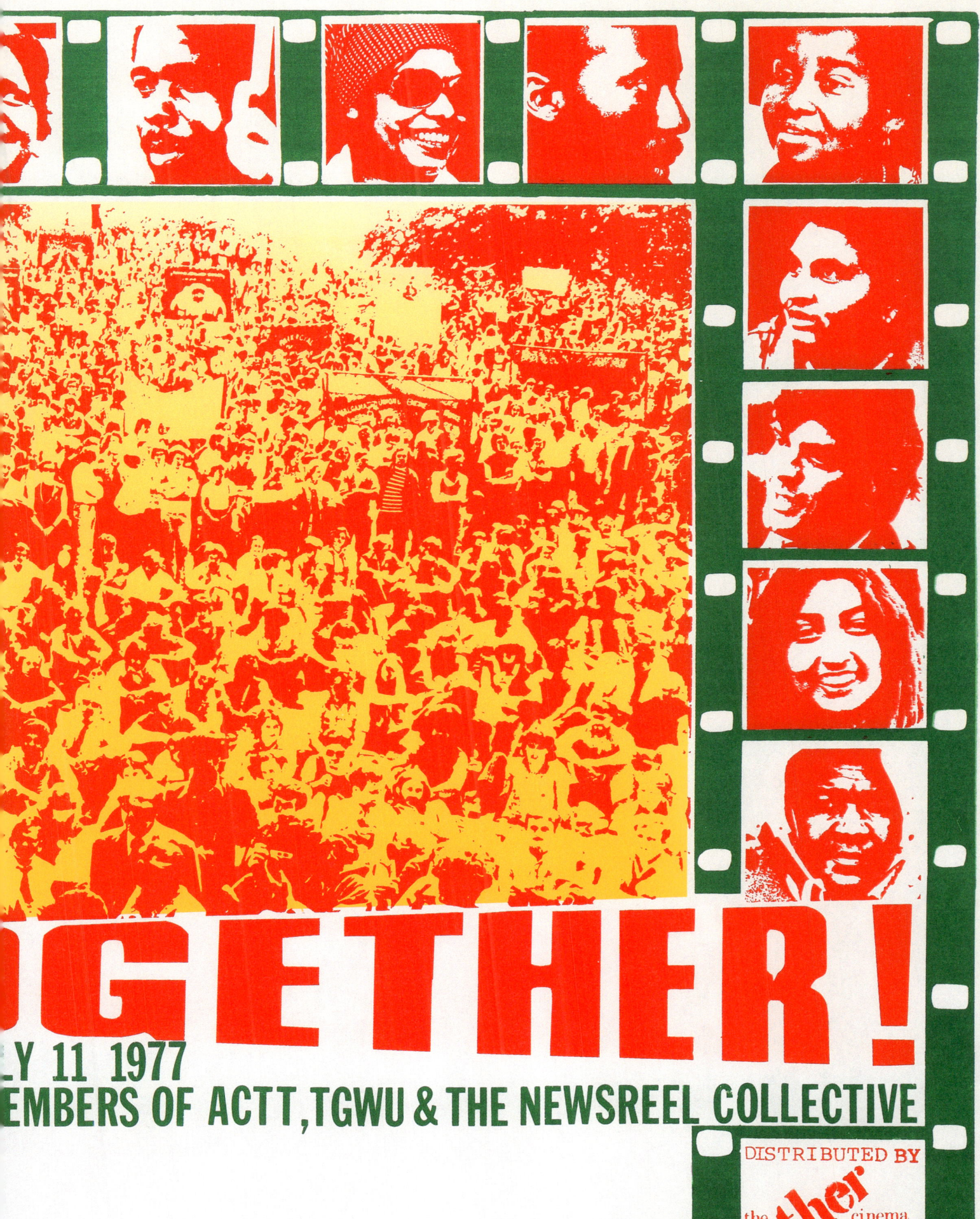

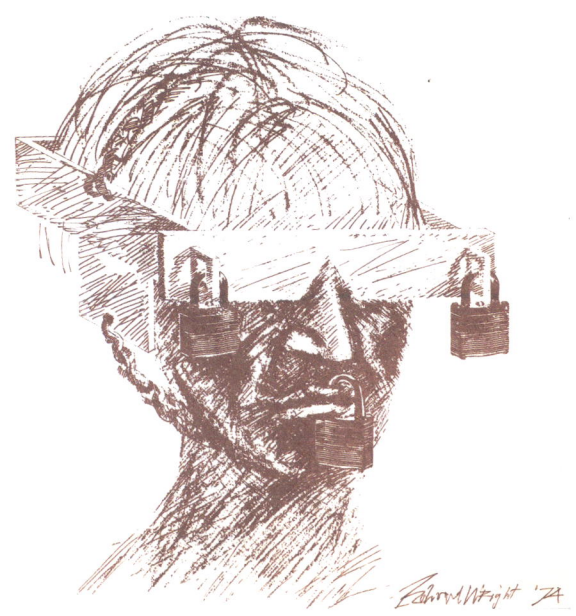
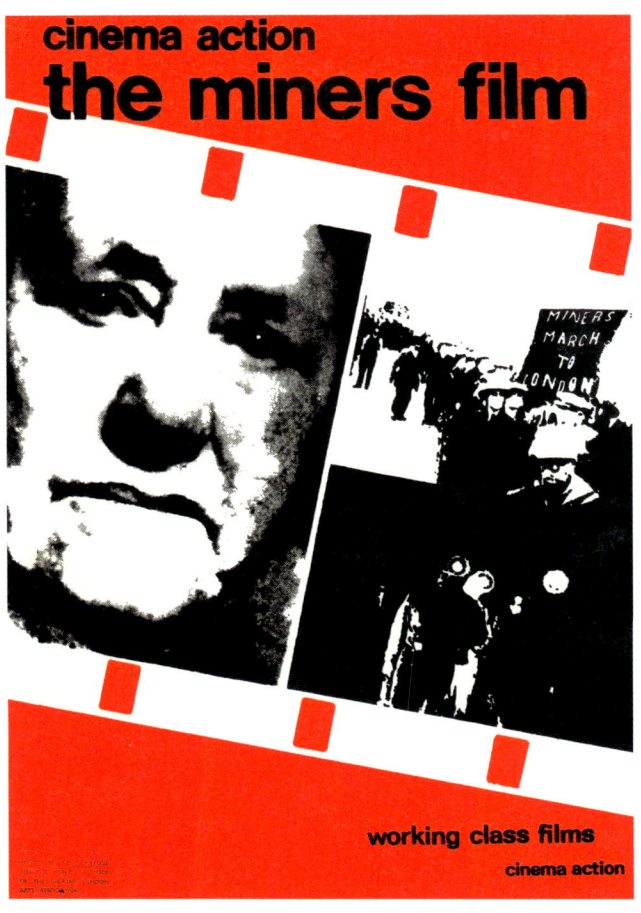

JUSTICE FOR FILIPINO WORKERS

Opposite

CULTURAL REPRESSION IN CHILE, 1974, Edward Wright

THE MINERS FILM, 1974, Steve Sprung

The Miners Film, by the left wing collective Cinema Action, represents the lives and struggles of miners as experienced and articulated through the voices of the miners and their families themselves.

JUSTICE FOR FILIPINO WORKERS, c.1980, Anon

Many migrant workers, frequently isolated by language and poor cultural integration into the wider society, experienced harsh and exploitative conditions. *Justice for Filipino Workers* is an example of a placard for an ad hoc protest attempting to bring attention to this problem.

Next pages

SOLIDARITY WITH THE PORTUGUESE WORKERS REVOLUTION, 1974–1975, John Phillips

From the outset, Paddington Printshop's posters reflected the global connections of the neighbourhood's migrant communities, whether long established such as the Irish, Spanish and Portuguese, post-war and first generation Caribbean, or relatively recent arrivals from Latin American. Early posters, predating the official opening of the Printshop, reflected our engagement with global political and social events. Examples included *Solidarity with the Portuguese Revolution,* which marked the 1974 military coup popularly known as the Carnation Revolution that overthrew the fascist regime of Estado Novo and Edward Wright's 1974 poster for Ariel Dorfman's discussion on cultural repression in Chile.

15 APRIL 86 TRIPOLI, 1986, John Phillips

The Printshop published and distributed numerous posters in support of social justice or protest against state sponsored violence. When, for example, on 15 April 1986 American planes stationed in the UK, undertook a bombing raid on 'terrorist targets' in Libya, the Printshop produced a poster featuring the image of a civilian casualty of the raid with the legend *Is this Child a Terrorist?* and, on the day following the raid, organised pasting the poster around the base from which the planes had flown.

TO IMPOSE MINERAL SANCTIONS, 1986, John Phillips

We referenced Sam Nzima's photograph of Hector Pieterson, the first casualty of the Soweto uprising on 16 June 1976, to contrast with a statement from White House Chief of Staff Donald Regan.

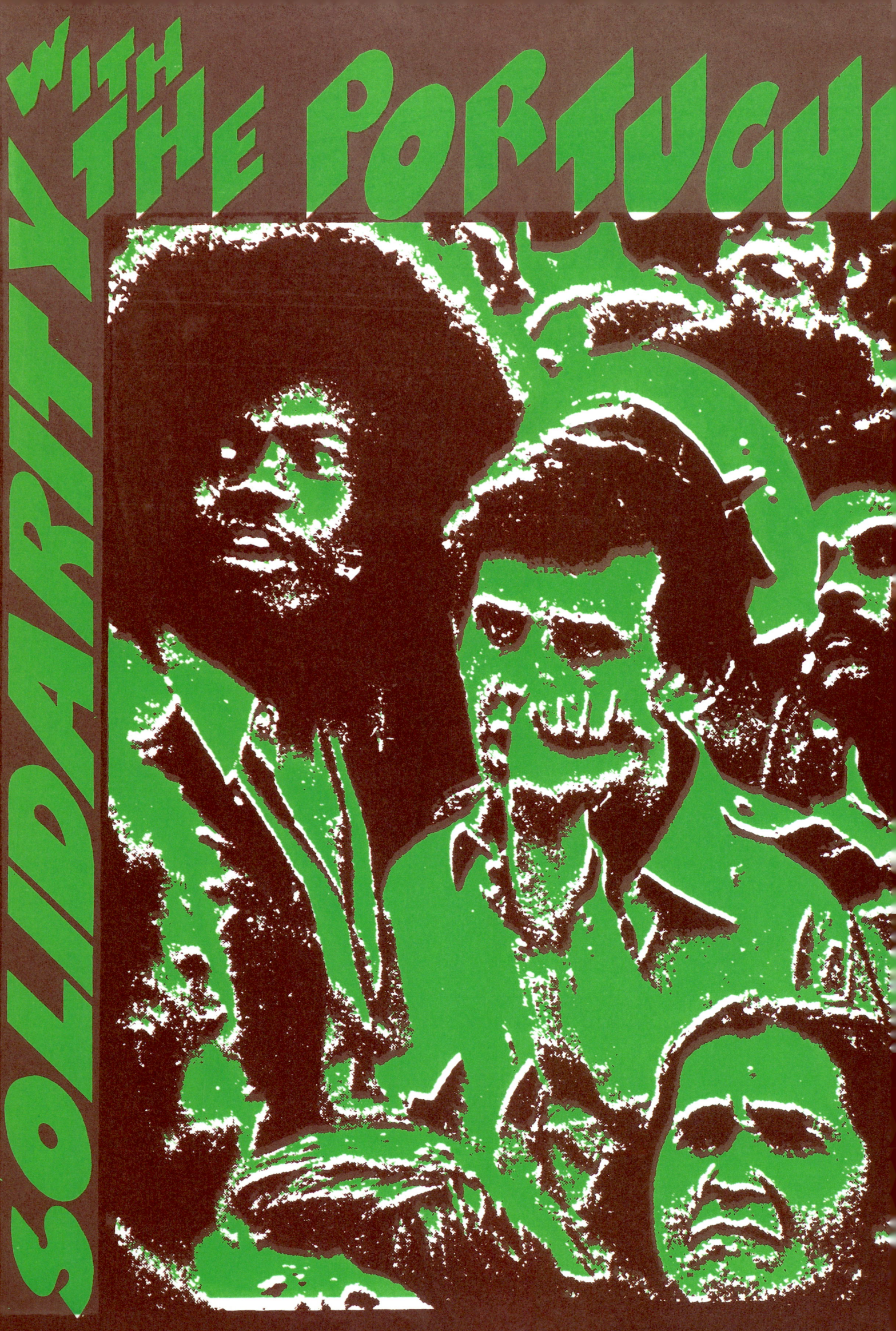

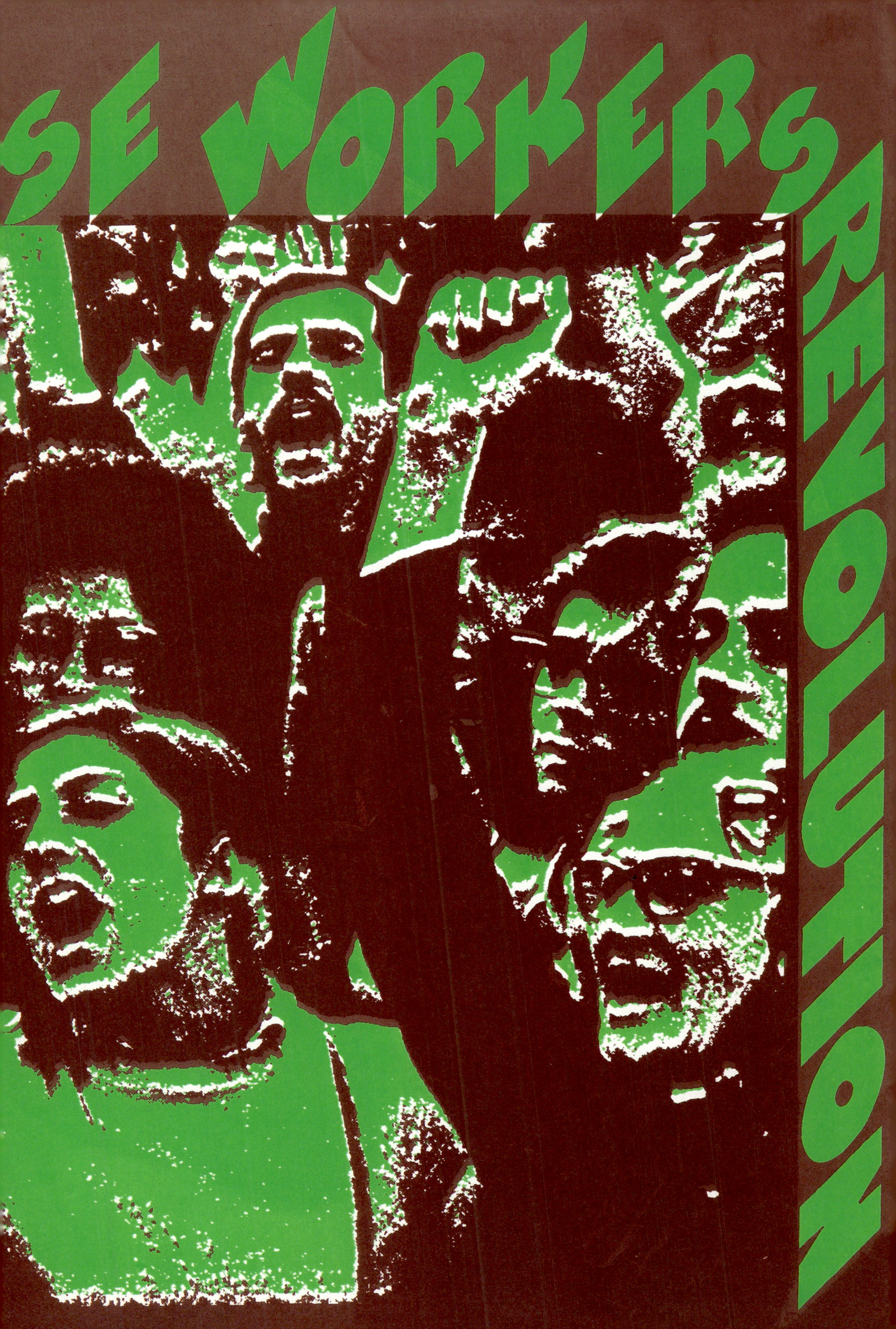

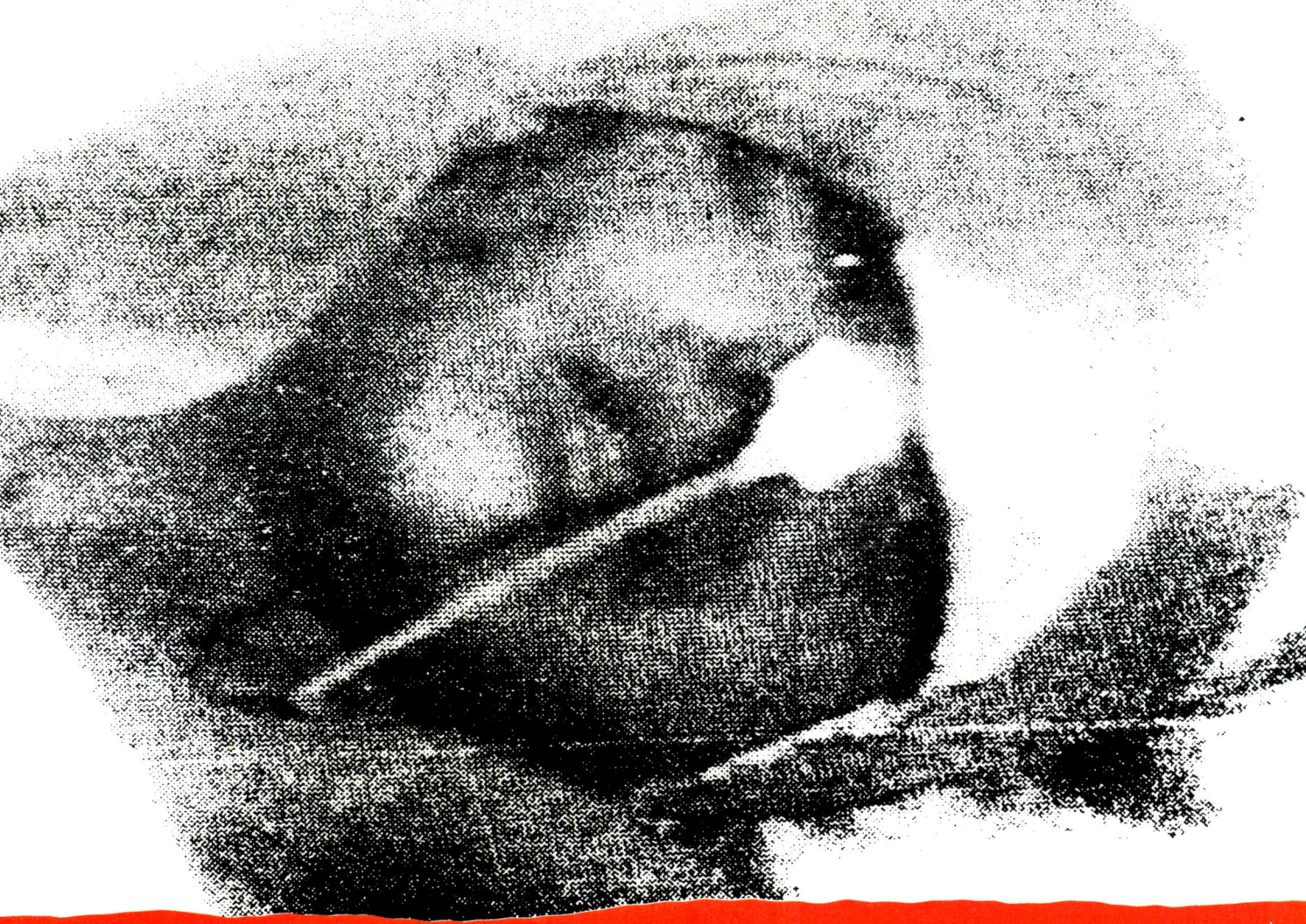

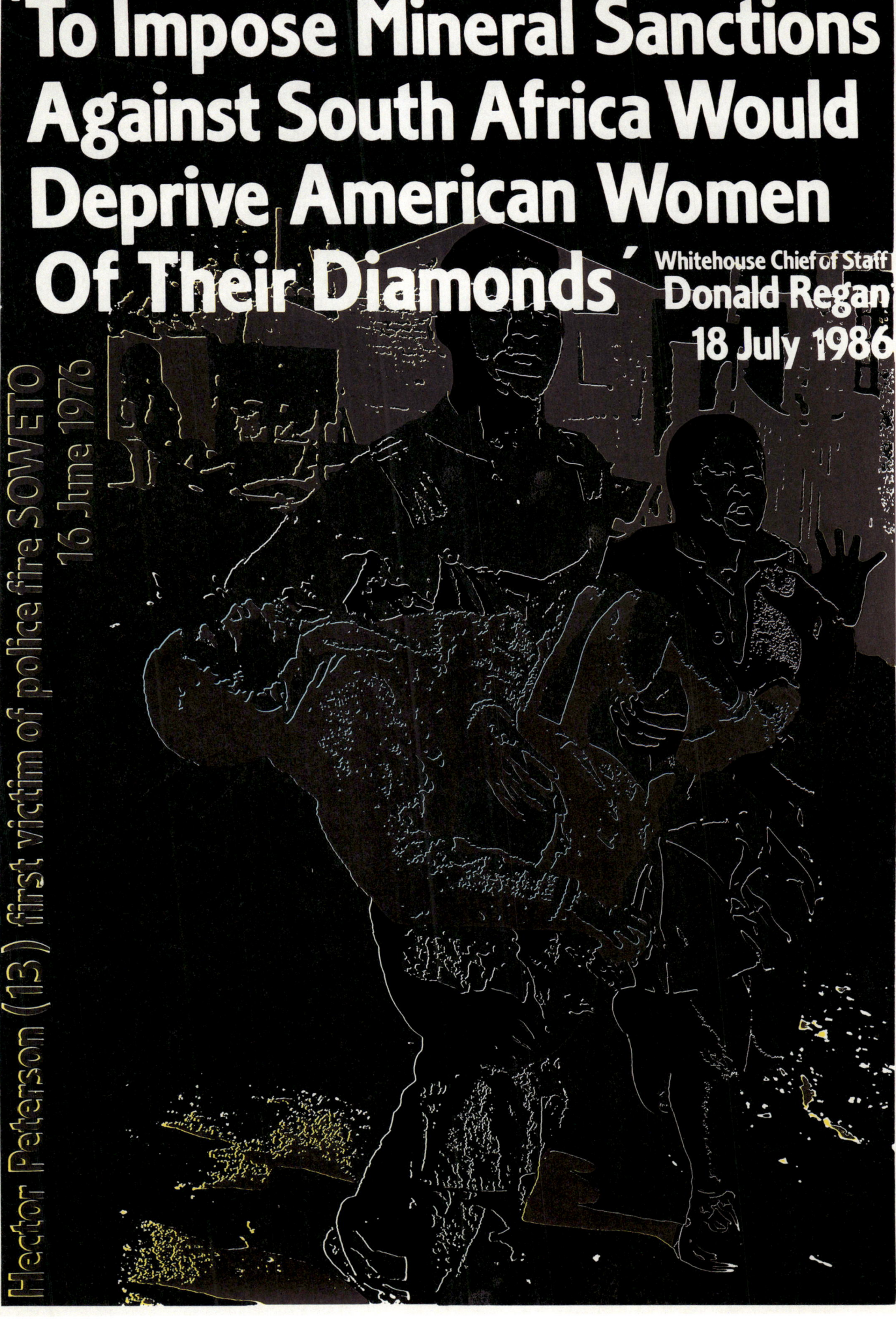

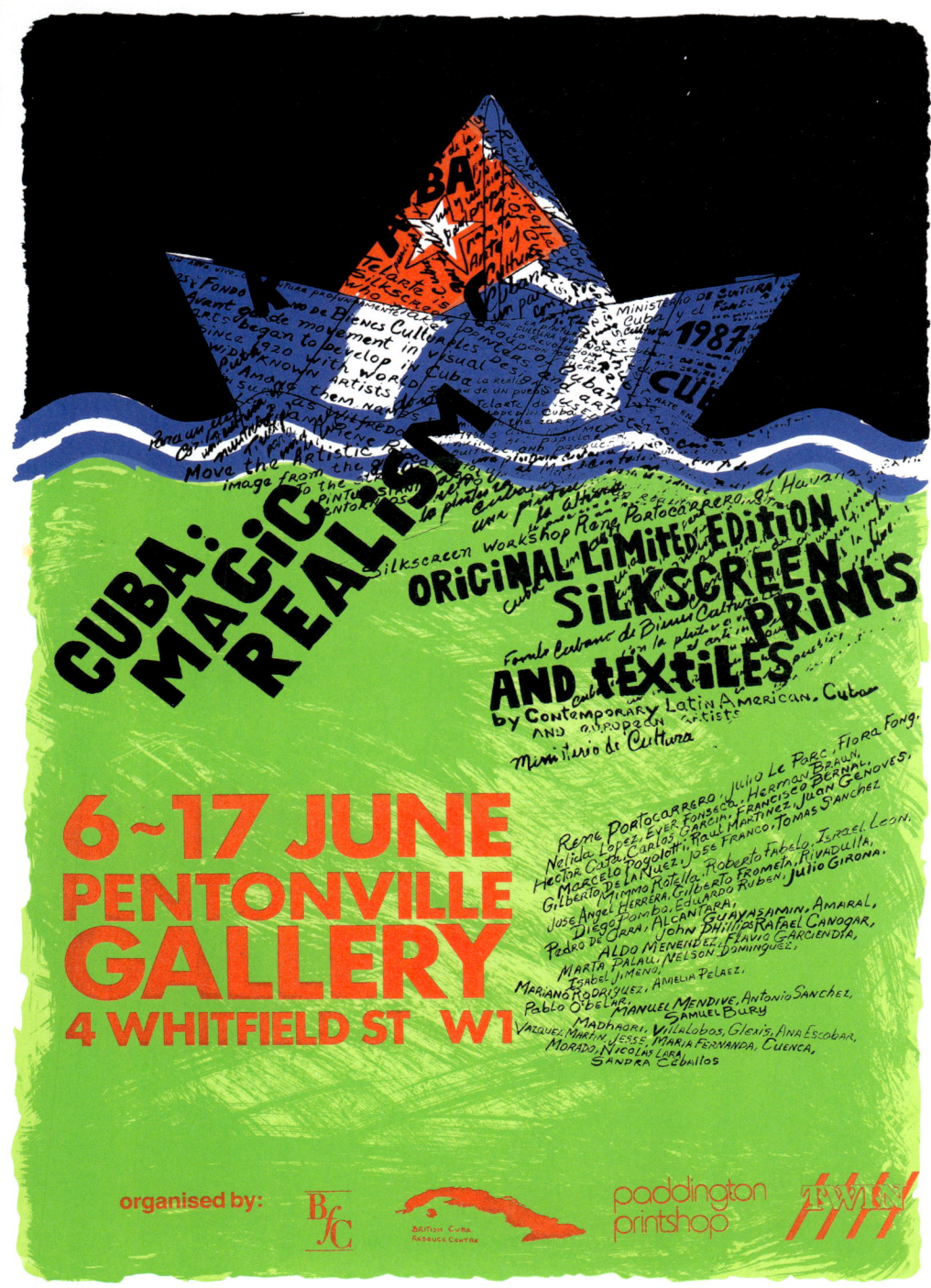

Above
CUBA MAGIC REALISM, 1988,
Aldo Menendez Gonzalez

Opposite
EL ARTE CUBANO, 1988, John Phillips
and Aldo Menendez Gonzalez

In 1988, the Printshop worked with the director of the René Portocarrero Printstudio (Havana) and the Cuba Solidarity Campaign to showcase contemporary Cuban printmaking. These posters were created during this period.

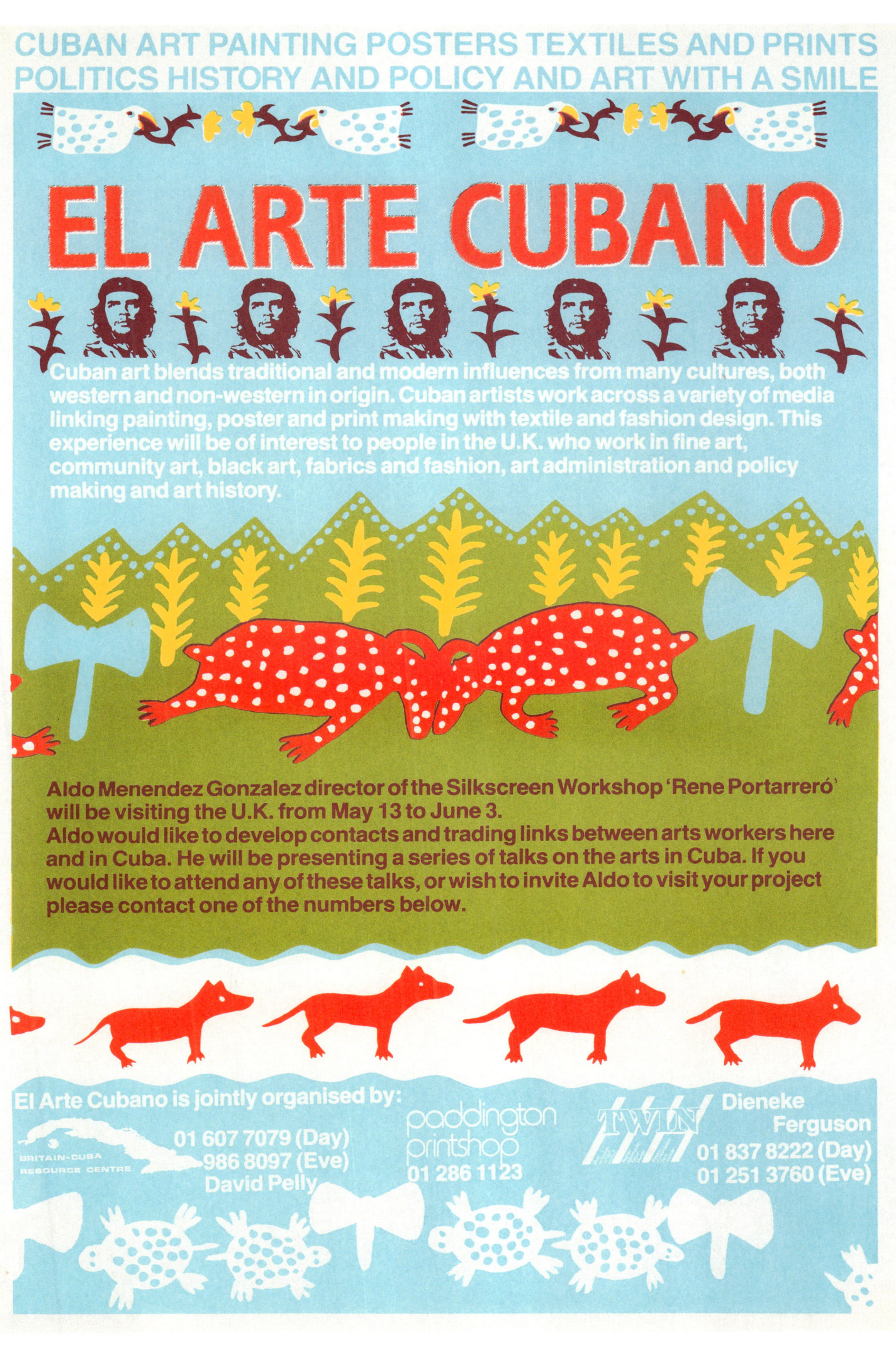

Next pages

BITTER FRUIT, 1986, John Phillips

THE ROTTEN APPLE, 1986,
John Phillips

These were the Printshop's contribution to the campaign to boycott South African produce in protest against the racist Apartheid regime. Cape and Outspan were the brands under which South African apples and oranges were marketed. Smaller versions of the posters were also made and distributed for insertion into supermarket displays.

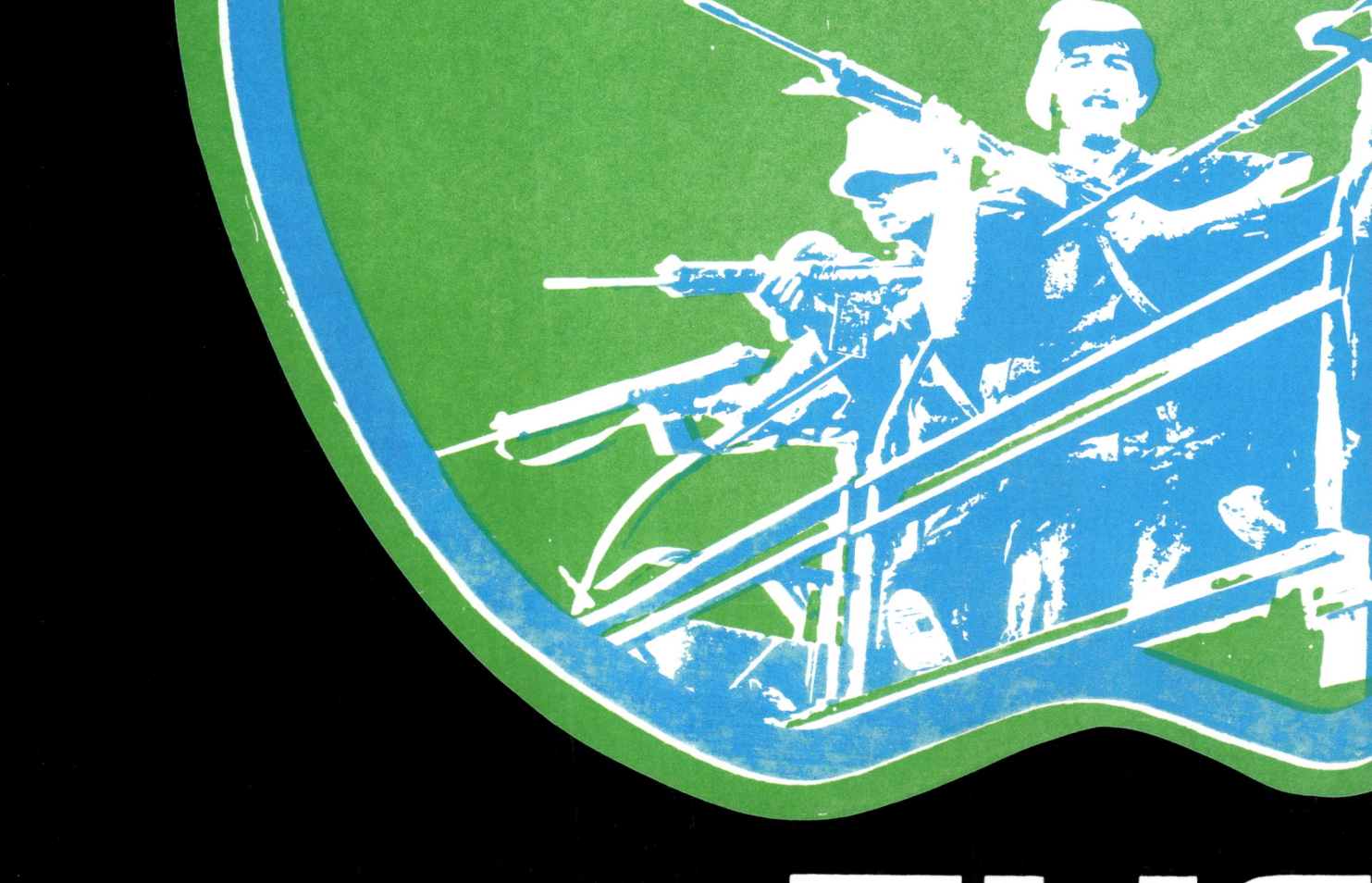

THE
ROTTEN A
REPUBLIC OF SOUTH AF

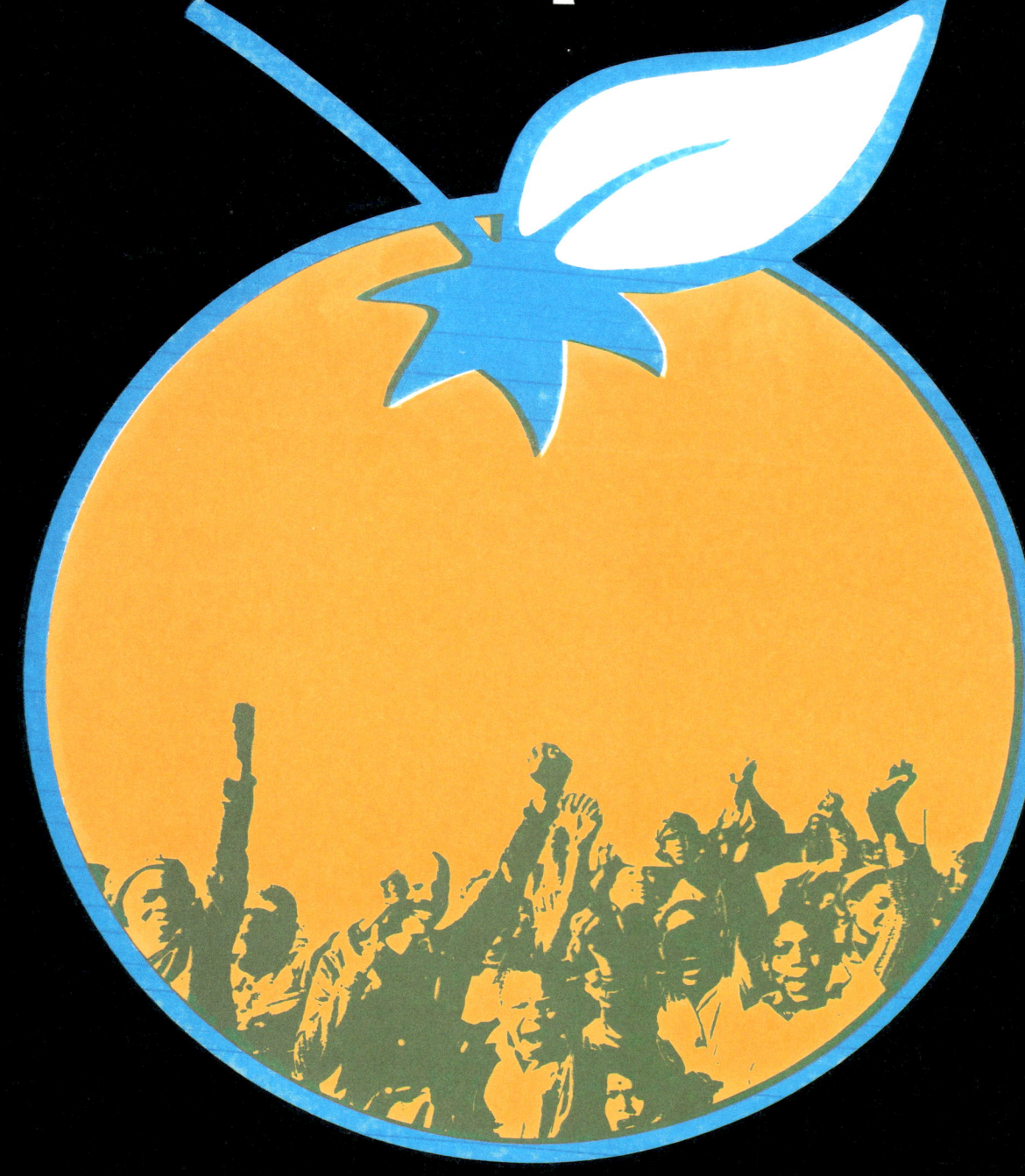

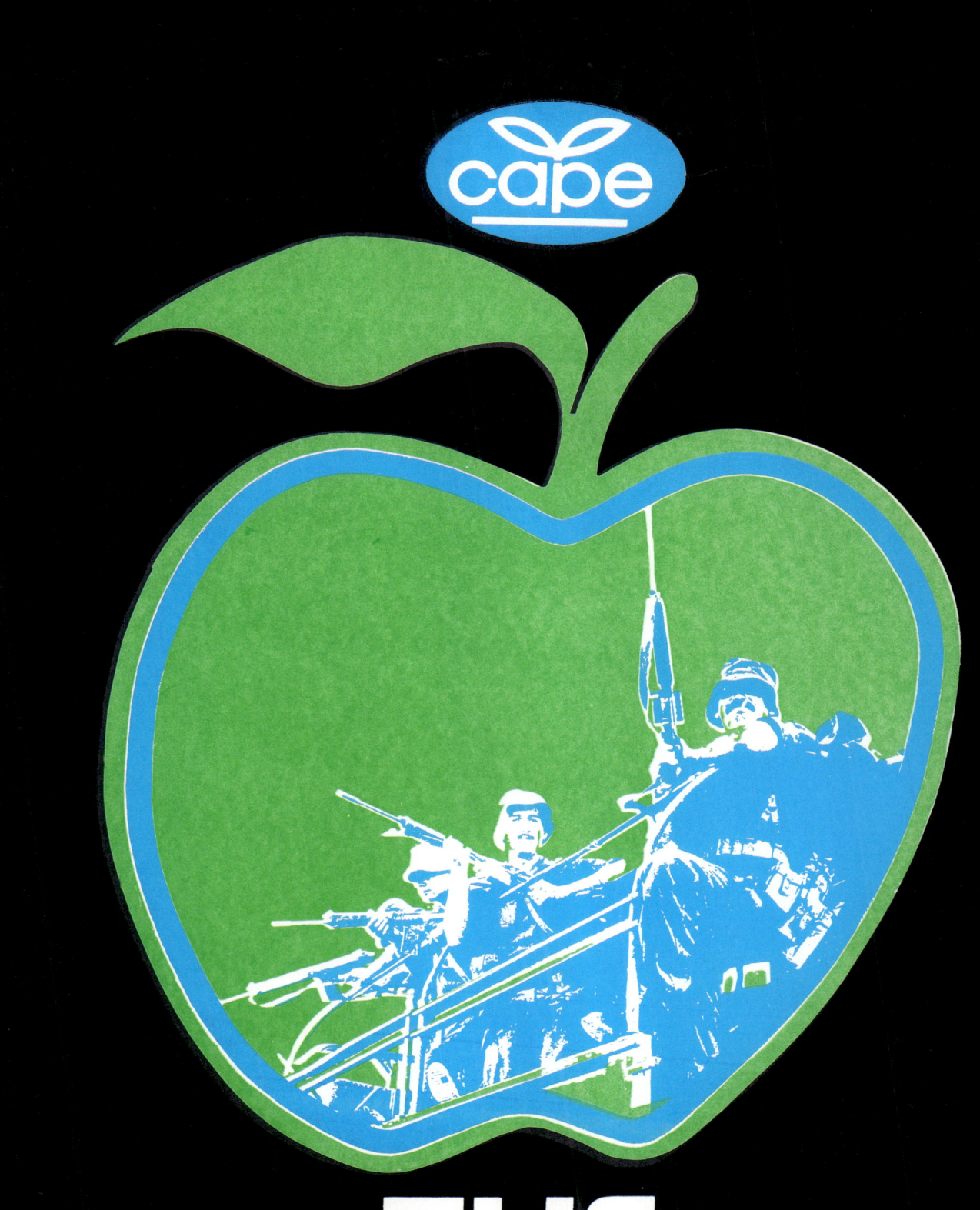

MERRY XMAS (LET'S HAVE ANOTHER ONE),
1982, Pippa Smith and Jay Talbot

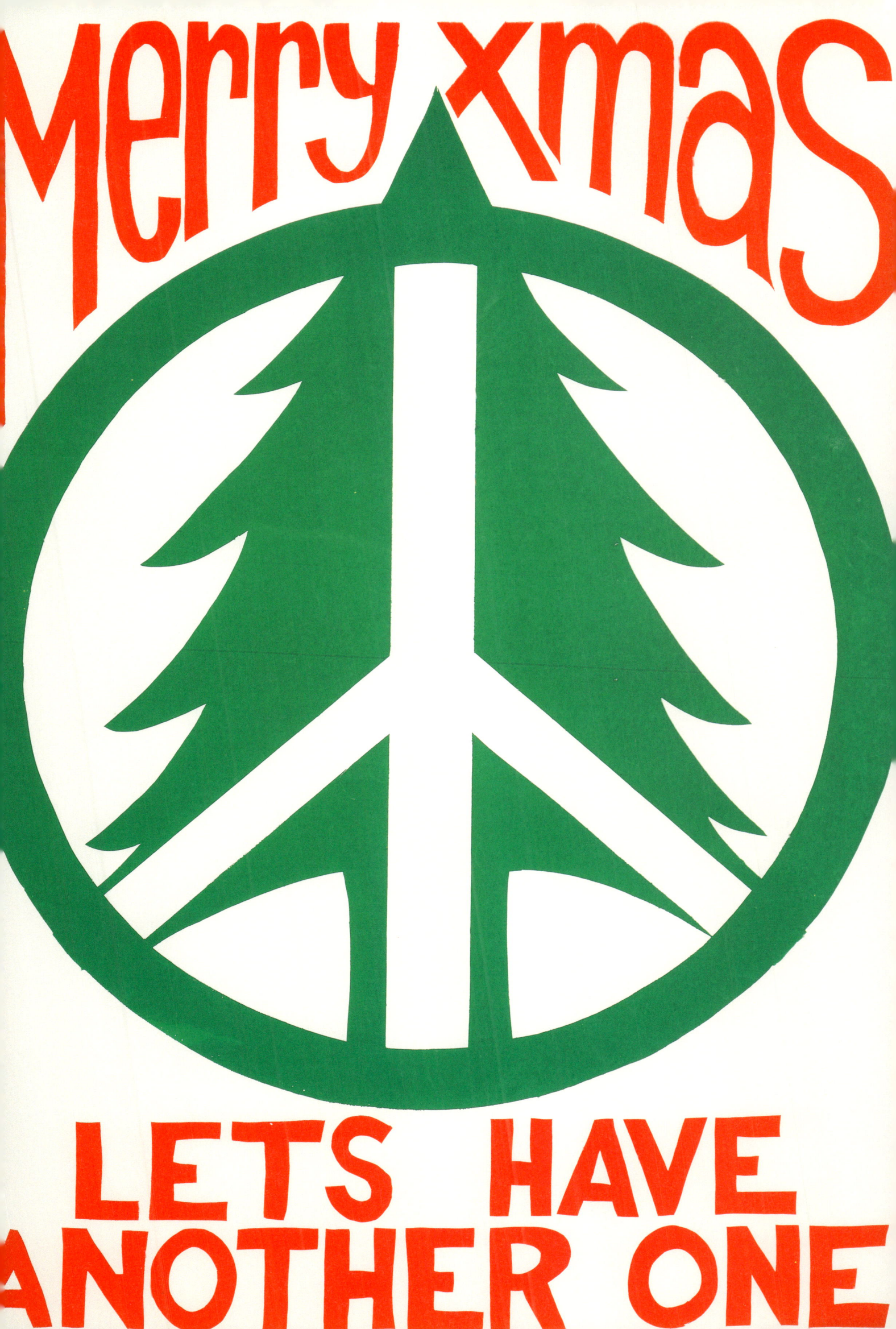

YOU, TOO, CAN IMPROVE YOUR GRAPHIC
DESIGN, c. 1982, John Phillips

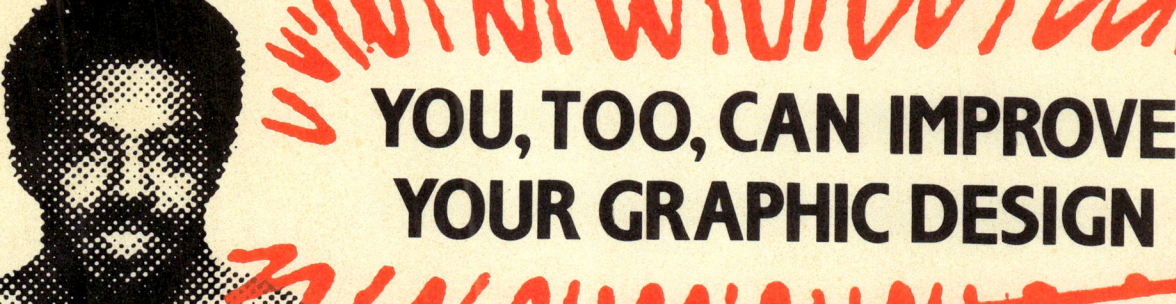

YOU, TOO, CAN IMPROVE YOUR GRAPHIC DESIGN

For further information send S.A.E. to Paddington Printshop, 1 Elgin Avenue, W9 3PR, or ring (01) 286 1123.

Do the leaflets and posters put out by your organization look less interesting than the small ads in yesterday's paper? Then why not do something about it? Paddington Printshop is running a series of graphic design workshops for people in the voluntary sector. These workshops can help you to cut costs, save time and communicate ideas more effectively.

Published in 2019 by Four Corners Books
56 Artillery Lane, London E1 7LS

fourcornersbooks.co.uk

Designed by John Morgan studio
morganstudio.co.uk

Print production by Martin Lee
Reprography by Flavio Milani
Printed in Italy by Printer Trento

Distributed in the UK by Art Data
artdata.co.uk

ISBN 978-1-909829-15-2

Text © John Phillips
Foreword © Andrzej Klimowski
Images © the artists and photographers
as credited

Every effort has been made to secure
copyright approval and ensure accuracy
but if there are omissions please contact
us at hello@fourcornersbooks.co.uk
and the corrections will be included
in any future editions of this book.